MYTHS AND REALITIES
IN THE DISTRIBUTION OF
SOCIOECONOMIC RESOURCES AND
POLITICAL POWER IN ETHIOPIA

Kasahun Woldemariam

University Press of America,® Inc.
Lanham · Boulder · New York · Toronto · Oxford

Copyright © 2006 by
University Press of America,® Inc.
4501 Forbes Boulevard
Suite 200
Lanham, Maryland 20706
UPA Acquisitions Department (301) 459-3366

PO Box 317
Oxford
OX2 9RU, UK

Library of Congress Control Number: 2005935102
ISBN 0-7618-3360-9 (paperback : alk. ppr.)

To the memory of
my sister, Tigab Reta,
my uncle, Alamnie Chanyalew,
and my cousins, Tigabu and Habte Alamnie

Contents

Figures and Tables

Figures

Tables

Abbreviations

AAPO	All Amhara People's Organization
ACC	Anti-corruption Commission
ADLI	Agriculture-Development Led Industrialization
AEUP	All Ethiopian Unity Party
AESM	All Ethiopians Socialist Movement
ANDF	Affar National Democratic Front
ANDM	Amhara National Democratic Movement
BMPDO	Bench Madji People's Democratic Organization
CAFPDE	Council of the Alternative Forces for Peace and Democracy in Ethiopia
CSA	Central Statistical Authority
CSO	Central Statistical Office
CUD	Coalition for Unity and Democracy
EDP	Ethiopian Democratic Party
EDU	Ethiopian Democratic Unity
EPDM	Ethiopian People's Democratic Movement
EPLF	Eritrean People's Liberation Front
EPRDF	Ethiopian People's Revolutionary Democratic Front
EPRP	Ethiopian People's Revolutionary Party
GDP	Gross Domestic Product
GER	Gross Enrollment Ratio

GNDM	Gurage Nationalities Democratic Movement
GPRDM	Gdeo People's Revolutionary Democratic Movement
HNDO	Hadiya National Democratic Organization
IMF	International Monetary Fund
KPDO	Ka'te People's Democratic Organization
KSPDO	Kafa Shaka People's Democratic Organization
MFA	Ministry of Federal Affairs
NEB	National Electoral Board
OPDO	Oromo People's Democratic Organization
OLF	Oromo Liberation Front
RDPS	Rural Development Policies and Strategies
SEPDF	Southern Ethiopia People's Democratic Movement
SNNR	Southern Nations and Nationalities Region
SPDO	Sidama People's Democratic Organization
TPLF	Tigray People's Liberation Front
UEDF	United Ethiopian Democratic Forces
WSLM	Western Somalia Liberation Movement
WGGPDO	Wolayta, Gamo, Gofa Dawro Konta People's Democratic Organization

Preface

The sources of conflict and cooperation and the distribution of socioeconomic resources and political power in many African countries are usually perceived and examined through a primordialist theoretical lens. Ethiopia is no exception. Almost every phenomenon that occurred in Ethiopia is depicted as revolving around ethnicity. Indeed, many scholars and policymakers singled-out one nationality group, the Amhara, as the ethnic group that monopolized the decisionmaking apparatus during the previous governments. Interestingly, without substantiating whether the "ruling ethnic group" had actually a monopoly of political power, many scholars and policymakers were quick to generalize that this group was also economically more powerful than any other ethnic group in the country. Consequently, the government of Meles Zenawi (1991 to present) adopted various policies and strategies, arguably, to correct injustices in the distribution of political power and socioeconomic resources among the different ethnic groups.

Even if the alleged "super-ordinate" ethnic group had a monopoly of political power, it does not necessary follow that the "ruling ethnic group" also devised strategies that were biased against the economic interests of "subordinate" ethnic groups. Yet, such deductive fallacies, erroneous generalizations, and the use of inappropriate theoretical lenses found their expressions in such protracted wars as between the central government, on the one hand, and secessionist and irredentist movements in northern, southern, and southeastern parts of the country, on the other hand. Irrespective of whether these movements were politically divisive or established to advance legitimate claims for the right to self-determination of people under "internal colonial rule," the thirty year wars had devastating consequences on the lives of the people and the relationships among the diverse ethnic groups in Ethiopia.

This book examines whether the alleged "super-ordinate" ethnic group in Ethiopia—the Amhara—had a monopoly of economic and political power during Emperor Haile-Selassie's era (Regent, 1916-1931, and Emperor, 1931-1974). It also analyzes the extent to which the military government of Mengistu Haile-Mariam (1974-1991) was bent on protecting the interests of the "ruling ethnic group" at the expense of politically and economically alienating other ethnic groups. From a holistic theoretical standpoint, the book further explores the redistribution policies and strategies of the Meles government and concludes with some policy-oriented recommendations and suggestions for further studies.

To be sure, competition for access to political power as a means to socioeconomic ends can be intense in a country such as Ethiopia where public and private goods and services are becoming increasingly scarce. It goes without saying that in a no-party or one-party political system, access to political power as an end, in itself, can also be a source of conflict between dominant and marginalized groups. Similarly, to the extent that the liberalization of the political market-place results in nothing more than a change in personalities, discontented segments of society would ultimately rise against the ruling elites to demand greater access to economic opportunities and political power.

To worsen the economic conditions of the people and make the resolution of conflict over resources more complicate, disenfranchized elites in Ethiopia and their protagonists in Western European academic and policymaking circles insisted that during the previous governments socioeconomic resources and political power were divided along ethnic lines. This reductionist and minimalist approach correlated Ethiopia's poor economic performance and political instability to the prevalence of a dichotomized social, economic, and political stratification. Consequently, there emerged a myth that one nationality group has historically dominated the decisionmaking apparatus and that this group enslaved, exploited, and discriminated against all other ethnic groups in Ethiopia.

In 1974, frustrated by the growing complacency of the ruling elites to the suffering of drought victims in Tigray and Wollo and by the lack of economic progress and political freedom, thousands of Ethiopians took on the streets and toppled one of the most revered dynastic rulers in Africa. Unlike the 1974 popular uprising, the collapse of the military regime in 1991 was partly influenced by exogenous factors, including the end of the Cold War and the United States' intervention as a mediator between the military regime and opposition groups. The withdrawal of public confidence towards the military regime and the moral bankruptcy of the armed force were more decisive factors than anything else. Even though these phenomena were fundamental and historically unprecedented, neither the internal nor the external currents of change created a fertile ground for the emergence of a truly accountable and transparent regime.

To be sure, Ethiopia is home to at least sixty ethnic groups with varying degrees of settlement patterns, economic and political aspirations, and religious beliefs. Of the more than eighty languages spoken in Ethiopia, the Amharic language serves as a medium of communication among the diverse ethnic groups. This language is derived from one of the oldest languages in the world, *Ge'ez*, and is associated with the Amhara ethnic group. Interestingly, when one gains insights into the meaning of the term "Amhara," one finds that it has been a social construct without distinct subjective and objective attributes of ethnicity. Until the recent surge of *ethnogogues* who invoke the subjective attributes of ethnicity to gain political power, the term was used to identify oneself as Christian.

The use of Amharic as the national and official language of Ethiopia has also been misconstrued as a vicious policy of domination and systematic erosion of the identities of non-Amharic speaking nationalities. Some political entrepreneurs and scholars insisted that Amharic was the language of power and the bureaucratic elites used this linguistic power to limit non-Amharic speaking ethnic groups from meaningful participation in the socio-cultural, economic, and political arenas. Continuing along a similar line of argument, some academics also contended that the Amhara claimed a disproportionate number of political offices and, consequently, had unobstructed access to economic opportunities and social services.

The socially constructed ethnic group has also been characterized as "Black Africa's imperialist ruler," which deliberately diverted a significant proportion of Ethiopia's resources to the development of the dominantly Amharic speaking provinces of Addis Ababa, Gonder, Gojjam, and Shoa to the impoverishment of the people in other provinces. Indeed, some influential leaders and scholars have long accepted the prevalence of a dichotomized inter-ethnic, economic and political power relationships, and sympathized with ethnoregional elites in Ethiopia. They asserted that the struggle for the right to self-determination by such groups as the Oromo Liberation Front is understandable, because these groups were discriminated by the more powerful ethnic group that monopolized political and economic power during the Haile-Selassie government. The military regime of Mengistu Haile-Mariam has also been indicted for allegedly allowing one nationality group to continue commanding the decisionmaking process and executing policies that were biased in favor of the "ruling ethnic group."

The transformation of myths into realities has essentially been achieved through the promotion of a paradigm that explains conflict and cooperation through the prisms of ethnicity. Through riddles, fictitious narratives, and manufacturing of historical facts secessionist group leaders were able to mobilize international political and military support and advance their tinted and divisive claims. The ultimate aims of satisfying their appetite for economic and political power were camouflaged in the doctrine of multiparty democracy, principles of market economy, and in the rubrics of asserting the right to self-determination and creation of ethnic enclaves as the final solution to ethnic conflict.

Even though there were no scientifically conclusive and empirically verifiable evidences to support the notion that geographically isolating each ethnic group would reduce the incidence of conflict, the Ethiopian government created ethnic Bantustans as a viable solution to the country's structural problems. During the transitional phase, the present regime authoritatively granted the secession of Eritrea without the consensus of Ethiopians. For the fist time since Africa's independence from colonial rule, African Head of States and Governments legitimized the birth of a new nation-state—Eritrea. To the disappoint of scholars such as Francis Deng, Edmond Keller, and James Scarritt, the separation of Eritrea from Ethiopia did not open the floodgate for other secessionist groups to assert their elite-centered self-determination rights. Three main reasons may be mentioned here as to why other African countries such as the Sudan did not follow the Ethiopian example to grant the right to self-determination of the people of Southern Sudan.

First, in the late 1990s, the Eritrean regime went to war with at least three of its neighbors, including Ethiopia, confirming that secession is not necessary and sufficient to end conflict. Second, the ethnic diversity of Eritrean society in what was once believed as a homogenous state has been recognized as inconsistent with the realities on the ground. There are at least nine nationality groups whose political rights and civil liberties continue to be threatened by Isayas Afeworki's regime in Asmara. Finally, indirectly related to the ethnic heterogeneity of Eritrean society is the question of whose rights to self-determination has been attained. While this question deserves a closer examination in future studies, suffice to say that the birth of a new nation-state did not produce tangible or non-tangible benefits for the majority Eritreans.

As a condition for the United States blessings of the transitional regime, Meles Zenawi and his counterparts also agreed to pursue a multiparty political system and adopt a constitution that mirrored the United States constitution and majority electoral laws. The liberalization of the Ethiopian political marketplace in the early 1990s created a suitable political atmosphere for the mushrooming of toothless political parties, congesting the marketplace with irrelevant development agendas and party platforms. With very few exceptions, many of the political parties were *ethnogogues*. They were inclined to stir up public emotions, thereby pitting one ethnic group against another and feeding into the erroneous assumption that the sources of conflict in Ethiopia were value-related, as opposed to interest-related. Such deductive fallacies, characterized by lack of theoretical and methodological rigor, reduced the sources of conflict and cooperation to their lowest denominator—ethnicity. Consequently, demands on the state for equitable redistribution of socioeconomic resources and political power have been made by establishing political parties with ethnic slogans and invoking subjective cultural attributes.

To examine whether one nationality group controlled the decisionmaking process and monopolized socioeconomic resources, what is appropriate is not a minimalist or reductionist paradigm. Rather it is a holistic theoretical frame of reference that would enable us to systematically analyze statistical data on the regional or provincial distribution of revenue and expenditure, education and health facilities, manufacturing industries, and construction of roads. A holistic approach would also enable us to analyze how one was appointed to a high-ranking public post during the Haile-Selassie and Mengistu governments. Furthermore, from a systems theoretical standpoint, we should be able to gain an in-depth understanding of how the behaviors of authoritarian regimes have been disguised in the shadow of multiparty democracy. Whether the development, democratization, and redistribution strategies of the current government are grounded on the Ethiopian realities can also be examined by adopting systems analysis as a theoretical framework.

The study is interdisciplinary in its theoretical and methodological approach and includes over twenty figures and contingency tables that are directly relevant to analyzing the distribution of socioeconomic resources and political power from the mid-1950s to 2005. The names and titles of high-ranking officials who were assassinated by the military regime, in 1974, and short biographies of officials who were executed during the first coup attempt against the Haile-Selassie government, in 1963, are also included in the appendix.

One of the book's important contributions to scholarship is its demystification of the notion that socioeconomic resources and political power were distributed along ethnic lines. Unlike most previous studies, this work combines quantitative and empirical data to produce as complete a picture as possible concerning the distribution of socioeconomic resources and political power in Ethiopia. Another area in which the book contributes to scholarship lies in its in-depth and comparative analysis of the dominant theories on the persistence of ethnicity and the sources of conflict in Africa.

In addition, the political environment in which the values of ballots are likely to depreciate and the factors that contribute to the erosion (or reconstitution) of social capital are also other distinctive features of the book. In this regard, the book is designed to help us gain greater understanding of whether ballots, as currencies in a centralized or liberalized economic market, serve as a medium of exchange between the electorate and political parties or candidates. It is also intended to provide some policy-oriented recommendations and to challenge the academic community to search for a suitable model for correcting maldistribution of economic and political power in plural societies such as Ethiopia.

It is hoped that the statistical data presented in the form of contingency tables and line graphs and their analysis would lead to the development of an equity model with practical relevance. Similarly, a list of high-ranking officers of the Haile-Selassie government who were executed by the military regime is included in the appendix with the hope of stimulating scholarly research that would fully investigate their biographies and how they were elevated to such important posts at that time.

This book may be used as a supplemental text for undergraduate and graduate courses in African studies, conflict analysis and resolution, African politics, political economy, ethnic and development studies, and democratization and development in Africa. Finally, even though this study covers a range of issues, a few qualifying statements are in order. As stated earlier, many scholars had little or no hesitation when they assert that there are core and peripheral cultural groups in Ethiopia. They insisted that the core cultural group had culturally, economically, and politically dominated the peripheral groups. Investigation of how the core cultural group socio-culturally disenfranchized all other ethnic groups is not one of the main focuses of the book. Also, for lack of biographical data, backgrounds of members of the 1960s coup leaders as well as biographies of members of the military government are not examined extensively and intensively.

Acknowledgments

I am deeply indebted to my family for their support, patience, and understanding. They sacrificed so much for so long while I devoted my time, energy, and resources to pursue undergraduate and graduate studies since I left my homeland in the early 1980s. No word can fully express how grateful I am to my mother, my sisters, and others in my extended family for encouraging me to explore new grounds in my scholarly journey.

I thank my wife, Sara Abate, for her confidence in me and for standing next to me in times of hardships. I am grateful for her love and advice on personal and professional matters. As my elders say, *Egzier Zefen Yawkal, Yegetmal*. She is truly a blessing from God. I also owe an unplayable debt to my late sister, Tigab, and stepfather, Abate Wube, for teaching me by example the rewards of patience, persistence, and humility. I am forever grateful for their guidance.

I also wish to express my gratitude to my former professors from the African Studies Department at Howard University and the School of International Affairs at Clark Atlanta University for their contribution to shaping and nurturing my intellectual and professional goals. They brought to the classroom an inimitable knowledge base, decades of practical experience, and unparalleled passion for a holistic approach to African Studies and International Affairs. Particularly, I extend my heartfelt gratitude to Professors Mbye Cham, Robert Cummings, Wilfred David, Robert Edgar, Ayo Langley, Sulayman Nyang, Luis Serapiao, and Almaz Zewde (Howard University) and the late Cedric Grant, Mustafah Dhada, and Herschelle Challenor (Clark Atlanta University).

I am especially grateful to Professors Dawit Abebe, Robert Edgar, and Ayo Langley and Ms. Robtel Pailey and Mr. Debay Tadesse for their insightful comments on the final version of the manuscript. My thanks also goes to the Librarians at the Addis Ababa National Archives, Central Statistical Authority in Addis Ababa, and the Addis Ababa University Institute of Development Research.

I also wish to thank Dr. Orlando Taylor, Vice Provost for Research and Dean of the Graduate School, and Gloria Lloyd, Coordinator of Financial Support and Grants Management, for their leadership and the care and attention they have given me throughout my matriculation at Howard University. I thank Professor Haile Gerima for his advice and generosity and for bringing together Ethiopians in the Diaspora and the academic community by organizing such activities as seminars and book-signing events.

Last but certainly not least, I wish to thank my colleagues at the University Press of America. I am grateful to Judith Rothman, Director, David Chao, Acquisitions Editor, and Catherine Forrest, Editorial Assistant, and others for their leadership, superb editorial expertise, and for coordinating the production and promotion of this book.

While acknowledging the contributions of my friends and colleagues to the conception and completion of this book, all errors remain the author's responsibility.

Chapter I

Introduction

For more than three decades, Ethiopia's basic economic welfare indicators such as Gross National Product (GNP) per capita remained constant and, in some cases, deteriorated significantly. The gap in the quality of life between the minority rich and majority poor continues to widen as policymakers and scholars search for a useful poverty reduction, redistribution of socioeconomic resources, and conflict resolution strategies and theoretical lenses. To make matters more complicated, some scholars and foreign aid agencies took a minimalist approach and argued that such extreme socioeconomic resources and political power maldistribution exists between the super-ordinate and subordinate ethnic groups in Ethiopia.[1]

In 1995, Ethiopia was the sixth poorest country in the world with the highest human poverty index. Not surprisingly, between 1989 and 1994, almost 34% of the total population of Ethiopia lived below the $1 per-day poverty line.[2] In 1995, almost 50% (or approximately 28 million) of the population of Ethiopia were between ages 15 to 64 and approximately 80% and 2% of the labor force were engaged in the agricultural and industrial sectors, respectively.[3] Two years after the overthrow of the Haile-Selassie government in 1974, GNP per capita was $100 and increased to $130 in 1987.[4] Since the collapse of the military regime in 1991, GNP per capita continued to decline from $120 in 1989 to $100 in 1995 and 2000.[5]

The significance of these economic welfare indicators can be appreciated when viewed from a historical perspective. The military government of President Mengistu Haile-Mariam took power immediately after the 1973 oil crisis, which exhausted Ethiopia's dwindling foreign currency reserve. In an effort to revitalize and transform the economy, the military government took a socialist ideological path and declared public ownership of the means and distribution of production, thereby denying the public any meaningful participation in the political and economic spheres.

Bilaterally and multilaterally, the international community vainly attempted to pressure the military government to respect the political rights and civil liberties of Ethiopians. Secessionist, irredentist, and nationalist groups were also engaged in guerrilla warfare against the central government, wreaking havoc on the lives of ordinary citizens and diverting the government's attention and the country's scarce resources away from investing in the people to procuring military hardware.

The widening of income gaps between the rich and the poor or, arguably, between members of the super-ordinate and subordinate ethnic groups and lack of improvement in the general welfare of citizens intensified the competition for scarce resources. Particularly, in plural societies faced with structural problems, political entrepreneurs, more often than not, magnify and transform the natural tendency of people to compete for equitable access to scarce resources into primordially rooted ethnic conflict.

The perception of inequity or distributive injustice must be internalized by marginalized group(s) for politically mobilizing one ethnic group of against another. Manipulating the wretched socioeconomic conditions of the majority, discontented group leaders and their sympathizers have been successful in creating a fertile ground for the development of essentialist perceptions against members of the "ruling ethnic group or groups" and deepening public disenchantment towards the state. In so doing, they transformed myths into realities and contributed to worsening the conditions of the majority poor and stimulated inter-ethnic tensions. It is now conventionally and uncritically accepted that "one nationality group, the Amhara,"[6] has dominated the Ethiopian socio-cultural, economic, and political systems. The Amhara has been characterized as "Black Africa's" imperialist ruler,[7] a "feudalist . . . ruling class,"[8] and a "remarkably basic, crude, and exploitative" imperialist ruling elite of Ethiopia.[9]

The indictment against the alleged "ruling ethnic group" ranges from characterizing it as an imperialist power to an outright conviction that this group enslaved and colonized other ethnic groups in Ethiopia. Both by design and default, any demand on the state is understood as a grievance on behalf of minority ethnic groups against the "ruling ethnic group." Demands on the state for equal treatment of minority groups (not necessarily in demographic terms but in terms of socioeconomic stratification) were therefore made by invoking subjective and objective cultural attributes and sometimes by manufacturing common historical experiences and misinterpreting statistical data.

In advancing a secessionist agenda, Ethiopian political elite and their proponents in Western European academic and policymaking circles found it convenient to ignore the absolutist and authoritarian nature of the two previous Ethiopian governments. As totalitarian and dictatorial regimes, the governments of Emperor Haile-Selassie and President Mengistu Haile-Mariam knew no ethnic, religious, geographic, or cultural boundaries in enforcing Imperial decrees and martial laws or in implementing their development policies. Overwhelming empirical data suggest that the governments of Haile-Selassie and Mengistu Haile-Mariam transcended ethnic, religious, linguistic, and other cleavages in appointing individuals to cabinet, civil service, and other high-level posts. Admittedly, the rigid political and economic systems of these two governments provided very little, if any, opportunities for upward social mobility and failed to respond to a growing demand for opening the political marketplace for competition.

Disregarding deductive fallacies, which correlated the totalitarian and dictatorial regimes with Amhara domination, the present government of Ethiopia adhered to the conviction that the Ethiopian socioeconomic and political systems have been characterized by superordinate/subordinate ethnic relationships. Ethiopia's poor economic performance, protracted conflict between the state and secessionist groups, the denial of political and civil rights of the majority, and almost everything else is seen through a narrowly constructed theoretical framework that regards ethnicity as an overarching characteristic of the challenges facing the people of Ethiopia.

Born out of the tinged references to the distribution of scarce resources are the policies and strategies of the Meles government. Rather than tackling the growing disparities between regions/provinces or, even better, between the minority rich and the majority poor, the policies and strategies of the government of Prime Meles Zenawi seek to rectify distortions among ethnic groups. The realities concerning the distribution of tangible and non-tangible resources are far from what has been presented in many of the literature on Ethiopia. Therefore, the erroneous assumption and conclusion on the prevalence of a superordinate/subordinate, dominance/dependence, paradigm "must be put into its proper perspective so that it does not inhibit progress."[10]

The Transformation of Myths into Realities

The Ethiopian Peoples Republic Democratic Front (EPRDF), which came to power in 1991, has taken a broad-based approach to

correct the historically distorted distribution of socioeconomic resources and political power. In 1993, supposedly to facilitate the
redistribution of resources and eliminate or reduce the incidence of
conflict, the current government of Ethiopia divided the country into
loosely defined ethnic regions based on four criteria: consent of the
people, language, settlement patterns, and identity.[11] These criteria
were designed to combine real or perceived segmental cleavages with
geographical isolation and apply the concept of "segmental autonomy"
under a federal system of government.[12]

Prior to the division of the country into regional states in a federal
system, there were fourteen provinces (including Eritrea which had a
population of approximately 3 million) and the capital of Ethiopia,
Addis Ababa.[13] According to the new division of the country, however,
Amhara, Oromo, and Southern Ethiopian Nations and Nationalities
constitute 27%, 36%, 19% of the population of Ethiopia, respectively.
There are six other regions (Affar, Benishangul/Gumz, Gambella,
Harari, Somali, and Tigray) and two self-governing cities (Addis Ababa
and Dire Dawa), respectively. In spite of the effort to place over fifty
ethnic groups in their own geographic enclave, all regional states
remain as ethnically heterogeneous as Addis Ababa and Dire Dawa.[14]

As indicated above, out of the more than fifty ethnic groups with at
least eighty languages, varying degrees of settlement patterns, economic activities, and political aspirations, many scholars accord a
privileged status to the Amhara as a super-ordinate group in the
Ethiopian socioeconomic and political stratification.[15] Members of the
alleged "ruling ethnic group" proudly accepted scholars' classifications, a mythology that placed them at the apex of Ethiopia's socioeconomic and political pyramid. The Amharas may have remained content
with the seemingly prestigious but patently meaningless position for a
number of reasons. Usually, most Ethiopians who believe in divination
and revere their leaders appeal to the Creator rather than engage in a
combative confrontation with their leaders and other ethnic groups to
bring about favorable changes in their living conditions.

Likewise, members of the "super-ordinate" ethnic group also over-
look their destitute economic conditions and political repression. This
was partly because there were no points of comparison against which to
measure their living conditions and partly because they uncritically
accepted their useless social position. It was after the enrollment of
students from the neglected regions of the country in colleges and
universities in Addis Ababa and abroad in the late 1950s that the
monarchy began to experience political resistance, riots, and demonstrations led primarily by members of the "ruling ethnic group."[16] In
this regard, Samuel Huntington may be correct in pointing out that an

"ignorant" traditional society or ethnic group could remain poor and stable.[17] Whatever the explanations are, Amhara elite are partly responsible for the predicament of the group and are as much responsible as secessionist groups for the economic and political crises that characterized Ethiopia over the past fifty years.

As far as other scholars and development specialists are concerned, they either remained simply disinterested in exploring the historical bases, logical consistencies, and empirical accuracy of previous researches or ignored the question of whether or not there existed super-ordinate/subordinate relations along class lines and not between ethnic groups. Some scholars, including Peter Nyong'o and James Scarritt, made oblique references to interethnic relations and the sources of conflict in Ethiopia. Their views and conclusions were based on questionable premises and when the data contradicted their hypotheses, they engaged in cherry-picking and remained "prisoners of paradigm."

Nyong'o, for instance, was of the view that numerous nationalities in Ethiopia "had been brought under the imperial rule of an essentially feudalist Amharic ruling class over the last hundred years." Nyong'o went even further to attribute ethnic conflict to the "Amhara-dominated feudalist ruling class" when he claimed that the regime had created a sense of relative deprivation among Eritreans, Somalis, Oromos, and Tigreans who have or would ultimately demand "the right to some form of self-determination." Interestingly, Nyong'o admitted that Emperor Haile-Selassie was ruling the country "with an iron fist," supposedly to protect the interests of the ruling ethnic group – the Amhara. Apparently, Nyong'o took the term "Amhara" for granted and did not seem to recognize that Haile-Selassie, though the Emperor had tremendous appreciation for the value of ethnic, linguistic, and religious diversity, was more Oromo than Amhara.[18]

Ted Robert Gurr and Barbara Harff had no hesitation in claiming that "the Amharas of the Ethiopian highlands" have "exercised direct influence over the social, cultural, and political lives of their dominions." For Gurr and Harff, the Amhara highlanders undermined the local economies of their subjects by introducing favorable economic activities for the dominant group and that "the conquered peoples were forced into servitude, slavery, or dependency."[19] James Scarritt, for his part, identified the Affars in northeastern Ethiopia, southeastern Eritrea, and northwestern Djibouti as minorities at risk. He also identified the "Amhara" with "imperialism" and insisted that minority groups in Ethiopia were at risk because of the Amhara-dominated imperialist rule.[20]

To the contrary, the military government of Ethiopia granted autonomy to the Affar ethnic group in 1975; thus, the Affar hardly qualify to Scarritt's characterization of minorities at risk. His claims would have been best placed if he entertained the question of whether the Affars in Eritrea and Djibouti and the Bilen, Kunama, Saho, and the Tigre in Eritrea could be considered minorities at risk. Additionally, he did not advocate categorizing the Somali groups in Ethiopia, Kenya, and Somalia, the Gambellas in Ethiopia and the Sudan, or the Massai in Kenya and Tanzania, to mention but a few of the most isolated groups, as minorities at risk in "Black Africa."[21]

Donald Rothchild also asserted that the military government of President Mengistu "allowed one nationality group, the Amharas, to largely dominate the decisionmaking process." He went on to count the number of Amharas that occupied important political positions in the ministries, Standing Committees, and Central Committee of the military regime and claimed to have found that almost all of them were dominated by the alleged "ruling ethnic group." Furthermore, in providing evidence to his contention, Rothchild noted that by the end of 1973, "some 70 percent of Ethiopia's industrial activities were concentrated in Addis Ababa and Asmara [the capital of Eritrea]."[22] Herman Cohen also pointed out that "the Oromos experienced linguistic, educational, and social discrimination from the more powerful Amhara ethnic group that dominated both the Haile-Selassie and Mengistu regimes."[23]

Clearly, there seems to be a deliberate effort at simplifying the sources of conflict as attributable to the concentration of economic and political power in Shoa and its capital city, Addis Ababa, even though the province is ethnically heterogeneous. Indeed, these scholars looked at the Ethiopian situation through the lenses of Western colonialism. As Solomon Gashaw rightly pointed out, "Shoan hegemony is commonly presented as Amhara domination. However, it is erroneous to lump all nationalities included in Shoa as Amhara."[24]

Many of the scholars mentioned here say nothing about the possible marginalization of the majority of the Shoan Amhara by the ruling class, which was as ethnically diverse as the country itself. There are also apparent paradoxes in the assertions of scholars on the primacy of one ethnic group over the majority in Ethiopia. For example, if the peoples of the predominantly Amhara provinces (Gojjam and Begemder) rebelled against the Haile-Selassie government, then the policies of the aristocratic government were as unfavorable to the aspirations of the Amhara as they were to the Affar, Gambella, Kaffa, Somali, Oromo, Tigray, Wolayta, and others. Alternatively, if Eritreans reaped benefits from the authoritarian regimes of the previous era, while the majority of Ethiopians were forced into wretched conditions, then the assumption about the hegemony of the Amhara becomes fundamentally flawed.

Moreover, in the 1970s and 1980s, approximately 2% of the population were employed in the industrial sector. Since the Amharas constituted about 20% of the population of Ethiopia in the 1980s,[25] it would be difficult to maintain that the industrial sector created employment opportunities for a significant number of peoples anywhere in the country let alone the Amharas. Lest we ignore statistical evidence, it is presumptuous to say that this group was the sole beneficiary of the government's industrial development policy.

However weak the analytical tools they employed, whether by design or default, such erroneous generalizations served as a framework for secessionist groups in Eritrea, Tigray, Wollega, and elsewhere to insist that they have been placed at the periphery of the Ethiopian politico-economic hierarchy. For over three decades, Eritrean secessionist groups were at war with the government of Ethiopia. Their separatist movement was in no way designed to bring about an improvement in the living conditions of the majority poor. It was supposedly to free the people of Eritrea from the oppressive regimes of Ethiopia. For the most part, the war appeared to be squarely placed between a "culturally homogenous" people of Eritrea with common historical memories and economic and political aspirations and what was portrayed as an "Amhara dominated" repressive regime of Emperor Haile-Selassie and, later, Col. Mengistu Haile-Mariam.

As Fouad Makki noted, however, there are "nine distinct ethnolingustic communities: Affar, Bilen, Hadareb, Kunama, Nara, Rashaida, Saho, Tigre and Tigrinya" in what was once perceived as a homogenous Eritrean society.[26] Once in power, Isayas Afeworki of Eritrea shifted his strategy from what he claimed as "fighting for freedom and equality" to politically repressing and economically marginalizing the Kunama, Affar, and other ethnic groups in Eritrea.[27] John Young also rightly complained that the government of President Isayas has "denied the nine nationalities living in Eritrea the right to independence."[28] Just as the peoples of Africa have begun to resent their post-independence political elite, there emerged a growing frustration among the peoples of Eritrea over the government's lack of respect for human dignity. Many have come to realize Isayas's hypocrisy and feel even more infuriated than ever before by the fact that he is ruling the country without a constitution.[29]

To be sure, by a political necessity, President Mengistu, Emperor Haile-Selassie, or any of the previous rulers may have surrounded themselves with a few Amhara nobles who were nothing but self-

serving elite. The Amhara's respect for the rule of law, said Donald
Levine, has earned them a unique place in the Ethiopian political
culture and, ultimately, a dominant role in the public sphere. The
Amhara, he argued, are "over-represented" in the school system where
"competition is not affected by ethnic considerations," the armed
forces, and the "great majority of important positions in the government." Levine also pointed out that the over-representation of the
Amhara in the school system, the armed forces, and in the public
services is, "for the most part [by] Amhara of Shoa Province."[30]

Joseph Lapalombara, in his examination of the North/South politico-economic disparity in Italy in the 1960s, suggested that "the further
South one moves, the greater the tendency to seek employment in the
bureaucracy." He concluded that "[t]his preference is directly related to
the lack of alternative job opportunities, to poverty, and to grim
expectations about one's economic future."[31] To the extent that the
Amharas accept their meaningless position in the Ethiopian political
pyramid, like the peoples of Southern Italy of the 1960s, they are
essentially "singing happy ballads" in the face of their socioeconomic
plight.[32] In other words, to the extent that a rigorous analysis of data on
the distribution of political power results in confirming the conventional belief that the Amharas were politically dominant, it is not
necessarily true that the Amhara also dominated the Ethiopian economic landscape.

Moreover, some scholars seem to ignore the authoritarian characteristics of the previous governments in Ethiopia when making their
assertions about the diversion of resources in favor of a particular
ethnic group or region. Emperor Haile-Selassie did not attempt to
renounce his policy of authoritarian rule. The first constitution of
Ethiopia, signed by the Emperor and members of the ruling class on
July 16, 1931, made it clear that "the person of the Emperor [is] sacred,
His dignity inviolate and His power incontestable."[33] This meant that
every individual, irrespective of his/her ethnic background, was
excluded from any meaningful participation in the decisionmaking
processes. This is a norm shared by many authoritarian regimes in
many African countries, a norm that has been conveniently abandoned
for the sake of making sweeping generalizations about the distribution
of socioeconomic resources and political power in ethnically diverse
societies such as Ethiopia.

Furthermore, although Edmond Keller's observation provides
some insight concerning the concentration of industrial activities in two
of the fourteen provinces, his view does not neatly fit the thesis of
Rothchild and others about the hegemony of the "ruling ethnic group."
To the contrary, Keller's work leads to a more fundamental question

about the legitimacy of Eritrea's claim for independence from the repressive regimes of Ethiopia and whether or not the previous governments made a concerted effort at excluding ethnic groups in any part of the country.

What is evident from the discussions so far is that the literature on the distribution of socioeconomic resources and political power among the various ethnic groups in Ethiopia falls short of empirical and logical consistency. Nor does it demonstrate the extent to which there were spin-off benefits to a particular ethnic group or groups during the authoritarian systems of the previous regimes, as Keller, Rothchild, and others maintain, or under the present multiparty political system in Ethiopia. Indeed, the literature on the distribution of socioeconomic resources and political power is nothing more than a political statement, which implicitly contributes to the perpetuation rather than resolution of conflict.

The cumulative effect of such sweeping generalizations based on narrow theoretical lenses and scant empirical data on the formulation of national development policy is profound. It has shaken the very existence of the country as one of the linguistically heterogeneous, ethnically diverse, and culturally and religiously rich nations of the world. It has also eroded the social basis of conflict resolution, development, and democracy.

Policies and Strategies of Redistributive Justice

In line with conventional belief and the perceived dichotomy in the distribution of tangible and non-tangible resources between the "super-ordinate" and "subordinate" ethnic groups, the present administration took such bold steps as promulgating a constitution, liberalizing the economic and political marketplaces, and creating "ethnically" defined regional states. Its purpose is, arguably, to rectify the historically distorted distribution of socioeconomic resources and political power among the diverse ethnic groups in Ethiopia.

By and large, the government's stated objectives are commendable, but its policy instruments for achieving distributive justice may indeed be inconsistent with the historical and contemporary realities of Ethiopia. First, the assertion that there existed a dominant/dependent relationship between the "ruling" and the "oppressed" ethnic groups during the Haile-Selassie government is highly questionable. Second, the notions that the military government allowed one nationality group to dominate the decisionmaking process and that the distribution of social services and manufacturing industries, among others, was largely concentrated in a few of the provinces dominated by the ruling ethnic group are as problematic as the first assertion.

Third, the current government has relied on the primordialist school of thought to implement its policies of distributive justice. The present government has created ethnic enclaves by dividing the country into regional states. The decision reflects the government's assumption that "[s]ocial tensions are ... less readily soluble in pluralistic societies than they are in stratified societies composed principally of an ethnically homogeneous populace."[34] The oversimplification of ethnic identity formation, persistence, and conflict is also manifested in the criteria for drawing boundaries for the administrative regions. Clearly, the division based on the criteria enumerated earlier has a potential to create regional sentiments, but it is inconsistent not only with the realities on the ground but also with the government's own criteria.

For example, does an individual who speaks *Affarigna* identify him/herself with the Affars in Eritrea or Djibouti? Do the Tigrays in Northern Ethiopia that have significantly close settlement patterns and speak *Tigrigna* like the peoples in Eritrea identify more with Eritrea than Tigray or Ethiopia? Answering these questions is not simply a matter of equipping oneself with analytical tools. This issue is so complex and contentious that even some members of the Central Committee (CC) of the Tigray Peoples Liberation Front (TPLF) openly criticized Prime Minister Meles (who belongs to the Tigray and the socially constructed Eritrean ethnic group), for caring less for Tigreans and more for Eritreans. Twelve of the dissenters within the CC, including two members of the House of Peoples Representatives, were expelled in 2003 allegedly for expressing disaffection against Meles for not pursing the war against Eritrea strongly enough and for adopting pro-capitalist policies that are inappropriate to Ethiopian realities.[35]

Fourth, during the 1990/91 London negotiation between opposition parties and the Derg, Meles Zenawi, then chairman of TPLF's Central Committee, pledged to establish "a transitional government representing all points of view [and] only after the adoption of a new constitution and the holding of an election could a new regime implement a program."[36] Consequently, it lifted the ban imposed by the military regime of President Mengistu on the formation of opposition parties which allowed the mushrooming of political parties, thereby undermining the establishment of opposition parties with ideologies and development agendas that crossed ethnic boundaries.

In March 1989, the TPLF merged with the Ethiopian Peoples' Democratic Movement (EPDM) to form the Ethiopian Peoples Revolutionary Democratic Front (EPRDF). The merger was TPLF's attempt to elevate its struggle from secession to a nationwide political movement against the military regime.[37] In May 1991, the EPRDF also incorporated the Oromo Peoples' Democratic Organization (OPDO) that essentially helped the grand coalition party to monopolize the political marketplace.[38]

The grand coalition among the three parties is a major departure from the stated objectives of the government; that is, ensuring equitable distribution of political power and protecting the interests and rights of minority ethnic groups. According to *Africa Watch*, those political parties that attempted to transcend "the system of ethnic federalism . . . continued to face severe restrictions" by the EPRDF, including denial of access to state-controlled media and harassment, imprisonment, and killings of candidates and voters.[39] Moreover, the creation of a political alliance between nationalist and formerly secessionist parties attests to the fact that the primordialist explanation for the sources of ethnic conflict is insufficient. Why the primordialist explanation for the sources of conflict in Ethiopia and in other African countries is inadequate will be closely examined in chapter two.

Fifth, the liberalization of the political marketplace has also resulted in the resurgence of an unprecedented number of political parties accentuating their commitment to defend the interests of their ethnic group. The disproportionately large number of political parties effectively narrows their political base and mitigates against the importance of overarching party platforms such as improving access to quality education and health services that are common concerns of the majority poor. During the May 2000 election, for instance, there were over sixty political parties competing for political space. As a result of the creation of the coalition party and fragmentation of opposition parties, the playing field in the political marketplace remained biased in favor of the EPRDF, thereby significantly minimizing the potential contribution of opposition parties in the development and democratization of Ethiopia.

Lastly, one of the factors that undermined the process of redistribution of political power and that has created much tension and confusion is the adoption of a majoritarian electoral law rather than a proportional representation system. Since each ethnic group's interests are perceived to be distinct from one another—hence the creation of political parties with ethnic emblems—a proportional electoral system seems to be more appealing, if not appropriate, to protect the interests of minority groups in segmented societies.

However, the Constitution and electoral law of Ethiopia clearly make reference to a majoritarian electoral system as the rule governing the competition for seats in the House of Peoples Representatives. Why this is more appropriate than a proportional representation system is defended by the Speaker of the House, Dawit Yohannes, who pointed out that Ethiopia's political and economic situation calls for the establishment of a strong government. Explaining the adoption of a majoritarian electoral system, Dawit went on to suggest that "if we had a proportional system we would have gotten a weak government and unnecessary problems.[40]

Ironically, members of the House of Federation are elected for a five years term in office. Its composition is determined according to "a system of proportional representation where each national and national-ity is entitled to at least one member and one additional representation for each one million of its population."[41] The adoption of a proportional representation system for electing members of the House of Federation is intended to reflect the government's interest in protecting "minority rights."[42] Clearly, the adoption of such an electoral system is rooted in the belief that the best way to ensure equity in the distribution of political power in ethnically diverse societies is to adopt a proportional representation system.

The implication of adopting two electoral systems, proportional representation to protect minority rights and a majoritarian system to establish a strong government, ultimately undermines the importance of the House of Peoples Representatives, which are directly elected by popular vote according to a majoritarian electoral law. This apparent paradox may also have a significant implication for shaping the behaviors of the electorate, party platforms, and multiparty election outcomes and the relationship between the executive and legislative organs, on the one hand, and the judicial branch of the government, on the other.

What has been said so far makes it abundantly clear that a reduc-tionist, minimalist approach has little or no value to understanding and explaining the sources of conflict and whether or not socioeconomic resources and political power were distributed along ethnic lines. One of the major problems identified in this study is the attempt by academics and policy makers to revolve almost everything else around ethnicity in studying a complex system such as the social system of Ethiopia. Furthermore, scholars and foreign development agencies seem to deny historical and statistical data simply because the data did not fit into their minimalist theoretical framework and political agendas. As a result, dynamic interactions that occur in any given social system in most parts of Africa have been seen through the prisms of ethnicity with emphasis on the notion of super-ordinate/subordinate cultural, economic, and political hierarchy.

What is needed therefore is a theoretical lens that would enable us to gain a broader and deeper understanding of the characteristics of the aristocratic and single-party political systems of the two previous governments. Such a holistic, systemic approach is useful in understanding and explaining the overarching criteria employed by the previous governments in appointing their high-level political leaders and allocating public funds for such projects as building schools, roads, manufacturing industries, clinics, and hospitals. The depth and scope of this study also requires a theoretical tool that captures and explains inter- and intra-component interdependencies and interactions that takes place in a liberalized political marketplace. It should also help us understand why achieving equitable redistribution of socioeconomic resources and political power has become more difficult and complex than what the current government originally thought.

Endogenous and Exogenous Forces of Change

Conventionally, policies of any form and substance are formulated based on a set or sets of theories and conjectures. That is, the realities of a given social system are jam-packed in a set or sets of theory from which policymakers seek to extrapolate some desirable policy outcomes. Some developing countries' intellectuals protest such a sequence as theory-then-policy approach and much of the root causes of Africa's lack of economic and political transformations have been explained as emanating from the codification of theories and realities. Indeed, with few exceptions such as during the liberation movement of Guinea Bissau and Cape Verde Islands, led by Amilcar Cabral, the subjugation of many Africans to confirm to foreign ideologies and theories has not only been commonplace but also a major source of socioeconomic havoc and political turmoil.

Ethiopia is no exception. For example, the military government imported an alien socialist ideology of Marxism-Leninism and subjected Ethiopians to live up to the expectation of German and Russian philosophers who never set their foot on Ethiopian soil or even entertained the working conditions of Africans under colonial rule. The outcome of uncritically accepting theories and ideologies by political leaders in many parts of the continent, generally, and in Ethiopia, particularly, has had a detrimental impact on the wellbeing of ordinary citizens.

Similarly, in a society that has possessed and developed a tradition of social and group safety nets, the present government of Ethiopia imported a free market economic theory and promotes individualism while encouraging citizens to identify themselves to a given ethnic group's norms, values, and political aspirations. One of the major flaws in the theory-then-policy precedent is also plainly illustrated by the government's prescription of free market economic principles and demarcation of regional state boundaries, arguably along ethnic lines. On the one hand, free market economic principles encourage competition not only within the nation-state but also regionally and internationally. On the other hand, ethnic markers as boundaries among regional states isolate ethnic groups in their own enclaves, thereby discouraging investment and competition across regional boundaries.

The protection of freedom of the press is another problematic area in which a wholesale adoption of free market principles and liberal democracy is compromized by the absence of qualified journalists and becomes a hindrance on the desire of policy makers to help cultivate a democratic culture. Freedom of the press has been the bedrock both as a measure of political development and as a component that contributes to political, social, and economic transformations. In Ethiopia, the former is more pronounced than the latter in the sense that freedom of the press has been misconstrued as freedom of media personnel to publish and distribute stories even if they are irrelevant to Ethiopian information consumers. Part of such chaotic media behavior is also attributable to the short-lived theoretical obsession which advocated for substantially minimizing the regulatory role of the state in all aspects of society.

Yet, from both theoretical and empirical standpoints, freedom of the press is the right of citizens to express their views, adversarial or otherwise, based on credible sources and acceptable ethical standards. There may have been a dilution of the current government's intention to liberate the press from the legacies of the repressive regimes that restricted freedom of consciousness and expression. Nonetheless, it also suggests that the government may have simply offered carrots with few or no sticks that are often used arbitrarily but introduced to demonstrate its commitment to live up to the expectation of primarily the donor community and perhaps to citizens of Ethiopia. Although this proposition is given due attention in subsequent chapters, suffice it to say that the theories that have been tested in Ethiopia may not necessarily be flawed, rather they may have been applied in an environment that lacks such fundamental ingredients as intellectual capital, bureaucratic efficiency, and ethics in journalism.

To the extent that existing theoretical tools which, more often than not, reflect the interests of advanced societies, are sufficient to understanding a complex social system, the emphasis should not be on inventing wheels. It should rather be on modifying preexisting tools so as to help us explore the socio-cultural, economic, and political landscapes of a developing country such as Ethiopia. The question of where and how concepts, paradigms, theories, and ideologies originated is really immaterial, because some of the theories that have been claimed by outsiders and imported by Africans may have originated in Ethiopia or elsewhere in Africa. For instance, who is to say that the law of comparative advantage and diminishing returns was first theorized in Europe? Some can argue that one of the earliest theorization and applications of the principles of specialization (gold and iron smelting, tool making, weaving, farming, cattle ranching and etc.) and comparative advantage can be found in ancient kingdoms such as Ethiopia where international trade once flourished.

Certainly, the primary concern here is not to stimulate debate over the question of intellectual property ownership or where such concepts, theories, and ideologies originated. What is more important to note is that, whenever possible, domestic realities should influence the framing of theories. Researchers also need to be more cautious in using theoretical lenses which appear relevant when they are indeed inherently defective and inappropriate to gain an in-depth understanding of a given social system.

The historical and contemporary realities of societies across the globe indisputably confirm that no condition, however enduring it appears, is permanent. The historical and contemporary realities of Ethiopia are shaped and reshaped by endogenous as well as exogenous forces of change. The changes that took place in the past and the potential forces that are likely to have an impact on society are conditioned by interlocking and dynamic interactions that occur within a set of boundaries and environments. In particular, there were factors in the socio-cultural, economic, and political systems that dictated decision regarding the allocation of economic and political power. Some were internal, while others were external to the social systems of Ethiopia. The elements that influenced changes in these systems may differ in their magnitude, scope, and outcome. Such complex, dynamic, and multivariate interactions among the socio-cultural, economic, and political systems in Ethiopia can appropriately be examined, explained, and understood by using a systems theory.

Framework of Analysis

The general system may be characterized as "a set of elements that are interrelated"[43] which may go through a "morphostatis" process, a process in which the structure of the system essentially remains intact despite forces or "disturbance" tending to change it. It may also undergo an adaptive process known as "morphogenesis" through which there emerges a change in the structure of the system.[44] As Wilfred David has argued, "[e]very system has a boundary and an environment." While the elements within the boundary of a system directly or indirectly interact with each other and affect the state of the system and the role of its components, "the environment is something outside the system's control [and may partly] determine the system's behavior and performance."[45] That is, isolated events or interactions between elements within a given system may not always bring about structural changes in the general system. A system may undergo a morphostatis or morphogenesis process, depending on whether the interactions between two or more components are significant enough to alter the behavior and performance of the system.

It is widely known that Ethiopia is recognized as the only African country that upset the European expansionist appetite for Africa's natural resources and manpower. Although Ethiopia did not fall under the colonial yoke, it hardly escaped suffering from the consequences of the scramble for Africa. Its indigenous social, economic, and political systems have been transformed, shaped, reshaped, and tainted by the colonization of its neighboring countries which also aggravated border conflicts between them.

During Italy's short-lived occupation of Ethiopia, economic activities essentially stagnated as most of the economically active citizens joined the patriotic movement to defend their country. The catastrophic social consequences of the war, which left behind many widows and countless children without parents, are well documented in Emperor Haile-Selassie's memoir. The Italian occupying forces also dismantled indigenous institutions and, as a result, a new cabinet comprising no more than ten officials was formed in May 1940. Despite these social and political obstacles, the government of Haile-Selassie stretched its scarce resources to rehabilitate war causalities, orphans, and to build new clinics and administrative institutions.[46]

European colonialism in Africa also appeared to have little effect on the sovereignty of Ethiopia, but the reality is simply a matter of degree. For example, the colonization of Somalia and Kenya by Britain and Djibouti by France directly and indirectly affects Ethiopia's territorial sovereignty and national security. There were border clashes between Ethiopia and Kenya which may be attributed to the transnational nature of the ethnic groups who inhabit the disputed areas. Additionally, there are the Somali people, both in Ethiopia and Somalia, who identify themselves as belonging to the same cultural and linguistic groups, but happen to be separated by the historical wrongs of colonial rule. As a result, there were at least two major wars between Ethiopia and Somalia in the late 1960s and mid-1970s which were partly rooted in the irredentist movement of Somali's of the Ogaden region and partly provoked by Mahammed Said Barre's desire to expand Somali's territory.

The early 1970s drought in Ethiopia is also a case in point since its causes may be endogenous or exogenous and its consequences are complex and dynamic. The causes of this drought may be attributed to the civil war, lack of political will to implement land redistribution policy, the use of rudimentary farming technologies, or acidic rainfall caused by industrial activities in Asia and Western Europe. Whatever tool one utilizes in examining the sources and impact of the drought on the people of Ethiopia, the early 1970s drought was certainly one of the major factors for the 1973 uprising which brought about fundamental changes in the political and economic systems of Ethiopia. The same is true with regard to the 1973 oil crisis, which distressed the general public and stimulated widespread demonstration against the Haile-Selassie government.

Another factor that contributed to the transformation of the Ethiopian political and economic systems was the end of the Cold War. The end of the Cold War significantly eroded the clientele/patron relationships between the military regime and the Soviet Union and was one of the major reasons for the downfall of the military regime. What is important to note is that the military regime had no control over what happened outside its "boundary" but had to either adopt or face the consequences of the dynamic interactions between the two superpowers (the United States and the Soviet Union).

The previous governments of Ethiopia were, therefore, confronted with numerous challenges arising from European colonial expansionism, the East-West competition for spheres of influence, and secessionist and irredentist movements in and around the country. All of these development, coupled with poor policy choices, exhausted the country's resources and caused tensions and hostilities within the ruling class and between groups in their struggle to claim their share of the national pie.

To be sure, the government of Meles Zenawi inherited manifold problems that necessitate broad-based approaches and strategies. The interlocking forces that thwarted the development of the country in previous decades may now be more effectively addressed when and if the socio-cultural, economic, and political realities of Ethiopia dictate the policies and strategies of the government. Joseph Stiglitz, for example, argued that the Ethiopian government has formulated sound macroeconomic policies designed to narrow the urban-rural development gap and open the political system for a greater participation of the people in the decisionmaking process. According to Stiglitz, the government had a sound rural development strategy with a focus on

alleviating poverty. Nonetheless, the International Monetary Fund
(IMF) told the Meles government to adopt policies that are logically
inconsistent with the development needs of the country.[47] The IMF may
be characterized as an external agent of change (positive or negative),
but it is an institution with the ability and the will to flex its financial
muscles to influence the domestic policies of Ethiopia. Given the
overbearing power of the IMF, the government of Meles would find it
extremely difficult to resist the IMF's policy prescriptions, however
irrelevant they may be, to cure Ethiopia's economic and social ills.

Likewise, the military government had to capture the social
movement to outlaw private ownership of the means of production and
adopt a socialist ideology, supposedly to dispense social and economic
distributive justice. Some of the elements of change may hinder the
implementation of sound macroeconomic policies. Other factors may
destabilize the political system; and, still others diminish the level of
trust and cooperation between groups. In other words, there are
numerous impulses of change that may originate or be induced
internally or externally and that these elements of change, collectively,
are best depicted, examined, and understood when one adopts an
appropriate theoretical framework such as the one presented here.

The model shown in Figure 1.1 is designed to help us interpret the
dynamics of the Ethiopian economic, socio-cultural, and political
systems. However, only some of the components of the systems are
included the model. Moreover, since the linkages between most of the
elements of the systems are obvious, only a few of the subtle relationships and interdependencies are illustrated here. The model in Figure
1.1 shows that there are linkages between the systems, indicated by the
arrows, through which the elements of the systems interact with each
other. Interactions between elements take place because the systems are
assumed to be open in the sense that "the behavior of the total system,
or any particular subsystem within it" is influenced by endogenous
linkages" and exogenous factors.[48]

To elaborate on the dynamic interactions and interdependencies
among the components of the general system, it can be said that in a
"plural society,"[49] group membership or identity may be based on the
elements in the socio-cultural system (language, religion, lineage,
kinship, and social memories of origin). It may also be based on a
combination of the elements in the socio-cultural with those elements
in the economic and/or political systems. And, depending on how the
leaders of these groups such as those in the input structure find it useful
to express their group identity (or influence changes in the other
systems), societal cleavages along these elements may be consolidated.
Indeed, some ethnic group leaders may invoke one of the elements (for

example, language as in the case of the Oromo) as a distinguishing characteristic of the group.

Generally, some elements are multifunctional while others perform specialized roles to maintain the status quo, "morphostatis," or change the structure of the general system, "morphogenesis." Language and religion may be two such examples of the former. Some elements of the socio-cultural system may directly or indirectly interact and influence changes within the system while others may be inconsequential to the proper functioning of that particular system or to the system as a whole, including economic and political systems.

Figure 1.1: Economic, Socio-cultural, and Political Systems Interactions

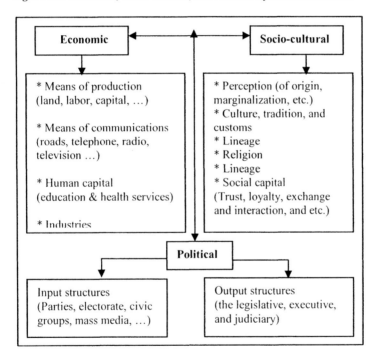

Source: Author.

The political system is divided into two spatial categories, "input and output structures."[50] The system may also be further divided into such categories as aristocratic, militaristic, and multiparty. The structure of the aristocratic rule was characterized not so much by the various properties in the economic system, but by the elements in its socio-cultural system. Even so, some of the components in the socio-cultural system (loyalty, lineage, and religion) were critical factors that shaped the structure, substance, and behavior of the aristocratic rule.

On the other hand, the structure and, consequently, the functional elements of military rule were largely influenced by the economic conditions of the society. That is, the elements in the socio-cultural system played little or no role in shaping the structure of the military government. Rather, the variables in the economic system were the major catalysts in the morphogenesis process that resulted in the formation of a single-party, dictatorial, political system. Unlike the one-party system, the multiparty political system emerged as a result of greater influence by some of the elements of the socio-cultural system such as the perception of relative deprivation and perception of common historical memories, origin, and experiences. In most cases, political elite help generate morphostatis or morphogenesis changes in the three sub-systems analyzed here.

Furthermore, some of the elements in one of the systems may strongly and closely interact with the elements in the other systems while others may not. For instance, mass communication may enhance the performance of the political system and strengthen or weaken the level of trust between actors in the economic and socio-cultural systems. In addition, if education is designed to facilitate greater awareness about the values, traditions, and aspirations of competing groups, then it can defuse some of the elements in the socio-cultural system that lead to conflict and animosity.

Education may also help voters to critically assess party agendas and the value of ballots; and through it, vital information on ways of improving farming techniques may also be acquired. Furthermore, any attempt to understand and explain why Ethiopia's economy remained stagnant or why the country experiences drought more frequently than other countries in the region must take into account whether or not land is designated as private or public property. It also needs to take into account whether the majority of the labor force is skilled, semi-skilled, or unskilled. The role of the input and output structures in the political system may also affect which production input requires closer attention and budgetary support.

In short, the model does not include all the possible elements and systems. It is nevertheless a useful model for a greater understanding and insight into some of the major elements that dictated how socio-economic resources and political power were distributed in Ethiopia. This holistic and systemic approach is also a useful tool to examine and explain some of the major forces that brought about two fundamental changes (in 1974 and in 1991). The framework is equally pertinent to critically examine the degree to which each of the systems facilitate or impede the present government's strategy to equitably redistribute socioeconomic resources and political power among the various ethnic groups or regions.

Notes

1. Donald Rothchild, *Managing Ethnic Conflict in Africa: Pressures and Incentives for Cooperation* (Washington, D.C: Brookings Institution Press, 1997), p.63. See also, United States Agency for International Development "Basic Education System Overhaul Program Assistance and Project Paper," (Addis Ababa: USAID/Ethiopia, September 1994), unpublished document.

2. United Nations Development Programme, *Human Development Report 1998* (New York: Oxford University Press, 1998), p.147.

3. World Bank, *The State in a Changing World* (New York: Oxford University Press, 1997), p.220.

4. See the United Nations Development Programme, *Human Development Report 1992* (New York: Oxford University Press, 1992), p.134.

5. World Bank, *The State in a Changing World*, p.214. See also, World Bank, *The Challenge of Development* (New York: Oxford University Press, 1991), p.204.

6. Rothchild, p.77.

7. James Scarritt, "Communal Conflict and Contention for Power in Africa South of the Sahara," in *Minorities at Risk, A Global View of Ethnopolitical Conflict*, ed. Ted Robert Gurr (Washington, DC: United States Institute of Peace Press, 1993), p.278.

8. Peter Nyong'o, "The Implication of Crises and Conflict in the Upper Nile Valley," in *Conflict Resolution in Africa*, eds. Francis Deng and William Zartman, (Washington, DC: Brookings Institution, 1991), p.98.

9. Herbert Lewis, "Ethnicity in Ethiopia: The View from Bellow (and from the South, East, and West)" in *The Rising Tide of Cultural Pluralism: The Nation-State at Bay?*, ed. Crawford Young (Madison: University of Wisconsin Press, 1993), p.162.

10. Wole Soyinka, "Of Sacred Cows ...," *Mail & Guardian* (Johannesburg) 26 July 2005.

11. "Ethiopian Constitution," July 25, 2000, at <www.sas.upenn.edu/Afri can _Studies/ Hornet/ Ethiopian_Constitution.html>.

12. Arend Lijphart, *Democracy in Plural Societies* (New Haven, CT: Yale University Press, 1977), p.42.

13. During the government of Emperor Haile-Selassie and, later, President Mengistu, Ethiopia was divided into fourteen administrative provinces.

14. See, the Prime Minster's Office, "1994 Population Census," (Addis Ababa: Office of the Prime Minister, 1999), unpublished document.

15. See, Rothchild, p.63; see also, Scarritt, p.278.

16. Teshome Wagaw, *The Development of Higher Education and Social Change: An Ethiopian Experience* (Michigan: Michigan State University Press, 1990).

17. Samuel Huntington, *Political Order in Changing Societies* (New Haven, CT: Yale University Press, 1968), pp.41-2.

18. Nyong'o, p.98. Also, Nyong'o did not seem to be aware of the distinction between the language and the recently constructed name of the ethnic group (Amhara).

19. Gurr and Harff did not make distinctions between the "Amhara colonial power" and European, Han Chinese, and Ottoman Turks colonial agents. From their comparisons, it is evident that they viewed the Amharas as alien rulers as were the Europeans in Africa, Asia, or Latin America. For specifics of their inference, see Ted Robert Gurr and Barbara Harff, *Ethnic Conflict in World Politics* (Boulder, CO: Westview Press, Inc., 1994), p.16.

20. Scarritt, p.278. See also, Eric. J. Hobsbawm, *Nations and Nationalism since 1780: Programme, Myth, Reality* (New York: Cambridge University Press, 1990), p.154.

21. Although the title of his chapter is about minorities at risk in sub-Saharan Africa, Scarritt preferred to use the term "Black Africa" as if there are no whites, Arabs, and Asians in "Black Africa" who may not wish to be lumped together as Blacks.

22. Edmond Keller quoted in Rothchild, p.77.

23. Herman Cohen, *Intervening in Africa: Superpower Peacemaking in a Troubled Continent* (New York: St. Martin's Press, LLC, 2000), p.23

24. Solomon Gashaw, "Nationalism and Ethnic Conflict in Ethiopia," in *The Rising Tide of Cultural Pluralism: The Nation-State at Bay?*, ed. Crawford Young (Madison: The University of Wisconsin Press, 1993), p.142.

25. Estimated from the 1994 regional population census. See, Prime Minster's Office, Data Processing Service Regional Affairs Sub-Sector, "Regional Population Census 1994," (Addis Ababa: Government Spokesperson, 1999). See also, World Bank, *The State in a Changing World*, p.220.

26. Fouad Makki, "Nationalism, State Formation and the Public Sphere: Eritrea," *Review of African Political Economy*, No. 70 (December 1996): 475-497.

27. See, for example, Lussier's discussion on the "Continued Victimization of the Kunama 1991-?," in "A Day to Celebrate a Mass Murderer," 4 December 1999, at <http://www.geocities.com/~dagmawi/News/News_Sep1_Awate.html>.

28. John Young, "Ethnicity and Power in Ethiopia," *Review of African Political Economy*, No. 70 (December 1996): 531-542.

29. "Letter to President Isayas From Eritrean Professionals And Academics," October 13, 2000, at <http://www.telecome.net.et/~walta/conflict/articles/article1407.html>.

30. Donald Levine, "Ethiopia: Identity, Authority, and Realism," in *Political Culture and Political Development*, eds. Lucian Pye and Sidney Verba (Princeton: Princeton University Press, 1965), pp.248-49

31. Joseph Lapalombara, "Italy: Fragmentation, Isolation, Alienation," in *Political Culture and Political Development*, eds. Pye and Verba, p.307

32. Ibid., p.305.

33. Harold Marcus, *Haile-Selassie I, The Formative Years: 1892-1936* (New Jersey: The Red Sea Press, 1998), p.117.

34. George De Vos, "Ethnic Pluralism: Conflict and Accommodation, The Role of Ethnicity in Social History," in *Ethnic Identity: Creation, Conflict, and Accommodation*, eds. Lola Romanucci-Ross and George De Vos (Walnut Creek, CA: AltaMira Press, 1995), p.16.

35. "Ethiopian ruling party confirms divisions," BBC World Service, March 23, 2001, 15:02 GMT.

36. Cohen, p.51.

37. Ibid., pp.22-3.

38. Ibid., p.23. See also, Africa Watch, "Ethiopia and Eritrea: Fratricidal Conflict in the Horn," August 4, 2000, at <http://www.iss.co.za/Pubs/ASR/7.5/Africa%25 Watch.html>.

39. Africa Watch, "Ethiopia and Eritrea: Fratricidal Conflict in the Horn," August 4, 2000. See also, "Intimidation and Harassment Escalates in the South," *Ethio Time*, March 11, 2000, quoted in "Ethiopian Election News-flash," May 9, 2000, at <http://www.mesob.org/elect/parties.html>.

40. Dawit Yohannes, quoted in Kjetil Tronvoll and Oyvind Aadland, *The Process of Democratization in Ethiopia – An Expression of Popular Participation or Political Resistance* (Oslo: Norwegian Institute of Human Rights, 1995), p.13.

41. "The Parliament of the Federal Democratic Republic of Ethiopia," April 9, 2000, at <http://www.ethiospokes.net/Backgrnd/b0409981.htm>.

42. Ibid.

43. Wilfred David, *The Political Economy of Economic Policy* (Westport, CT: Praeger Publishers, 1988), p.175.

44. Walter Buckley, "A Systems Model of Societal Regulation," in *General Systems and Organization Theory: Methodological Aspects*, ed. Arlyn Melcher (Ohio: Kent State University Press, 1977), p.20. See also, David, *The Political Economy of Economic Policy*, p.189.

45. David, p.175.

46. Emperor Haile-Selassie, *Hewotiena YeEthiopia Ermja*, II Tiraz, (My Life and Ethiopia's Progress, Vol. II) (Addis Ababa: Berhanena Selam Printing Press, 1941), p.323.

47. Joseph Stiglitz, *Globalization and Its Discontents* (New York: W.W. Norton & Company, 2002), pp.28-31.

48. David, p.176.

49. Lijphart, *Democracy in Plural Societies*, pp.3-4.

50. Ibid.

Chapter II

The Nature and Resolution of Conflict

Separatist, secessionist, and irredentist movements in Angola, Ethiopia, Mozambique, Nigeria, Somalia, Sudan, Zaire (now the Democratic Republic of Congo) and civil unrest in many African countries in the 1960s signaled the need for a systematic investigation of the sources of inter- and intra-state conflict in Africa. Until the collapse of the ethnically homogeneous state of Somalia, in 1994, many scholars and African as well as non-African policymakers were of the view that ethnic heterogeneity is the source of conflict in Africa. The 1994 genocide in Rwanda seemed to reassert the notion that the main reason for the prevalent violent conflict in heterogeneous societies in Africa is the essentialist perception of ethnic groups against one another, but not the instrumentalization of ethnicity. The present government of Ethiopia was carried away by the growing current of ethnic assertiveness and secessionism of the early 1990s and took the view that the segregation of ethnic groups into their own enclaves is the final solution to ethnic conflict.

Even though one of the realities of African countries—ethnic pluralism—may have helped many observes and scholars to explain away the nature and sources of conflict, some continue to grapple with the basic question of why ethnicity persists in the first place. The persistence of ethnicity has been explained from a primordialist and instrumentalist theoretical standpoint. However one explains the persistence of ethnicity and conflict, Africa remains the only continent faced with the need to develop effective conflict resolution mechanisms.

If one considers the division of administrative regions and the mushrooming of political parties, arguably, to resolve conflict and rectify inequitable distribution of economic resources and political power in Ethiopia, one is left with the impression that ethnic identities are inborn attributes that persist even under adverse circumstances. The very purpose of geographically isolating ethnic groups also leads us to believe that ethnic conflict is irreconcilable and that a viable solution to distributive injustice in political power is through the formation of political parties with ethnic emblems. However, as the subsequent chapters theoretically and analytically demonstrate, political elite play key roles in helping ethnic identities to persist and in steering the source of conflict over access to economic resources and political power towards what appears to be irreconcilable differences and hostilities between primordially distinguishable ethnic groups.

To the extent that ethnic conflict is irreconcilable, it seems reasonable to assume that the numerous political parties that mushroomed following the liberalization of the political marketplace in Ethiopia in the early 1990s would find it difficult to converge towards a common goal. It would also appear that the leaders of these elitist political parties would be unable to submerge their parochial sentiments and narrow political perceptions in favor of achieving a national development objective. Yet, the liberalization of the political marketplace and the formation of the Ethiopian Peoples Revolutionary Democratic Front (EPRDF) transcend cultural barriers to democracy and underscore the fact that, after all, the diverse ethnic groups in Ethiopia were not as antagonistic as we were led to believe.

Indeed, in spite of the current government's "instrumentalization" of ethnicity for political gains, it seeks to promote foreign private investment in Addis Ababa as an exemplary city in which a large number of ethnic groups live in harmony.[1] This should have reminded policymakers of the present government that it is not geographical isolation but formal and informal interaction among competing forces that minimizes the incidence of conflict and enhances peaceful coexistence between groups. To be sure, there are arguments and counterarguments on whether the various ethnic groups in Ethiopia and other African countries are locked in an irreconcilable, primordially rooted, zero-sum game. Theoretical arguments, empirical evidences, and numerous statistical data seem to suggest otherwise. The purpose of this chapter is, therefore, to examine how ethnic identities are formed and transformed and to analyze the sources of conflict as well as the strategies of conflict resolution in plural societies such as Ethiopia.

The Formation and Persistence of Ethnicity

Proponents of the primordialist theory hold that ethnic identity is formed naturally and that every child is born into a distinct ethnic community or group. As such, each ethnic community or group exhibits unique cultural markers and "a strong psychological sentiment of belonging to the group"[2] as well as belief in the similarity of their historical experiences and religious practices. Thus, subjective and objective cultural attributes and behavioral features not only distinguish one ethnic group from another, but the need to protect and promote these attributes is also given as explanations for the irreconcilably of ethnic conflict with a state. In other words, as it is almost impossible to manipulate the human genetic markers, cultural markers are perceived as static, which always distinguish one ethnic group from another. Therefore, ethnicity cannot be wished away and that ethnic conflict can only be managed but not resolved. According to John Furnivall, the management of ethnic conflict in plural societies included the imposition of external forces such as colonial rule.[3] Yet, no empirical data supports the notion that colonial subjugation of indigenous Africans was an effective means of ethnic conflict management or resolution. Indeed, the colonization of Africa did not mitigate the incidence of conflict; rather, it perpetuated and shifted the sources of conflict over access to resources to what appeared to be ethnic in nature.

Advocates of the instrumentalist theory emphasize the role of political entrepreneurs and social engineers in the formation and persistence of ethnic identity and ethnic conflict as well as in the resolution of ethnic conflict. Paul Brass argued that "strong psychological sentiment" and other subjective ethnic markers are too arbitrary and "make it impossible to determine how a group of people arrives at subjective self-consciousness in the first place." Moreover, objective and behavioral ethnic markers may help distinguish one ethnic group from another in a simple society where these traits are "all-pervasive and more evident" than in a complex society. Many of the features that once characterized a simple society have either overlapped, defused, or disappeared due to fundamental transformations of the social and economic landscapes in the past one hundred years.[4] Consequently, any attempt at explaining the formation and persistence of ethnicity as primordially rooted is not only simplistic but it also fails short of taking into account contemporary realities in many developing counties. Thus, the objective, subjective, and behavioral features need not be considered as inflexible symbols of ethnic identities.

Charles Keyes also pointed out that within a particular society there could be two major types of social structures: "symbiotic" and "ethnic minorities" or more precisely "ethnic enclaves." Under the "symbiotic" social structure, different ethnic groups perform different "political-economic functions." At times, the boundaries defined on the basis of "ethnic division of labor" between the various groups may be fixed, while in other cases it may be flexible, depending on the specific objectives a group seeks to achieve. On the other hand, "ethnic enclaves" may assimilate or, if the membership of these groups is sufficiently large, may seek to organize themselves into an autonomous or independent political entity.[5] In addition, an ethnic group may be distinct from other ethnic groups in a plural society, but this does not mean that there is cultural homogeneity within that group. "A culturally homogenous group can be internally divided into descent groups" and still maintain its distinctiveness from other ethnic groups. Furthermore, the absence of the two most visible "emblematic" features of ethnic identity, a common language and religion, does not shake the foundations of the instrumentalist nature of ethnicity. For example, as Keyes noted, slavery, "massive killings in the Holocaust," the systematic and often outright subjugation of Native-Americans and Australian-Aborigines,[6] and the Arab-Israeli conflict deepened a sense of common historical experiences within each group.

Furthermore, the formation of ethnic identities that transcend geographical, linguistic, and religious boundaries can be internalized through "a variety of forms: stories both oral and written, songs, artistic depictions, dramatizations, and rituals." Once internalized, ethnic identity essentially becomes "a variable in social action" and a potent instrument of interest aggregation, especially, when "access to the means of production, means of expropriation of the products of labor, or means of exchange" is determined in terms of ethnic affiliation. As such, ethnicity becomes a factor that contributes to the formation, consolidation, and persistence of ethnic identity. "In other words, ethnicity is a factor in some social contexts because it is perceived by people as a means to overcome . . . alienation."[7] As Robert Bates noted, the ability to extract resources from the public sector or even shielding the group from excessive intervention of the government are determining factors in the persistence of ethnic groups.[8]

In short, ethnic identities are neither static nor intrinsic and are formed and transformed due to changing social and economic circumstances. Indeed, ethnic identities are results of complex and dynamic interactions between members of a community and between groups. Ethnicity may be an inborn attribute and, yet, some attributes persist while others diminish in importance. The persistence of ethnicity, therefore, is a social construct and ethnic identity persists so long as it serves to differentiate one ethnic group from others or as a means of aggregating collective interests. It also needs to be noted that the fact that there are diverse ethnic groups in each African country does not establish a correlation between the incidence of ethnic conflict and ethnic diversity.[9] People simply do not tear themselves apart "on account of coming from different ethnic groups,"[10] but they do so in response to a sense of marginalization or when ethnicity becomes a political instrument.

The Sources of Conflict

In situations where an ethnic group maintains some of its unique cultural features, language, and/or religion, these cultural features are bound to be exploited by elite in their competition for scarce resources including political power. If a widely spoken language becomes an official language of a country, primarily to facilitate the process of economic development, then opposition groups may "emphasize slight differences of dialect which will serve the same purpose of differentiating the group from others."[11] For example, Oromo elite, "[f]inding themselves in a situation that demands ethnic political solidarity, not found in Oromo tradition . . . strive to 'create' a national identity by invoking shared cultural elements, such as language."[12]

In the late 19th century, Shoan Oromos, in alliance with Amhara and Tigray aristocrats, expanded their territorial acquisition southward to incorporate the largely pastoralist communities (Arsi) of Arussi province in southern Ethiopia. According to Karl Eric Knutsson, the Shoan Gala (Oromos) and northern Amharas, which were immigrant communities in Arussi, "shared a basically common value system dominated by Orthodox Christianity." However, there were visible differences between the two immigrant communities. The Shoan Oromo tended to be bilingual, polygamous, and "exhibit a dual pattern of both Orthodox Christianity and ecstatic tribal cults led by the *kallus,*" while the Amhara are monolingual, monogamous, and strictly adhere to Orthodox Christianity. Despite these differences between the two groups, the Arsi identified them as essentially belonging to the same group and referred to them "either as Sidama (the Arsi word for Amhara)" or as Shoan people. Knutsson also observed that although the Shoan Oromos did not identify themselves as Amhara in their "intercommunication" with the Arsi people, "they certainly dichotomized the lowland cattle people from themselves and acted towards them as did the Amhara."[13] Consequently, these immigrant communities have come to be recognized, not as two different ethnic groups, but as an ethnic group known as Sidama.

A territory, which could dictate the characteristics of an ethnic group's social organizations and economic activities, may also be invoked to claim distinctiveness of one group from others. For instance, many of the cultural features including language, religion, customs, and dance among the people in the Tigray region are quite similar to the cultural attributes of most ethnic groups in Eritrea. But, separate territory provided one of the justifications for Eritrea's secession from Ethiopia as well as for the absorption of the Affars into Eritrea based on an arbitrary territorial boundary set during Italy's brief occupation of Ethiopia, including Eritrea. Furthermore, the inculcation of secessionist sentiments among Eritrean elite and the protracted civil war between the central government of Ethiopia and separatist groups in Eritrea illustrate the making of Eritrean identity and the erroneous overture that colonial rule defuses internal rivalry.

Furthermore, even though the Haile-Selassie government seem to have allocated dis-proportionally larger funds to Eritrea for its economic and military strategic importance, cultural, linguistic, and religious similarities between the peoples in the province of Eritrea and Tigray have come to be de-emphasized by the former and overemphasized by the latter. In other words, even though the majority of the people in both provinces speak Tigray and have almost identical cultural markers, these similarities were conveniently ignored by Eritrean elite in their attempts to create an Eritrean national identity. More often than not, Eritrean elite exhibit an attitude of superiority vis-à-vis their relationship with the people of Tigray province. On the other hand, just as the colonial (under)development policy created a sense of relative deprivation, so did the government of Haile-Selassie between the people of Eritrea and Tigray provinces.

Until the mid-1990s, Eritrea was known as ethnically homogeneous region that was denied of access to economic resources and political power and, generally, the right to self-determination. After the separation of Eritrea from Ethiopia in 1993, the notion of ethnic homogeneity and the perceived marginalization of the people in that region, which was widely accepted by advocates and opponents of Eritrea's claim for self-determination, became manifestly inconsistent with the realities of that region. Indeed, there were never any ethnic group known as "Eritrean," and one wonders as to whose right to self-determination has been achieved as a result of the separation of Eritrea from Ethiopia. Additionally, is there any theoretical argument and/or empirical evidence why the majority Ethiopians did not participate in the referendum over Eritrea's right to self-determination, as do Canadians in response to grievances over the right to self-determination of Quebec?

Nevertheless, as Tekle Woldemikael argued, in spite of the fact that there exists a range of similarities and differences within the people of Eritrea, they are dichotomized as Christian highlanders and Muslim lowlanders. There are multiple variations within these highland and lowland communities in terms of "languages, religions, castes, ethnic ties, regions, and ways of life," and they are "overlapping, intersecting, [and] complex arrangements."[14] When the leadership finds it necessary, any of these cultural variations are invoked either to consolidate or weaken group solidarity. For instance, the Kunama and Nara ethnic groups in Eritrea are believed to be the original inhabitants of western Ethiopia and southern Sudan. These two groups rarely intermarry and there is a dominant/dependent relationship between them. While the Nara, the dominant group, "are entirely found in Eritrea, the Kunama have spread into Tigray and Begemdir provinces of Ethiopia."[15] Clearly, it is difficult to assert that these two groups share common historical memories that unite them together or with the larger Eritrean society. Nonetheless, neither Eritrean nor Tigray secessionist groups recognized the often conflicting and diverse ethnic groups within these provinces.

In some respects, this is also true in the case of the Arsi and "Sidama," on the one hand, and the Arsi and Laki, on the other hand. In the case of the former, there are not ecological boundaries that serve as an instrument of differentiation between the two groups. The Arsi are "sons of the soil,"[16] while the Sidama are immigrant communities. In the case of the latter, the Arsi and Laki are homeland communities and yet they articulate their differences largely based on agricultural "technological advancement" which sets the dichotomization of ethnic identification in motion. While differences may have existed prior to the emergence of the immigrant communities, those with better farming tools have been able to retain and expand control over farmlands, increase productivity, and become a favorable ally to the Sidama groups, making open conflict between the Arsi and Laki a common phenomenon.[17]

Hiroshi Matsuda's study of the Koegu, Kara, Nyangatom, and other groups in the lower Omo river basin in southern Ethiopia demystifies the notion that ethnic group identities are inborn and rigidly defined. He demonstrated that although the Koegu are the original inhabitants of the river basin area and the Kara are the immigrant community, "the two groups are not distinguishable from each other by appearance, body ornaments, clothing, hair-style, or anything else."[18] The Koegu "have no cattle and depend on cultivation, fishing, hunting and gathering," while the Kara are mainly subsistence farmers. Although there are taboos, disdain, and contempt between the two groups, they established an alliance—Karo—and fought against outsiders including the Nyangatom (until 1988) and the Turkana that inhabit the lands along the border between Ethiopia and Kenya. While their economic activities complemented each other's needs, intermarriage did not take place between the two groups. Taboos and disdain may be responsible for the absence of intermarriage between the two groups, because the Kara characterize the Koegu as "baboons," "'stinking people' who usually ate fish, and 'poor people' who had no cattle."[19]

On the other hand, although there were intermittent conflicts between the Koegu and Nyangatom, the two groups, perhaps to reduce tension between them, had a long history of intermarriage. It is interesting to note that alliance and alignment shifted from rivalry to cooperation and vice-versa between the three groups discussed above. The "leaders of the two groups [Kara and Koegu] had quarreled over the distribution of goods brought to them by aid organizations and the government of Ethiopia" in October 1988, which resulted in the shifting of the alliance between the Kara and Koegu to Nyangatom and Koegu groups. Matsuda also noted that the Nyangatom had been frequently raided by the Turkana who are also pastoralists. For the Nyangatom, like the Massai of Tanzania, their identity is largely defined by possession of cattle. The possession of cattle is so significant in the cultures of the Nyangtom and the Massai that even the subjects of songs, riddles, and stories are cattle. The Karas, on the other hand, insist "in regarding themselves as pastoralists, [although] they have no cattle, only a few goats and sheep, and subsist mainly by cultivation."[20] This perception, which may be termed as the *Kara paradox*, brought them in conflict not only with the Turkana but also with the Nyangatom group. This conflict of interest in symbols of identity may be responsible for the establishment of an alliance between the Koegu and the Nyangatom against the Turkana.

The Somalis in Ethiopia, Kenya, and Somalia, the Affars in Djibouti, Eritrea, and Ethiopia, and the Massai in Kenya and Tanzania are a few of the ethnic groups that attempt to maintain cultural, behavioral, and subjective attributes to separate themselves from others. In the late 1970s, there were efforts by the military government of Ethiopia to resettle communities from arid and drought-stricken areas of the north to fertile lands of the south, which is largely occupied by pastoralists. The northerners resisted the settlement program, insisting that it would fundamentally alter their way of life such as moving from subsistence to cash crop farming. In addition, the military regime's efforts to enhance its access to one of the largest sesame farmlands in Setit Humera (formerly in Gonder province) by changing seasonal roads into all-weather roads, was viewed as a military strategy to help speed the deployment of armed forces to subdue the region.

Aili Mari Tripp also noted that the Tanzanian government, in the 1960s, had attempted to abolish "the traditional dress of the Massai men without consulting them." The villagization program in Tanzania also included the forced settlement of "backward pastoralists" so that they could benefit from public services, including health and education programs. The settlement of the pastoralists would mean, on the one hand, redefining Massai identity by something else other than ownership of cattle. On the other hand, it was supposed to increase availability of farm lands for subsistence and cash crop producers which, according to Tripp, was designed to favor cultivators and increase government revenue.[21] For the Kara, Turkana, Koegu, Massai, to mention but a few, "[e]conomic factors contribute in a complex manner to ethnic definitions and identity maintenance"[22] and, consequently, define the nature of conflict between groups.

Secessionist groups in Tigray and Eritrea also formed a strategic alliance in the 1980s against the military regime. Following the collapse of the military regime in 1991, the military alliance expanded to include diplomatic and economic cooperation between the two states, which later collapsed due to the "border conflict" between Ethiopia and Eritrea in 1998. The formation of an alliance took place despite the Eritrean elite's long held repugnance toward the Tigrays as wanderers and a poverty- and drought-stricken people. And yet, in spite of some observable aversions between the elite of the two groups, they were able to cooperate against a common enemy—the Derg. There were also cross-ethnic marriages between the diverse ethnic groups in Tigray and Eritrea; witness, for instance, the consanguineal relations between Prime Minister Meles Zenawi and President Isayas Afeworki. The prevalence of cross-ethnic marriages suggests that taboos and disdain are manufactured largely for the purpose of strengthening group solidarity and may be abandoned in the absence of external threat. Similarly, the formation of alliances among the various political parties and between secessionist parties of pre-1991 Ethiopia suggest that ethnicity is a social construct and could be submerged for strategic reasons.

Management or Resolution of Conflict

Secessionist movements in Congo, Ethiopia, and Nigeria and civil unrest in many African countries in the 1960s signaled the need for a systematic investigation of the sources of conflict. The realities of African societies—ethnic pluralism—served as a building block for the development of various paradigms, including communalist, plural-society, and the modernization-assimilation gap to explain the sources of conflict and propose ways of dealing with ethnic conflict. Common to these paradigms was the assumption that multi-ethnic societies are prone to violent conflict which, in turn, impedes economic development and political stability. The resulting policy frameworks were, therefore, designed to resolve conflict through the gradual elimination of ethnic diversity, such as through assimilation or separation of ethnic communities, which may have once lived together peacefully, into ethnic Bantustans. Secessionist movement leaders and advocates which, more often than not, rely on primordialist explanation of the sources of ethnic conflict, insisted that a lasting solution to conflict in multi-ethnic societies is the assertion of self-determination. Consociationalism, internal colonialism, and hegemonic exchange paradigms gained some currency as theoretical frameworks to explain the sources of ethnic conflict. Consociational and hegemonic-exchange paradigms favor the management of ethnic conflict through an emphasis on elite cooperation and equitable distribution of political power among elite with the view to regulate and reduce the frequency of ethnic conflict.

Ethnic pluralism is a result of conquest and annexation, European colonial rule, decolonization, nation-building, and migration.[23] These historical processes are major factors for the present multi-ethnic characteristics of African societies. Migration is one of the phenomena that contributed to ethnic diversity in industrialized and developing nations over the past one hundred years while conquest and annexation are phenomena within which small communities become absorbed into a demographically larger and politically and militarily more sophisticated group.

One may find international law an appropriate point of departure to explaining the extent to which conquest and annexation are responsible for ethnic diversity and heightening ethnic conflict in Africa. Having recognized the importance of international law in the formation of nation-states, through conquest and annexation, one finds discussion of the colonial legacy and the nationalist movements of the 1960s virtually inescapable in discourses that seek to identify the sources of conflict in Africa. The historical processes will be discussed briefly followed by an examination of the various approaches to ethnic conflict management.

Rising above Parochial Sentiments

For over seventy-five years, European colonial rulers played one ethnic group off against another to prolong their direct and indirect subjugation of the peoples of Africa. The British and Belgian policy of indirect rule, for instance, recognized "traditional authorities," with varying degrees of autonomy but always under "supervision and statutory" regulations by the colonial administrators. French and Portuguese colonial policy, on the other hand, implemented a policy of assimilation with the view to dismantling traditional political systems and creating a culturally European-Africans in Africa. The colonial policy of direct and indirect rule was partly dictated by the extent to which "the traditional political system" was clearly articulated and defined. Where "the traditional political system was less articulated," such as the Ibo in Nigeria and the Kikuyu and Luo in Kenya, the colonial policy of annexation and domination was more direct than in other situations. In other words, "direct rule has been employed in those areas where the government commands effective authority; indirect rule in the case of the more powerful chiefdoms."[24]

These differential colonial policies within a given territory and across regions not only derailed the process of the development of indigenous political systems but also favored individuals and chiefs belonging to a particular ethnic group, thereby germinating the seeds for a system of social and economic stratification based on ethnicity. Consequently, any movement against colonial rule had to overcome the deep-rooted divisions between ethnic groups and garner popular support to shake off the shackles of colonial rule. As Crawford Young argued, during the struggle for independence, "excessive preoccupation with ethnicity indeed risked playing into the hands of the imperial enemy."[25]

In the immediate aftermath of independence, as during the liberation struggle, many African leaders attempted to rise above primordial sentiments and seize the nationalist spirit to promote national, regional, and continental integration. Kwame Nkrumah's Pan-Africanism, Julius Nyerere's home-spun socialist ideology of *Ujaama* with an emphasis on class rather than ethnicity, and Leopold Senghor's theory of negritude are testimonies to African leaders' efforts to dampen the forces of ethnic cleavages. The decision to headquarter the Organization of African Unity in Ethiopia was designed as an illustrative emblem of successful resistance to colonial rule. Writings by African leaders and intellectuals on the glories of "the medieval kingdoms of Ghana and Mali" and Cheikh Anta Diop's view of "Africa as sources of civilization"[26] were intended as expressions of pride and remarkable achievements by the peoples of Africa. All of these were calculated strategies to promote unity and common political outlooks.

African leaders and scholars drew lessons from the experiences of the United States and the Union of Soviet Socialist Republics on the benefits of unity in accelerating the modernization process and were more preoccupied with the notion of integration, nation-building, and modernization and less with the question of ethnic division.[27] African leaders and scholars firmly believed that the rate of ethnic conflict depreciates as the rate of "modernization" accelerates.[28] Conversely, the absence of significant inroads in the provision of education and health services, increase in per capita income and industrial employment, and greater participation of citizens and the media in the decisionmaking process tend to fan conflict between the ruled and their rulers.

Neither modernization nor nation-building was achieved, and the result was the evaporation of the euphoria that followed independence and the rise in the rate of civil unrest, political instability, and economic stagnation. At the center of these social, political, and economic phenomena is the authoritarian state that dictated how, when, and where goods and services are produced and distributed. The impact of the centralization of economic and political resources on deepening the crises in Africa is well articulated by Naomi Chazan. She observed that dwindling and maldistribution of resources and chronic poverty have resulted in "self-encapsulation," cynicism, and alienation. These, in turn, have weakened the "symbolic significance" and viability of the state.[29]

Deliberate emphasis on primordial differences between groups conceals the weakening of the "symbolic significance" and viability of the state. Consequently, the ruling class became associated with a particular ethnic group, shifting the focus of the sources of the crises from the ill-conceived public policy to primordially rooted ethnic hostility. In other words, the sources of conflict in many African countries have been perceived as "value-related" (conflict between cultural groups) rather than "interest-related" (conflict between the state and social, economic, and political organizations).[30] Eghosa Osaghe, for example, claimed that every ethnic group in Africa is primordially rooted and therefore "cannot be eliminated, suppressed or wished away."[31] However, it needs to be noted that the main reason for attributing conflict to differences in values is that the elements of culture are subjective and could easily be manipulated by political entrepreneurs.

It should also be recognized that the sources of conflict may not be easily isolated as either "value-related" or "interest-related, because value-related conflicts may, by design, converge with interest-related conflicts. There are a number of cases where such a convergence has taken place. For example, European colonial rule had both a primordial and instrumental component to it. Colonial rule had a primordial element, in the sense that it was designed to replace African traditional values with Western culture. The exploitation of Africa's human and natural resources to the benefit of the colonial rulers was also an interest-related objective of colonialism. The Ethiopian and Tanzanian governments' policy of villagization in the 1960s and 1970s, though intended to improve the economic conditions of the people, was viewed as a threat to the very survival of the groups concerned, both economically and culturally.

Is Conflict a Zero-sum Game?

The emphasis on the management or resolution of ethnic conflict is not simply a semantic difference between primordialists and instrumentalists. These terms—management and resolution—define the theoretical underpinnings between primordialists and instrumentalists. From the primordialist point of view, ethnic conflict is inherent in the nature of things and, therefore, can only be managed but not resolved. Some even go as far as suggesting that conflict, after all, is not entirely undesirable for it is "the root of personal and social change."[32] As Mohamed Rabie noted, conflict management is a process in which parties to the conflict and third parties as a mediator devise strategies to "bring conflict under control" while conflict resolution is a process to end conflict.[33]

In addition, Rabie asserted, to say that a conflict is resolved is to suggest that the outcome of the settlement is fair and equitable to all parties involved in the conflict. However, due to "the multiplicity of parties and issues involved," parties to the conflict cannot be fully satisfied with the outcome of the negotiation.[34] This is the same as saying that competition is adversarial and cooperation is non-adversarial. Irrespective of these distinctions, "conflict is seldom objective, meaning that the gain of one party is the loss of the other."[35] In other words, whether the sources of conflict are value- or interest-related, adversarial or non-adversarial, parties to a conflict are locked in a zero-sum game either in absolute or relative terms.

If competition and conflict are perceived and internalized as irreconcilable, then each contending group tend to eliminate one another as the ultimate solution to distributive injustice. Expression of anger or hostility occurs when a person internalizes that his or her rewards (output) are not proportional to his or her contribution (input) and that others have been rewarded more than their contribution to the social exchange. In his critique of George Homans' equity theory, Morton Deutsch argued that "the basic concepts of the equity theory—'outcomes' and 'inputs'—are deplorably vague."[36] It is difficult, for example, to measure with greater precision the outcomes from investment in networking that takes place between individuals and social groups. An individual may invest in building trust with another person in the hope of improving his/her leverage in future competition with an adversarial or non-adversarial person (or group). Those at the receiving end of this social exchange may not necessarily have similar expectations from or reciprocate in the exchange, making the concept of distributive injustice more difficult to measure than it already is.

Conflict viewed as irreconcilable differences between competing groups makes the concept of equitable redistribution of resources almost meaningless. Furthermore, the notion that ethnic conflicts are irreconcilable is at odds with the capitalist conception of competition for political power and access to public resources, and runs opposite to the capitalist system of development and democratization that has been embraced by post-Cold War African leaders. It is a Leninist conception of conflict, which sought to promote the dictatorship of the proletariat and the emergence of a classless society—communism. According to Vladimir I. Lenin, conflict between the proletariat and the capitalist class is irreconcilable and the end of exploitation of the majority by the minority can only come about by dismantling the state apparatus.[37] A recent interpretation of the Leninist conception of conflict from an essentialist, antagonistic, point of view is the theory of internal colonialism. Let us now closely examine the various paradigms of conflict management/resolution.

Paradigms of Conflict Management

Michael Hechter suggested that a society could be divided into core and periphery cultural groups (super-ordinate and subordinate cultural groups). Regardless of the instrumental nature of ethnic identity and ethnic consciousness or favorable allocation of resources to formerly neglected areas, the peripheral cultural groups take an essentialist perception of their relations with the culturally dominant group or groups.[38] For subordinate groups, which may have been subjected to internal colonial rule, the question is not simply acquiring material resources but maintaining their cultural identity that may, in some cases, be threatened by the expansion and deepening of the modernization process. Modernization, however conceptualized, creates the basis for redefining new cultural boundaries, group loyalties, patterns of competitiveness, and collective self-awareness where none existed before.[39] Where it did, it is more firmly established by imposing new rules and obligations to discourage the pursuit of individual interests and protect group identity and solidarity.[40]

In underdeveloped societies, ascription rather than role differentiation is emphasized in characterizing inter-ethnic adversarial or non-adversarial relations, thereby compartmentalizing political, civic, and economic institutions on communal grounds. Since states in underdeveloped countries "cannot cope with social mobilization and are unable to satisfy the aspirations they generate," elite and ethnoregional leaders find the communal setting convenient for agitating resentment against the state. Disputes may arise between the state, on the one hand, and

elite and ethnoregional leaders, on the other hand, over the allocation of
resources and appointment of public officials, even if the redistribution
policy is based on "corrective equity." Eritrea is a case in point where
separatist movement leaders, "motivated by the search for power, privilege and economic gain,"[41] exploited ethnic symbols and historical
memories to assert the right to self-determination, even though the
province received a significant proportion of industries during the
Haile-Selassie government.

Proponents of the plural society approach argued that whether one
prefers to look at conflict from the standpoint of internal colonialism or
communalism, the fact remains that multi-ethnic societies are politically unstable and, consequently, cannot develop economically. Proponents of the plural society approach suggested that the inability of the
state to check competition between groups for access to economic resources and political power is the cause for the fragmentation of society.[42] Therefore, fragmented societies, as John Furnivall argued, could
be held together by the iron fist of colonial rule.

Since colonial rule is no longer an alternative, M.G. Smith posited
that plural societies could be held together in one of three ways: uniform, equivalent, or differential incorporation.[43] Uniform incorporation
may lead to assimilation, while differential incorporation is based on
super-ordinate/subordinate relationships among ethnic groups. For obvious reasons, peripheral cultural groups are unlikely to accept ether
methods of managing conflict. To a certain extent, as Ganguly and Taras maintained, equivalent incorporation seemed to hold the key for
bringing about stability and viable democracy in multi-ethnic societies.[44] However, since regions within a state are not equally endowed
with natural and human resources, those with greatest potential in natural and human resources may dispute equivalent incorporation (consociational formula) as biased against the interests and survival of their
group.[45] From the plural-society approach, it can be inferred that neither uniform, equivalent, nor differential incorporation are suitable
models for resolving ethnic conflict. Consequently, states in plural societies seeking to hold fragmented societies together must put up barriers to mitigate against inter-ethnic interactions, such as the kind of segregationist policy adopted by the current government of Ethiopia.

Consociational Democracy

Any attempt at managing or resolving conflict must take into account the dynamic forces that led to conflict in the first place. Arend
Lijphart argued that in a plural society, a society divided by segmental
cleavages such as religion, ideology, language, territory, culture, race,

or ethnicity, the tendency for conflict between the different segments of the population is greater. Such tendencies for conflict, however, are "counteracted by the cooperative attitudes and behaviors of the leaders of the different segments of the population." Therefore, "elite cooperation is the primary distinguishing feature of consociational democracy."[46] However, as Eghosa Osaghe noted, "it is unusual to find people tearing themselves apart simply on account of coming from different ethnic groups, even if the groups combine but do not mix."[47]

There is a growing interest in exploring whether the existence of multiethnic groups within a given society is responsible for the persistence of conflict. For example, Paul Collier, Ibrahim Elbadawi, and Nicholas Sambanis argued that "the relatively higher incidence of wars in Africa is not due to ethno-linguistic fragmentation, but rather to high levels of poverty and, especially, to failed political institutions." Ethnic diversity is less likely to be a cause for intensified and frequent conflict in Africa, "provided that ethnic groups are formally integrated into the political process."[48] In other words, the structure of cleavage is an important element that determines the intensity and incidence of conflict. For example, if "the religious cleavage and the social class cleavage crosscut to a high degree, the different religious groups will tend to feel equal." On the other hand, if the two cleavage structures coincide, then "one of the groups is bound to feel resentment over its inferior status and unjustly meager share of material rewards" and, therefore, the incidence of conflict between the two groups is intensified.[49]

Lijphart argued that "A game is a good game when the outcome is in doubt and when the stakes are not too high."[50] In fragmented systems, in which individual or collective interests are articulated on the basis of non-crosscutting affiliations, for instance, along ethnic, religious, cultural, language, and other primordial emblems, the stakes are too high. It can be inferred that the political game in such a system is a "bad game" and the outcome of the competition for the right to rule is predetermined. "Political parties are the principal institutional means for translating segmental cleavages into the political realm."[51] Thus, political parties may invoke segmental cleavages to agitate the politically useful cleavages and deepen the degree of conflict. They may also place greater emphasis on crosscutting cleavages and overarching loyalties such as nation-building and nationalism to reduce the incidence of conflict and bring about political stability.

There is the assumption in Lijphart's *Consociational Democracy* model that political parties are reflections of the nature of interests in a given society. Some heterogeneous societies may have overlapping memberships in a social group while memberships in others are sharply defined in accordance with the number of groups that define their affiliation in variety of ways. If memberships in a social group are over-lapping, then political parties tend to "adopt moderate positions" in an effort to increase their support and probability of winning the political game. In contrast, if membership in a social group is defined along primordialist attributes in multi-ethnic societies, then political parties dissipate to represent the diverse interests of the groups. Consequently, "[t]he larger the number and the smaller the size of the parties in a system, the less effectively the aggregation function will be performed."[52]

In less fragmented but ethnically diverse societies, or even in the most homogeneous societies such as Great Britain and Sweden, a grand coalition may be necessary in times of crisis—World War I, World War II, and the Gulf War.[53] Julius Nyerere also observed that it is an accepted practice in times of emergency for opposition parties to sink their differences and join together in forming a national government.[54] Such an emergency is nowhere more apparent than in Ethiopia and other African countries where the establishment of a viable democratic system is threatened by the promotion of unproductive cultural, linguistic, and ethnic elements. As a result, if Lijphart's thesis on the factors affecting the effectiveness of political parties is accepted, political parties in Africa are performing a minimal role in articulating the interests of their constituents and in contributing to emergence of a viable democratic system.

To enhance the effectiveness of political parties in responding to internal or external threats, "the formation of a grand coalition cabinet or an alternative form of elite cartel is the appropriate response to" fragmentation of the system into "hostile subcultures." Lijphart stressed that consociational democracy is a viable alternative to a two-party or multiparty majoritarian system when certain interrelated conditions are satisfied. Elite must have the willingness to tolerate and accommodate diverging interests, to transcend cleavages, to have a commitment to the maintenance of the system, and to have an understanding of the stakes for opting-out or -in of the coalition. Although many scholars attributed African conflicts to "distinct lines of cleavages," Lijphart saw such cleavages in a positive light and argued that "distinct lines of cleavages" are, in fact, "vital to the success of consociational democracy" as it is the foundation of elite cooperation and internal cohesion of the subculture.[55]

Internal cohesion of the subculture is a leverage to a party that seeks to represent the political interests of a social group vis-à-vis other competing forces, including the state. When a group is in the majority or if there are two groups with evenly matched subcultures, the leaders of the group in each of the two cases may prefer to achieve their goal by domination rather than cooperation.[56] The tendency to opt-out of a grand coalition scheme is also greater among groups of dominant or minority subcultures which may lack internal cohesion. When the subcultures are all minority groups, elite tend to take a pragmatist perception and harbor less fear and mistrust toward competing groups. In such cases, dissent, allegiance, or cooperation is expressed through political parties that are formed along class in seeking access to political power and public resources to their constituents.

Hegemonic Exchange

Donald Rothchild, in his effort to refute consociational democracy and propose an alternative model, begun with the assessment of African economic realities. He argued that in middle-Africa, distributable resources are scarce and, as a result, the competition for favorable allocation of resources is intense. Rothchild noted some of the weaknesses of consociational model when he said:

> Consociational democracy's expectation of open party contestation, irrespective of hard- or soft-state circumstance, appears to run at cross purposes with the African dominant elite's general perception of the need, during a transitional period at least, for a unitary state and party control.[57]

In addition, the experiences of many African leaders during the struggle for independence suggest two critical points: First, they were able to "sink" their ideological, strategic, and other differences for the common good—liberating their people from colonial rule. Second, they were willing and able to enter into "hegemonic political exchange" with the colonial powers to shake off the colonial yoke. During the colonial period, some traditional political institutions were accorded legitimacy within the parameters of the colonial political structure and received favorable treatment from the colonial power. This enabled them to be formidable threats to post-colonial states in Africa.[58]

Nonetheless, the process of independence was more accelerated when liberation movements formed a unified front against the colonial powers than when they were fragmented along ideological or regional lines. That was in the 1950s and 1960s when differences between the colonial powers and liberation fronts and movements were clearly visible on both sides. After independence, some African elite followed a similar pattern in that they were undermining ethnic or class-based political participation in an attempt to promote national consciousness and solidarity. Those countries that adopted a single-party political system, for instance, Uganda under Milton Obote, Zambia under Kenneth

Kaunda, Kenya under Jomo Kenyatta, and Cote d'Ivoire under Houphouet-Boigny, improved the legitimacy of the state through "state-facilitated coordination" of hegemonic exchange.[59]

State-facilitated hegemonic exchange takes place between the state and ethnoregional spokesmen "on the basis of commonly accepted procedural norms, rules, or understandings."[60] The informal mechanism of hegemonic exchange differs from the formal process described above in that there are no set rules and procedures to govern the exchange process. In effect, it is "behind-the-scene negotiation" which requires credibility and trustworthiness between the negotiating parties. Credibility and trustworthiness are results of repeated interactions, be they formally or informally, between competing or rival groups.

The state, recognizing its limitations, grants some autonomous status and economic incentives to ethnoregional leaders in exchange for "support and compliance with the state's regulations." Another objective of the state in crafting hegemonic exchange strategy is not simply to extend the legitimacy of the state beyond the confines of the metropolitan areas, which in and of itself is a profound weakness of contemporary African states. It is also to reduce "the scope for open manifestations of vertical as well as horizontal inter-group conflict." The state, through the formal procedures of conflict management, is also engaged in mediating inter-group conflicts and co-opting ethnic-based factions to maintain or bring about political stability. Therefore, from the point of view of the state, hegemonic exchange is a political necessity.[61]

Just as the state weighs its alternatives and constraints, ethnoregional groups also evaluate the costs and benefits associated with engaging in hegemonic exchange with the state. Until recently and only in the case of Ethiopia, the international community discouraged ethnoregional secession. The state, lacking in effective coercive mechanisms, took advantage of the international community's reluctance to entertain self-determination claims by secessionist movements as leverage to induce ethnoregional groups to formally or informally engage in political exchange with the state. For self-proclaimed ethnoregional spokesmen who may wish to reward themselves with political power, perhaps even benefit from "the goods of modernity, they have little option but to operate within the confines of the state" and exchange support and compliance for autonomy and public resources.[62]

At the sub-regional level, the people at the periphery exert pressure on their representatives to gain access to public resources. Consequently, ethnoregional leaders play critical roles in linking the periphery with the center and become regarded as defenders of the interests of their people. Recognition of mutual need is, therefore, a necessary condition for formal and informal hegemonic exchange between the state

and ethnoregional leaders. To be sure, government authorities and ethnoregional leaders do not always perceive hegemonic political exchange as a positive-sum game. Government authorities and ethnic
group leaders may harbor essentialist perceptions of each other, making
the process of hegemonic exchange "extremely difficult to initiate and
sustain."[63] For instance, the right to self-determination has been perceived by many African governments as a non-negotiable demand, with
the exception of the government of Ethiopia during the transitional period in the early 1990s.

Summary and Concluding Remarks

Arend Lijphart and Donald Rothchild have developed consociational and hegemonic-exchange approaches, respectively, to provide a
conceptual framework for the integration of ethnic groups into the national political process. Both Lijphart and Rothchild place a high pre-
mium on the state and the African elite for reducing and managing conflicts over social, economic, and political resources. The essence of
their argument for the formation of a grand coalition, a result of elite
cooperation, lies in their fundamental premise that a majoritarian system of democratic model may be inappropriate for societies that are
deeply fragmented on the basis of ethnic, religious, and class cleavages.
In particular, as Rothchild argued, the consociational model leaves out
informal mechanisms of mutual accommodation, negotiation, and cultural norms and traditional systems of exerting pressure on the state that
are central to conflict resolution in post-independence Africa.

In addition, the consociational model presupposes the legitimacy
of the state and its administrative capacity to enforce rules, norms, and
regulations to govern competitions in the political game. The consociational model also assumes some degree of productive economy and
institutional capacity to lift the burden off "the decisionmaking apparatus" and willing and able elite to implement development policies effectively and to "solve the political problems of their country."[64] In
other words, for the consociational model to be an effective tool for
managing conflict, countries must improve their economic productivity
and institutional capacity, preconditions that are lacking in many African countries, making the consociational model almost useless. Moreover, opposition political parties in Africa are usually perceived, at
least from the point of view of the state, as obstacles to national integration with nonnegotiable demands and diverging priorities and interests.

Rothchild, on the other hand, appeared to be sympathetic to African governments and is cognizant of traditional methods of conflict

management and economic and institutional underdevelopment. Nonetheless, the informal procedure of hegemonic exchange between the
state and ethnoregional leaders is an arbitrary method of conflict management and distribution of public resources. Nepotism, corruption, and
inequitable distribution of resources are likely to result from "behind-
the-scene" negotiation and mediation between competing forces. In
addition, the hegemonic exchange model does not differentiate the intensity of conflict in societies where a group is in the majority or if
there are two groups with evenly matched subcultures, as Lijphart
rightly pointed out.

Moreover, the formation of political parties as group interest ag-
gregators allows some degree of upward social mobility. And, since
election is one of the core components of the consociational model,
political parties that are able to extract resources from the state are rewarded while others are punished through voting mechanisms. However, in the hegemonic exchange model, there were no considerations
of how ethnoregional leaders come into the political scene in the first
place. A more grave weakness in the model is that once these ethnoregional leaders come into the political scene, they are there to stay just
as central government authorities are. In other words, since distributable resources are extremely scarce, once ethnoregional leaders secure
some form of legitimacy and power, they retain such privileged status
and power as long as tensions and conflicts exist between members of
the group and the state or among competing ethnic groups.

Rothchild suggested that the effectiveness of these ethnoregional
leaders may be measured by their abilities to draw on resources that are
available from the state. This is an important point to note, but the
model does not provide an alternative means for peripheral groups who
may believe that they are not receiving their fair share of the national
pie. What happens, for example, when a new generation of elite and
ethnoregional leaders emerges in the political arena that may have divergent outlooks on how their people are being ruled? Co-option may
be a temporary solution, but such an arbitrary system is inconsistent
with long-term objectives of bringing about political stability and economic development.

The assumption that the state can be an arbitrator and mediator to
manage conflicts between competing groups is simply unrealistic. For
various reasons, the state may in fact instigate conflict, directly or indirectly, between competing ethnoregional groups and among ethnic
groups within a region. It may do so directly by its "unofficial practice"
of recruiting individuals for civil service positions, providing favorable
treatment to a particular region under the guise of "corrective equity,"
and by responding to "powerful ethnoregional demands."[65] Indirectly,

the state may play one ethnic group off against another to create breath-
ing room for itself, enhance its credibility, and, ultimately, consolidate
its hold on power. In short, the state is not an "impartial umpire"[66] even
if the conflict appears to be between non-state actors.

Furthermore, ethnic conflict is not a zero-sum game where the
gains of one group are derived at the expense of another. The transformation of conflict from interest-related to value-related, or a combination of both, and from cooperation to antagonism is not necessarily
dependent on whether the state is soft or hard in executing its resource
distribution and conflict resolution policies. Africa provides a mixture
of examples where one finds states with enormous capacity and resources to reduce and resolve conflicts and, yet, unable to contain inter-
group and state-ethnoregional conflict. There are also soft-states which
effectively reduced and resolved inter-ethnic and state-ethnoregional
conflict over the distribution of economic resources and political
power.

The ability of states to maintain and promote peace and stability is
partly dependent on the political will and commitment of the leadership. It is also partly dependent on whether the creative minds of policymakers, traditional leaders, and indigenous civic association leaders
are explored and exploited for the benefit of the society concerned.
Short of entertaining the views of traditional leaders and enabling
emerging political elites to express their views, however adversarial it
may be, would be purely a bandage to fix structural problems. It should
also be noted that the crowding-out of indigenous civic organizations
and the growing inclination of many African states to align themselves
with foreign "development" or aid agencies erode their internal legitimacy and ability to play the role of umpire.

Notes

1. "The Regions of the Federal Democratic Republic of Ethiopia," 4 December 1999, at <http://www.ethiospokes.net/Backgrnd/b0311981.htm>.

2. Rajat Ganguly and Raymond C. Taras, *Understanding Ethnic Conflict:
The International Dimension* (New York: Addison-Wesley Educational Publishers, 1998), p.9.

3. John Furnivall, *Netherlands India: A Study of Plural Economy* (New
York: Macmillan Publishers, 1944), p.448.

4. Paul Brass, *Ethnicity and Nationalism, Theory and Comparison* (Newbury Park, CA: Sage Publications, 1991), pp.18-9.

5. Charles Keyes, ed., *Ethnic Change* (Seattle: University of Washington
Press, 1981), pp.12-13.

6. Ibid., pp.7-9.

7. Ibid., pp.9-12.

8. Robert Bates, "Modernization, Ethnic Competition, and the Rationality of Politics in Contemporary Africa," in *The Politics of Cultural Sub-Nationalism in Africa*, eds. Donald Rothchild and Victor Olorunsola (Boulder: Westview Press, 1983), p.161.

9. Ted Robert Gurr's data show that sub-Saharan Africa has cultural (2.1), political (1.8), and economic (1.8) differentials as opposed to the global mean 2.5, 1.83, and 2.24, respectively. The region has much lower cultural, political, and economic differentials than Asia, Latin America, Western Europe and Japan (except in political differentials, 1.2 for this region), and North America and the Middle East. For analysis of the data, see Ted Robert Gurr, *Minorities at Risk: A Global View of Ethnopolitical Conflicts* (Washington, DC: United States Institute of Peace Press, 1993), pp.38-43.

10. Eghosa Osaghe, *Ethnicity and Its Management in Africa: The Democratization Link* (Lagos, Nigeria: Malthouse Press, 1994), p.3.

11. Brass, p.15.

12. Katsuyoshi Fukui and John Markakis, *Ethnicity & Conflict in the Horn of Africa* (Athens, OH: Ohio University Press, 1994), p.9.

13. Karl Eric Knutsson, "Dichotomization and Integration, Aspects of inter-ethnic relations in Southern Ethiopia," in *Ethnic Groups and Boundaries, The Social Organization of Culture and Difference*, ed. Fredrik Barth (Boston, Massachusetts: Little, Brown and Company, 1969), p.92.

14. Tekle Woldemikael, "Eritrean Nationalist Movements," in *The Rising Tide of Cultural Pluralism, The Nation-State at Bay?*, ed. Crawford Young (Madison: The University of Wisconsin Press, 1993), p.182.

15. Ibid., p.184.

16. Rajat Ganguly and Raymond Taras, Understanding Ethnic Conflict: The International Dimension (New York: Addison-Wesley Educational Publishers, 1998), p.9.

17. Knutsson, p.93.

18. Hiroshi Matsuda, "Annexation & Assimilation: Koegu & their Neighbours," in *Ethnic & Conflict in the Horn of Africa*, eds. Katsuyoshi Fukui and John Markakis (Ohio: Ohio University Press, 1994), p.53.

19. Ibid., p.54.

20. Ibid., pp.52-58.

21. Aili M. Tripp, "The Political Mediation of Ethnic and Religious Diversity in Tanzania," in *The Accommodation of Cultural Diversity*, ed. Crawford Young (New York: St. Martin's Press, 1999), p.52.

22. George De Vos, "Ethnic Pluralism: Conflict and Accommodation, The Role of Ethnicity in Social History," in *Ethnic Identity: Creation, Conflict, and Accommodation*, eds. Lola Romanucci-Ross and George De Vos (Walnut Creek, CA: AltaMira Press, 1995), p.21.

23. Ganguly and Taras, p.12.

24. James Coleman, "The Politics of Sub-Saharan Africa," in *The Politics of the Developing Areas*, eds. Gabriel Almond and James Coleman (New Jersey: Princeton University Press, 1960), pp.257-8.

25. Crawford Young, "Evolving Modes of Consciousness and Ideology: Nationalism and Ethnicity," in *Political Development and the New Realism in Sub-Saharan Africa*, eds. David Apter and Carl Rosberg (Virginia: University Press of Virginia, 1994), p.73. See also, Julius Nyerere, "African Socialism: Ujamaa in Practice," *Black World* (March 1974): 211-18.

26. Young, p.69.

27. Kwame Nkrumah, *Revolutionary Path* (New York: International Publishers, 1973), pp.222-3.

28. Robert Bates used the conventional definition of modernization as "education, per capita income, urbanization, political participation, industrial employment, and media participation." He may also have added the provision of health services and improvement in transportation and communication systems as variables in measuring modernization. See Robert Bates, "Modernization, Ethnic Competition, and the Rationality of Politics in Contemporary Africa," in *The Politics of Cultural Sub-Nationalism in Africa*, eds. Donald Rothchild and Victor Olorunsola (Boulder, CO: Westview Press, 1983), p.152.

29. Naomi Chazan, "Ethnicity in Economic Crisis: Development Strategies and Patterns of Ethnicity in Africa," in *Ethnicity, Politics, and Development*, eds. Dennis Thompson and Dov Ronen (Boulder, CO: Lynne Rienner Publishers, 1986), pp.137-58.

30. Mohamed Rabie, *Conflict Resolution and Ethnicity* (Westport, CT: Praeger Publishers, 1994), p.22.

31. Osaghe, p.5.

32. Rabie, p.21.

33. Ibid., p.50.

34. Ibid., p.25.

35. Ibid., pp.50-1.

36. Morton Deutsch, *Distributive Justice, A Social-Psychological Perspective* (New Haven, CT: Yale University Press, 1985), p.25.

37. Viladmire I. Lenin, 2nd ed., *The State and Revolution, Marxist Teaching on the State and the Task of the Proletariat in the Revolution* (London: Communist Party of Great Britain, 1925).

38. Michael Hechter, quoted in Alexis Heraclides, *The Self-Determination of Minority in International Politics* (Portland: Frank Cass, 1991), p.8.

39. Rene Lemarchand, "Ethnic Violence in Tropical Africa," in *The Primordial Challenge, Ethnicity in the Contemporary World*, ed. John F. Stack, Jr. (New York: Greenwood Press, 1986), p.190.

40. Michael Hechter, *Principles of Group Solidarity* (Berkeley: University of California Press, 1987), p.41.

41. Ibid.,p. 9.

42. Stephen Ryan, quoted in Ganguly and Taras, p.15.

43. M.G. Smith, quoted in Ganguly and Taras, p.16.

44. Ganguly and Taras, p.16.

45. John Furnivall, quoted in Ganguly and Taras, p.16.

46. Arend Lijphart, *Democracy in Plural Societies* (New Haven, CT: Yale University Press, 1977), p.1.

47. Osaghe, p.3.

48. Paul Collier, Ibrahim Elbadawi, and Nicholas Sambanis, "Why Are There So Many Civil Wars in Africa? Prevention of Future Conflict and Promotion of Inter-Group Cooperation," Paper prepared for the UNECA Ad Hoc Experts Group Meeting on "The Economics of Civil Conflicts in Africa," (Addis Ababa) April 7-8, 2000. Unpublished document.

49. Lijphart, *Democracy in Plural Societies* (New Haven, CT: Yale University Press, 1977), p.75.

50. Lijphart, "Consociational Democracy," in *Consociational Democracy: Political Accommodation in Segmented Societies*, ed. Kenneth McRae (Toronto: McClelland and Stewart Limited, 1974), p.79.

51. Lijphart, Democracy in Plural Societies, p.88.

52. Lijphart, "Consociational Democracy," pp.72-3.

53. Ibid., p.78.

54. Nyerere, quoted in Lijphart, p.78.

55. Lijphart, p.84.

56. Ibid., p.81.

57. Donald Rothchild, "Hegemonial Exchange: An Alternative Model for Managing Conflict in Middle Africa," in *Ethnicity, Politics, and Development*, eds. Dennis L. Thompson and Dov Ronen (Boulder, CO: Lynne Rienner Publishers, 1986), p.95.

58. Ibid., p.68.

59. Ibid., p.72.

60. Ibid.

61. Ibid., pp.71-83.

62. Ibid., p.84.

63. Ibid., p.89.

64. Lijphart, p.81-2.

65. Rothchild, p.95.

66. Osaghae, p.7.

Chapter III

Political Market Liberalization

One of the most important differences among emerging democracies is whether there is a fairly balanced playing field for political parties to compete in the political marketplace. This aspect of political democracy is one of the key components of what Guillermo O'Donnell referred as "horizontal accountability." Another critical element of political democracy is the extent to which a given political system is designed to provide citizens the opportunity to hold their representatives accountable, individually through regularly held elections and collectively through civic engagement, the media, and other agents of accountability. These may be broadly termed as instruments of "vertical accountability."[1]

In the final analysis, both forms of accountability, directly and indirectly, define what democracy is and is not. While democracy is simply defined as "rule by the ruled,"[2] O'Donnell noted that some scholars insist for a more inclusive definition of democracy or distinction between social and economic justice and political democracy. He maintained that democracy should be defined on the basis of some form of balance between the two extremes without, of course, excluding some of the universal and critical elements that are necessary for the consolidation of democracy. The rule of law, he argued, is one such variable that must be taken into account in distinguishing political systems with or without substance.[3]

Stated differently, O'Donnell was on the view that some elements of a political system are too critical to exclude while others may be less important in differentiating one system from another. In his view, the definition of democracy should be less rigid so as to take into account the economic and cultural differences that exist among nations. This may seem an attempt to settle the debate between those who emphasize such preconditions as culture or economic development as a springboard to leapfrog from non-democratic to democratic rule. More importantly, O'Donnell is on target in recognizing the usefulness or irrelevance of some of the local, as opposed to universal, criterion to define or measure progress towards democracy.

Samuel Huntington is one of the leading scholars who viewed democracy from a cultural perspective. He maintained that any discussion about democracy must begin with an elaborated synthesis of whether or not democratic culture is inherent in a given society. In one of his seminal works, *Political Order in Changing Societies*, he argued that there is a dialectical relationship between the culture of society and political institutions. Deficiency in mutual trust is a "formidable obstacle to the creation of public institutions"[4] that are key to formulating and implementing such policies as economic and political liberalization. "Historically," Huntington observed, "there has been a strong correlation between Western Christianity and democracy."[5] Arend Lijphart and Carlos Waisman also insisted that cultural factors are the main impediments in the transition to democracy. They argued that many of the developing countries in Latin America and the transitional economies in Eastern Europe have a "weak democratic tradition, and thus the legitimacy of the new political institutions is fragile."[6]

Comparatively, if Christianity has a strong correlation with democracy, then Ethiopia and Egypt, not just the city-states of Greece, would have been the birthplaces of liberal democracy. Francis Fukuyama, in examining political developments in Asia, argued that there is not a theoretical explanation why some cultures are conducive to democratization and the establishment of effective political and economic institutions while others are not. Fukuyama insisted that, after all, Confucianism has not been an impediment to creating capitalist societies in Asia. According to him, Christianity played very little role, if any, in Asian societies' political culture or for these societies to become a dominant economic force in the world. It is, therefore, conceptually irrelevant to rigidly attribute democracy with cultural or religious heritage.[7]

Furthermore, if Christianity is one of the preconditions for democracy, then it would have been impossible to conduct fair and free elections, for example, in Mali, Nigeria, and Senegal where 90%, 50%, 92% of the population are respectively Muslim.[8] Similarly, if one is to expect democracy to prevail in the Middle East, then one has to induce the conversion of the majority in that region to Christianity well before one can even talk of toppling charismatic leaders in Iran and Saudi Arabia. Fortunately, however democracy is brought about, most scholars are conscious of the fact that democracy's core and defining elements include both the protection of political rights and civil liberties.

Axel Hadenius saw democracy from a different set of theoretical lenses. In *Democracy and Development*, Hadenius investigated the extent to which democracy is associated with a country's economic performance. One of his findings suggests that the greater the military expenditure, the lower the economic performance and, consequently, the probability of success in institutionalizing democratic rule. He also observed that there is a positive correlation between the rate of investment in social and economic sectors, on the one hand, and democracy, on the other. For example, "the literacy rate in the population appears as the most decisive" factor for democratization. However, Hadenius noted that his study of the relationship between economic performance and democratization is inconclusive. He argued that in many developing countries the connection "between modernization and democracy is far more weaker than has been reported in earlier studies."[9]

Brian Smith maintained that the two greatest threats to democracy in developing countries are militarism and religious fundamentalism. According to Smith, militarism and religious fundamentalism are invoked in response to a new order that favored the concentration of material resources and political power in the hands of a few ruling elite.[10] Ironically, what Smith identified as the two greatest threats to democracy are also institutions that inculcate respect for hierarchy, order, and promote a culture of discipline. There may be some components in military and religious institutions that could be transformed into useful elements for politically socializing former military officers and religious fundamentalists. These characteristics of military and religious establishments that could contribute to the consolidation of pro-democratic political culture may include mutual trust, resolve and conviction to a cause, and a sense of interdependency.

Some of the explanations and, indeed, the distinctions made between Western and non-Western religions arise from the notion of the separation of church and state. Implicit in conventional assumptions regarding these institutions is that they are inherently conflicting. Religion has often been the watchdog of political and economic corruption where the clergy is dissociated from the ruling clique. In other cases, especially in most parts of Africa, religion has been an effective instrument of suppression. As Smith argued, religion and militarism have been two of the greatest impediments to democracy in developing countries, because they were instruments of coercion and control. As instruments of control and domination, both may have also contributed to the erosion of public confidence toward the political system.

What can be inferred from the discussions so far is that there is really nothing inherently conflicting between militarism and religion, on the one hand, and the flourishing of democratic institutions, on the other hand. Indeed, many of the Presidents or Prime Ministers of the oldest democracies in the world (for example, France, Great Britain, and the United States) were Generals in the navy or the airforce. In the United States, the majority of individuals elected to the Presidency or the Congress have served in the armed forces at various capacities. One can also find similar instances in other nations where elected officials were *almost* career officers in the armed forces.

Of course, there were and still are junior military officers such as Idi Amin Dada of Uganda, Hosni Mubarak of Egypt, and Flight Lieutenant Jerry Rawlings of Ghana, and Mengistu Haile-Mariam of Ethiopia who insisted that politics and economics do not mix well. They claim that priority should be given to building an economically well-off society before they allow the expression and exercise of political rights. There are also those leaders in Africa such as President Olusegun Obasanjo and Jerry Rawlings who came from a military background and took courageous leaps to move their respective country closer to democracy. Furthermore, it was during Emperor Haile-Selassie's era that Ethiopians were first introduced to parliamentary elections and, at least from a conceptual but not from a practical standpoint, the notion of government by the people.

If one accepts the proposition that cultural differences are socially constructed, then it is possible to deconstruct those aspects of non-democratic cultures and economic behaviors to lay the foundation for political democracy. In this regard, Robert Dahl's in-depth analysis of the United States political system is instructive. He argued that accepting limits that are beyond the control of human beings, "limits that are imposed by nature's laws," is a sign of wisdom. "But to accept as real, limits that are imposed only by our minds, is not wisdom but self-inflicted blindness."[11]

Dahl went on to state that the new capitalist order has also displaced the agrarian order, which was "extraordinarily congenial to democracy," in a way the framers of the United States Constitution never dreamed of. The private sector took the economic leverage and autonomy away from the United States farmers, directly, by transforming the means of production and shifting the production relations in their favor. It also denied the economic freedom of the majority indirectly through the "president, who could increase, organize, and exploit all the political resources of the office"[12] to advance the interest powerful corporations in the country. The major obstacle to democracy is, therefore, a "self-inflicted blindness," accepting economic deprivation and political

repression under the guise of satisfying the economic and cultural preconditions to democracy.

To be sure, the majority of African governments were as guilty as
the colonial rulers in suppressing political freedom which, according to
Claude Ake, thwarted economic growth and development as well.[13] To
keep themselves in power, African leaders deliberately stimulated ethnic divisions in an attempt to undermine public demand and pressure
for accountability of government officials. "Besieged by a multitude of
hostile forces that their authoritarianism and exploitative practices had
engendered," African elite "were so involved in the struggle for survival that they could not address the problem of development."[14] Collier and others concurred with Ake when they stated that "improvements in the political front are prerequisites for stable economic growth
and other development policies."[15]

Formulating policies and devising strategies for one segment of the
social system, as if progression or regression of a sub-system has nothing to do with the performance of other sectors, clearly demonstrates
lack of vision and commitment on the part of policymakers. It seems
advisable, especially for developing countries, to harmonize relations
among the economic, socio-cultural, and political systems as entities in
a collective whole.

For over one hundred years, the peoples of Africa demanded political and economic freedom, but it was only after the end of the bi-
polar world that their demands brought about changes in political attitudes among authoritarian regimes. Even so, many of the countries that
recently liberalized their political marketplace are neither economically
developed, had a long tradition of pro-capitalist mentality, or are
strictly followers of Western Christianity and its accompanying values,
behaviors, or ethics. Thus, the global resurgence of democratic movements in developing countries is a serious challenge to scholars who
associate democracy with either the level of economic development or
Western tradition and religion or both.

The implementation of economic liberalization policy by many African governments was truly a departure away from the conventional
belief that Africans are captivated by "anti-capitalist mentality." In the
political realm, Africans are not simply insisting for political openness
and the institutionalization of a multiparty political system but, more
importantly, for the adoption of a political system that ensures that both
political parties and voters are meaningfully participating in the political marketplace. Even though most people in developing nations yearn
for self-rule, it is worth noting that their demand for government by the
people seems to be on hold until such preconditions as the transforma-

tion of their underdeveloped economies and traditions, cultures, and religions are satisfied.

The fact that Ethiopia is one of the poorest countries in the world should not lead scholars and policymakers to opt for a repressive regime that would, arguably, lay the foundation for the democratization of that country. No regime in Africa was as dictatorial and repressive as the military regime of Ethiopia was and, yet, Ethiopia is neither democratic nor economically advanced. Furthermore, there is no guarantee that economic development is a necessary and/or sufficient condition for democracy. The conceptual incarceration of most scholars is even more apparent when one considers the differences that exist among Western nations in their level of economic advancement and diversity in their cultural and religious practices.

In order to promote the wholesale adoption of Western democratic systems and cultural norms, the diversity of the social, economic, and political systems that exist among many developing nations has been seen as a curse. This is particularly so for many of the African countries which are perceived not only as culturally backward but also as societies with rudimentary economic and political institutions. Such presumptuous and crude generalizations are often made in the absence of evidence and scientific study on the voting patterns of the electorate or how differences in institutional capacities, religion, level of economic advancement, and/or culture contribute or hinder the consolidation of democracy in Africa.

The Competition for Political Power

When political parties enter into the political marketplace, they are usually driven by the desire to gain access to political power with the objective of advancing their personal and/or the collective interests of their constituents. Under ordinary electoral circumstances, the total number of votes cast in favor of a party is a good measurement of a party's achievement in the competition for access to political power. Thus, "the electoral market"[16] is part and parcel of the competition for political power. To the extent that the value of a ballot does not depreciate as a result of a highly imperfect political market, the electorate partly determines who wins and loses in the competition for political power. The electorate cast their ballots with the hope that the political party or the candidate of their choice will voice and protect their interests in the legislative and other decisionmaking organs of the government. In light of what is being stated here, the driving force for political parties to compete amongst each other is to rise to political power.

One of the most complex problems facing scholars is, however, explaining the motivations and patterns of voters in different political markets—competitive, less competitive, or highly imperfect. For example, to what extent does the parties' platform influence the decisions of the electorate to cast their ballots for one party rather than another? How do we know that voters are provided with credible information that would enable them to make meaningful choices and decide which political party to vote for? Another crucial subject of interest is the management and regulation of the political marketplace within which "political ideas" are exchanged for ballots. That is, is the judiciary or the electoral board sufficiently independent and have the capacity to manage the national political market and regulate the behaviors of political parties that may undermine the spirits of democracy? And, finally, what does the competition for political power and the voting behaviors and motivations of the electorate mean for conflict resolution and democratization in Ethiopia and in other democracies in transition?

Critics of the Ethiopian political process often focus their attention on access to mass media and the various strategies adopted by the ruling coalition party to frustrate opposition parties from participating in the elections. Researchers, domestic- and foreign-based civil society organizations, and election observers have also been more interested in assessing the fairness of the political marketplace and the outcome of elections than entertaining the question of what motivates voters to participate in elections in the first place. More often than not, elections in many parts of Africa are perceived as "ethnic voting," block voting, or "ethnic census."

While this characterization may hold true in some cases, the ramification and the ways in which such elections are conducted (characterized as "ethnic voting" or the survey of ethnic groups through their voting pattern) has not been critically examined. Furthermore, little or no attention has been paid to investigating whether the essence of a party's platform differs from other party platforms that are competing for political power within a given political marketplace. In the following sections, we will examine the nature of political party platforms and how institutions could facilitate a level playing field in the political marketplace as do in the economic arena. Ultimately, one of the objectives of the following sections is to stimulate further investigation of the electoral process and the voting patterns of African societies under different economic standards and culture.

Since the liberalization of the political marketplace, following the end of military rule in 1991, three multiparty elections were held in Ethiopia in May 1995, 2000, and 2005. During the first multiparty election, there were at least thirty political parties that fielded candidates to compete for seats in the House of Peoples Representatives (HPR). During the second election, that number more than doubled. The third parliamentary elections had some distinguishing features that disturbed the balance of power between the ruling coalition and opposition parties. How these elections differed from one another is closely examined in Chapter VII. The political environment in which these elections were conducted has ignited debates among observers of Ethiopia's transition from a single party authoritarian to a multiparty political system.

For example, Paul Henze and Fasil Nahum argued that the government of Ethiopia has succeeded remarkably in establishing democracy.[17] John Harbeson and others maintained that the assertions about the achievement of the government are not supported empirically. Harbeson was of the view that for all practical purposes, Ethiopia is under a bureaucratic authoritarian regime with virtually all "the forms of democracy but little of its substance."[18] From Harbeson's observation, it can be inferred that the political market is highly distorted in favor of the ruling party and that the electorate has little or no influence on the outcome of elections.

However, according to Henze, one of the remarkable achievements of the current government of Ethiopia is that "[t]he peasants who make up approximately 85% of the population have been freed to make their own decisions about which crops to plant and when and where to sell their produce."[19] This suggests that a political party with a banner such as "Long Live the Ethiopian Peasants" would have the greatest chance of winning an election. However, voters do not always participate in elections with narrowly defined expectations. For example, most citizens of the developed world cast their ballots during elections primarily because it is their civic duty to do so. But, it would be unwise for a political party not to devise a platform that captures the attention of the electorate and seize the political current.

In a majoritarian system such as the United States where the Electoral College ultimately determines the outcome of Presidential elections, a single ballot is worth much less than where the outcomes of elections are decided by popular vote. Clearly, the electoral law of a given country provides some insight into how a candidate achieves his/her political objectives. Where the rule of law prevails, candidates are bounded by the electoral laws of the country to promote their political agenda, convince the electorate, and possibly attract enough votes to win the election.

In a fairly liberalized political marketplace and where the electorate is sufficiently informed about "what would benefit him most, what the government is doing, and what other parties would do if they were in power,"[20] rational electorates may regulate monopolistic practices by using ballots as a form of sanction. (A more in-depth analysis of ballots as currencies in a liberalized political market will be presented in chapter eight). To the extent that the "political taste" of the electorate is not fixed and that the society is not divided along sharp segmental cleavages, political parties compete with one another for "selling their political ideas" designed to alter, primarily, the political taste of non-agitator voters.[21] For example, the focus of the issues debated among political parties in the United States depends on whether a candidate is running for the Presidency or senatorial positions. Presidential candidates have to demonstrate leadership skills in both domestic and foreign policy matters.

For senatorial candidates, the focus of their agenda varies according to the social and economic situation of their constituents, but like Presidential and Prime Ministerial candidates, they, too, have to convince the electorate that they possess leadership skills. Even more crucial are socio-economic factors that define the characteristics of political parties and set the tone of inter-party competition. For instance, there may be politically relevant identities such as those based on ascription (race, language, culture, and so on), class, or any combination of these identities.[22]

The fact that Senator Jessie Helms served in the United States Congress for as long as he did, despite his segregationist views, says a great deal about how the majority of people in North Carolina collectively identify with his position on race relations. In other parts of the United States, a senatorial candidate from Idaho, for instance, cannot be politically-wise and be elected if he/she opts for a reduction or elimination of agricultural subsidies. A candidate from Texas or California cannot, by economic necessity, ignore the Latino community and expect to win the race. On social issues, some Presidential and senatorial candidates in the United States have made reducing the crime rate by a certain percentage their campaign slogan. Others made improving the quality and increasing the quantity of health and educational services the center of their campaign platform.

The debate among most candidates is not whether crime rates and the quality and quantity of educational and health services should go up or down, but it is on how best to address these social problems. Candidates, irrespective of their ideological inclination, agree on the fundamentals but differ on the specifics and strategies of addressing economic, social, and foreign policy issues. However the focus of a candidate's agenda diverges from or converges with the agendas of others, the main objective is to convince the electorate that he/she has the best ideas for leading the country as a President or a senator.

In some African countries, elections are viewed as merely formal exercises, in the sense that there are not qualitative or quantitative returns *per se* for the electorate. Giovanni Sartori and Donald Horowitz have, for example, characterized the 1994 South African election as "ethnic voting" or a "racial census" in which party programs and incumbent performances were insignificant factors in determining electoral outcomes.[23] Robert Mattes and Amanda Gouws provided evidence to the contrary to show that there were cross-racial and cross-ethnic voting patterns in the 1994 multiparty election in South Africa.[24] Their observation is a critical point to the consolidation of democracy in an ethnically divided society such as Ethiopia. That is, sinking racial, ethnic or primordial differences in general seems to be the bedrock for the transformation of a one-party to a multiparty democratic system.

Robert Weissberg, taking a similar view as Sartori and Horowitz, insisted that in the United States, a sizable defection among white supporters of the Democratic Party is caused by the "party's inability to be all things to all party members on the issue of race." And, "this race-policy-caused defection is frequently the difference between defeat and victory."[25] On the other hand, he observed that the "Democratic-controlled Congress passed several landmark civil rights bills and beat back numerous attempts to circumvent pro-black Supreme Court decisions."[26] However, given the percentage of the black population in the United States, it is very unlikely for the Democratic Party to retain the majority of seats in the United States Congress by simply advancing the rights of blacks.

To say that a pro-black policy of the Democratic Party is the cause of defection of its white supporters is to deny the existence of overlapping memberships that brought the Party to dominate Congress in the first place. It is also important to note that, whether voting patterns are along racial, ethnic, religious, or other lines, party platforms do, more often than not, reflect the interests of the target electorate. As John Wiseman argued, the electorate shapes political agendas and decides the outcome of elections "through periodic elections in which the mass of the population is able to choose both the policies and the personnel of the future government." Moreover, the electorate in some African countries "can and does vote out MPs who are perceived to have performed poorly."[27]

Whether an electorate participates in the political process with the expectation for social and economic returns, as an expression of civic duty and political rights, or to show "loyalty and solidarity,"[28] the electorate's preference is taken into consideration when political parties compete for power. The transitional government of Ethiopia had the following expectations of political parties in the democratization of the country. The government forthrightly recognized that political parties play a significant role in the day-to-day process of building democracy. Political parties generate alternative views to protect the rights and interests of society and that they have to strive to have their views accepted by the public and translated into actions.[29]

However, under a highly imperfect political market, it is pointless to argue that the driving force for the participation of voters in the political process is the maximization of interests, be they social, cultural, economic, and/or political. The ideal type for a highly fragmented society is, of course, for political parties and the electorate to transcend sharp cleavages to maximize the benefits from participating in elections. As Lijphart succinctly put it, "the leaders of social groups with heterogeneous and overlapping memberships will tend to find it necessary to adopt moderate positions." Furthermore, the tendency to adopt "middle-of-the-road attitudes," a consequence of overlapping memberships, contributes to political stability.[30]

In the case of Ethiopia, overlapping membership of the electorate seems to be undermined by the proportional electoral law and the division of electoral districts and administrative regions based on arbitrary and unrealistic ethnic markers. In addition, there are very few political parties that rise above parochial attachments and sentiments in an effort to effectively compete for political power. Their efforts to transcend segmental cleavages seem to be deliberately undermined through the proportional electoral rules and by the preoccupation with avoiding the cost of opting out of the political process.

The discussion above suggests that a party's platform is one of the most important *visible* strategies in the competition for political power, at least until the final phases of the political campaign. In some cases, in casting their ballots for a candidate, voters may be influenced by charisma and cultural factors than by a party's platform on how to address socio-economic issues. In other cases, voters pay particular attention to a candidate's leadership experiences and skills. It also suggests that party platforms, voting patterns, and the political environment within which political parties compete for power varies across national and regional levels. The implication of the dynamic interaction among political parties and between political parties and the electorate within diverse political settings is that there is a need for a country-specific and sufficiently independent institution for managing the political marketplace.

Regulating the Political Marketplace

The political marketplace is by definition a forum in which political parties exchange "political ideas" for ballots with the objective of gaining the maximum possible votes to win elections. The value of ballots and information about a political party's agenda may be distorted under a highly imperfect political market, which usually leads to conflict and disruption of the market, in particular, and the political system, in general. Thus, market-enabling institutions are necessary for stabilizing the political marketplace.

The following discussion focuses on judicial independence as a political market-enabling institution and draws some parallels between its role in the economic arena with that of the political. Judicial independence is defined as "the insulation of judges and the judicial process from partisan pressure to influence the outcomes of individual cases."[31] Institutions, in general, and the judiciary, in particular, are vital for ensuring a level-playing field in the economic and political marketplace.

The World Bank Report, entitled *Building Institutions for Markets* (2002),[32] is a renouncing of the Bank's and its twin financial institution's (the International Monetary Fund) long-held beliefs that "the market can do no wrong." In its 1997 Report, the World Bank suggested that in an "era of free market economy," the choices are many and must be tailored to the circumstances of each country.[33] In a rebuttal to the notion of "the market can do no wrong," the Malaysian Prime Minister, Mhathir Mohammed, stated that "the creed of the market is to surrender your independence to those who know best." He added that "the swing from the government knows all . . . to the market can do no wrong . . . is as extreme as communism and socialism of yesteryear."[34]

Institutions harness competition among domestic private sectors and maneuver policy instruments to undermine the ability of foreign private sectors' monopolistic practices. Policymakers in Ethiopia and in other African countries may draw relevant lessons from the following two cases on the role of institutions in harnessing and/or undermining competition. For example, the United States Trade Representative complained that the "European Community grants export subsidies . . . on a wide range of agricultural products." These subsidies were designed to protect farmers who are engaged in wheat, diary, and certain fruits productions as well as some manufactured products, including pasta.[35]

On May 18, 1998, the United States Department of Justice filed a lawsuit against Microsoft Corporation alleging that it "has engaged, and continued to engage, in a broad course of conduct that improperly maintains Microsoft's monopoly in desktop operating systems and unlawfully retains trade."[36] The Department of Justice further argued that "Microsoft Corp. has used its unparalleled dominance in the computer industry to bully and squelch rivals"[37] Therefore, to level the playing field, the Department of Justice decided to split Microsoft into two "Baby Bills."

For the political market, like the economic marketplace, to be fairly competitive there must be institutions that are capable of monitoring, regulating rather than controlling, and stabilizing the market. That is, when situations arise that lead to a highly imperfect competition among political parties, institutions such as the judiciary and electoral board must be sufficiently independent from executive coercion, have the capacity to regulate unfair and predatory practices, and impose sanctions without fear of retaliations.

Unfortunately, there has been little, if any, comprehensive and systematic investigations of the role of the judiciary and the electoral board in monitoring and regulating the political marketplace and the degree to which they function with little or no interference from the executive branch of the government of Ethiopia. An initial assessment by Human Rights Watch on the Ethiopian political environment, in general, and judicial independence, in particular, suggested that "judges who try to uphold the rule of law are frequently defeated by local officials who refuse to comply."[38] In one of its reports, Human Rights Watch also observed that "[o]pposition activists, editors of the private press, and leaders of labor organizations who continued to challenge the EPRDF's monopolization of political space were systematically targeted through harassment and repeated detentions."[39]

Assessing the extent to which the judicial branch of government is insulated from external pressures, especially by the executive branch of governments in developing countries, is a complicated matter. This is partly due to the numerous actors that are involved in the judicial process and largely because of financial and human capital constraints. There are, however, standard criteria for measuring judicial independence; namely, the number of cases in which the government loses and the procedure for appointing, promoting, and removing judges.[40] "When judges have life-long tenure," the World Bank argues, "they are both less susceptible to direct political pressure and less likely to have been appointed by the politician currently in office."[41]

On the other hand, if the head of the executive organ, the Prime Minister, has practically an unlimited term in office, then it is difficult to adopt the "life-long" tenure-ship as one of the measurements of judicial independence. However, the procedure for appointing, removing, and promoting judges seem to be appropriate criteria for analyzing the extent of judicial independence in Ethiopia. Examining the structural transformation of the organizational rearrangement of the Federal Government, which is designed to release the various Ministries from the direct control of the Prime Minister's office, is yet another approach that could shed some light on the issue of judicial independence in that country. The emphasis should be less on the organizational skeleton of the government as it relates to judicial independence and more on the substance that is embedded in the structure. One of democracy's distinguishing features from any other systems of government is strengthen both horizontal and vertical accountability.

Horizontal and vertical accountabilities reinforce one another and are the major defining characteristics between democracy with and without substance. Separately, each may be relevant to maintaining the stability of the political system, but political stability should not be an end, in and of itself, in claiming success in the transformation of a one-party to a multiparty political system. Because, a system can be stable while embodying internal contradictions, contradictions that may permeate through the boundaries of other sub-systems, including socio-cultural and economic, which could contribute to or cause the collapse of the state.

Maintaining a stable political system requires a mechanism through which to channel and link one part of the system with others. Here, a symbiotic relationship or mutual trust between political elite is a precondition for the continuity of the system with or without a fundamental alteration in the internal composition and external structure of the political system. Having satisfied some of the most important preconditions, there can be horizontal accountability between, for example, the executive, judicial, and legislative branches of the government. Even if the preconditions are not satisfied, the system may continue to exist, but it exists in a fragile state.

Vertical accountability, on the other hand, seems to be more important to maintaining political stability and, above all, consolidating political freedom. However, while both elements of democracy could exist independent of each other, it is highly unlikely to have vertical accountability without horizontal accountability. This is perhaps one of the main reasons why some scholars advocate hegemonic exchange, elite cooperation, or power-sharing as an important initial phase in the process towards democracy and conflict resolution. This is not to say that horizontal accountability is the bedrock for democracy and that the political elite primarily determine how the system should behave. Vertical accountability may not be as critical in the initial stage of the transformation of the political system, it is nonetheless key to understanding whether the governing elite are restrained from undemocratic practices. When a transitional phase ends largely depends on the internal conditions of each society.

The role of the judiciary and mass media in the development and democratization of Ethiopia is so critical that one has to at least introduce the subject and suggest a few pointers for future research. The judiciary is one of the major components of any government. In Ethiopia, as in most other countries, the judiciary has overarching functions that cut across the socio-cultural, political, and economic systems. As such, it represents the most important images of the government. For instance, the legitimacy of the state may be eroded if the state fails to improve the economic welfare of its citizens, if its development policies are not grounded on the realities of the people, or if it muzzles freedom of speech. Disputes over election procedures and outcomes, corruption, and nepotism are other causes for the erosion of the legitimacy of the state. On the other hand, if the independence of the judiciary is meaningfully protected, then the judiciary essentially plays its role in maintaining a stable political system and insuring that the rights of citizens are not violated.

A clear separation of power between the legislative, executive, and judicial organs of the Federal Government enables the government to regain public confidence and consolidate its internal legitimacy. Furthermore, the effort to insulate the judicial process from partisan pressure through structural reform may be a step in the right direction to implementing a free market economic policy. A demonstrated commitment by the executive to distance itself from interfering in the functions of the judiciary may inadvertently but positively result, for example, in accelerating domestic investment and capital formation and the flow of foreign private investment. As chapter four suggests, cheap labor and abundant natural resources do not sufficiently capture the attention of investors. Because, the private sector also looks to see the extent of judicial independence as a measure of impartiality and fair trials over a possible dispute between an investor and the state, labor unions, or other parties.

When judicial independence is maintained, it encourages a spirit of invention and innovation that may be expressed through a medium of communication such as the mass media or in the actual production or emulation of equipment and technologies necessary for social and economic advancement. Given the insulation of judges and the judiciary from factional pressures, the judiciary could also keep the state in-check to ensure that it restrains itself from violating the civil and political rights of citizens. Ultimately, judicial independence reinforces the process of socio-economic development and democratization by protecting freedom of expression, encouraging invention and innovation, and guaranteeing a fair and an impartial trial and decisions on criminal and civil cases.

Given that there is a clear separation of power between the executive, legislative, and the judiciary, mass media may also be shielded from unreasonable restriction of its activities by the executive branch of the government. The media is a vital bridge between the public and political leaders and could also serve as a channel for the transfer of knowledge. Invention and innovation, for example, are expressed in different ways: physically producing tools and equipment or through publications of scholarly works which may be applied to improve the social and economic conditions of the people. In this regard, new research findings could be interpreted and conveyed to the public through radio and television programs or other means of mass communications. Providing these and other basic services to the public, of course, requires not only constitutional guarantee of freedom of speech, upholding the constitution, and enforcing the laws of the land but also rise of journalists who are critical and objective and live up to the expectation of the people.

In a country where these and other conditions are met, radio could be an effective means of communications between the people and the government, political parties and their constituents, and among civil society organizations. This is true for a country such as Ethiopia where the majority of the people are functionally illiterate and its annual per capita income is one of the lowest in the world. Unlike newspapers where the cost of one issue often equals the cost of a breakfast and where newspaper circulation is limited to urban areas, the importance of radio as an instrument of mass communication cannot be underestimated. Through radio, it is possible to instantaneously transmit news, comments and opinions, and to reach the rural and urban areas at the same time. It narrows the gap in quantitative and qualitative information consumption between the rural and urban areas and between the majority poor and the minority rich segments of the society.

Freedom of expression is exercised when the mass media conveys the views of the people without fear of harassment and persecution by the state. Consequently, the role of mass media in conveying new ideas and stimulating views and opinions becomes creatively improved. Therefore, on the one hand, the degree to which the judiciary is independent from executive coercion contracts or expands the legitimacy of the state. On the other hand, the social, economic, and political developments of Ethiopia are firmly embedded and enhanced where there are legal and institutional protections to shield the mass media from arbitrary and retaliatory measures by the state.

To the extent that the structural reform of the cabinet affects the organization and accountability of mass media organizations, the role of the media may also change from shaping public opinion, in line with that of the ruling party's ideology, to a vertical and horizontal channel of integration between the general public and leaders. In turn, the contribution of the mass media to the transformation of the socio-cultural, political, and economic systems is contingent on the degree to which the judiciary is independent from the coercive pressures of the executive organ. Even so, the mass media is a vertical and horizontal link among the various systems and components of the Ethiopian society when media personnel are reasonably impartial in their reporting and when the issues discussed over electronic and print media are relevant to improving the general welfare of society.

While the critical and integrative role of the mass media is widely recognized by numerous segments of the society and is one of the key elements of the input structure of the general system, its performance contribution to social, economic, and political development in Ethiopia is over-valued and under-investigated. The state-sponsored three-day symposium, in January 2003, to discuss the role of mass media in the development and democratization of Ethiopia caused great distress and uproar by the international community and the Ethiopian Free Press Journalists' Association.[42] For instance, a report by the Committee to Protect Journalists stated that Ethiopia "has a dismal press freedom record" and that the "government is planning alarming changes [to the] press laws that would severely restrict the rights of Ethiopia's already beleaguered private press corps."[43] Amnesty International also noted that the "Ethiopian Government has . . . intensified its attacks against the private press, which have put it at the forefront of repression of the press in Africa, despite its claim to welcome a free and critical press."[44]

Apparently, the government of Ethiopia did not find the free press to be objectively "critical." After ten years of medium- to high-level tolerance towards the media, the government was clearly and understandably getting impatient with the lack of journalistic ethics, professionalism, and accurate reporting. According to the government, the private media, mainly newspapers and journals, have been exceedingly irrelevant as a medium of communication among intellectuals, policymakers, and the public, in general, to advance alternative views on issues concerning the development of the nation.[45]

Members of the Ethiopian private press took the view that the conference on defining the role of media in Ethiopia illustrated the government's inability to endure harsh but constructive criticism by the independent media. They insisted that the independent media "have been rendering services as alternative sources of information."[46] The

perception among critics of the government seems to be that press freedom must be upheld even if editorial as well as news reporting and
analysis and opinion pieces are irrelevant to the country in question.
While the government preferred a regulated press freedom, human
rights activists, academics, and others contended that the right to freedom of expression through the mass media is not dependent on the benevolence of the state.

Summary and Conclusion

The level of a country's social and economic development needs to
be taken as two of the multivariate factors of democracy. For instance,
a reliable and expanded means of communication, a free and socially
responsible mass media, and an electorate that is functionally literate
facilitate the transformation of a single-party into a multiparty democracy. Here, expanded networks of communication are crucial as there
can be reliable communication networks in major cities but not in rural
areas where the majority of the people in developing countries live. If
these social and economic factors are limited to a few major cities, the
legitimacy of the state is questionable by the very fact that the state is
"soft" and unable to govern and draw its legitimacy from a significant
proportion of the masses.

Additionally, it needs to be noted that political parties play key
roles as sources of legitimacy by linking the state with the people and
vice-versa. Their role becomes more enhanced when the political marketplace is fairly competitive and when the electorates possess both
carrots and sticks to enable them to reward political parties based on
their performance. However, even if the political marketplace is regulated by a truly independent institution and the ruling party is less inclined to meddle with the workings of the market, the social and political environment under which political parties come into the political
scene may compromise the electoral process. It may also undermine the
ability of the electorate to use their carrots and sticks appropriately and
effectively as instruments of reward and punishment. For example,
most of the political parties in Ethiopia flourished as a result of the liberalization of the political market which may be an indication of their
opportunistic stance in the political process, lack of commitment and
vision, and weak organizational capacities and leadership skills of the
political leaders. With the exception of a few parties, most of them
were created in response to ethnic sentimentalism, thereby significantly
reducing the possibility of mobilizing popular support and cross-ethnic
party membership.

The problem is not that each political party would be constrained by the lack of sufficient political support to make meaningful contributions to the consolidation of democracy, because it is possible to resolve such quantitative shortcomings by adopting an appropriate electoral law. However, to the extent that political parties do not sink their ethnic sentimentalism, the electorate in each "ethnically" divided electoral zone is given no alternative but to vote for the same party and the same candidate with the same political agenda in almost all future elections. This may lead to a greater degree of ethnic sentimentalism, cohesion, and irrational consumption of "political ideas," making elections symbolic exercises of political rights. Implicit in such an election is that candidates are almost always rewarded largely because they come from the same ethnic group as the electorate. Such electoral rules, party platforms, and electoral patterns and behaviors essentially dilute the essence and meaning of election and create the conditions for nepotism and corruption. In this regard, the Ethiopian mass media has a social and moral obligation to show that the sacrifices of those who fought and died for political and economic freedom would not be in vain.

Sadly, neither the media nor the judiciary has so far been able to carry out its duties and responsibilities. Part of the reason has to do with the obsession of the executive to control what is produced and disseminated through electronic and print media. Two other reasons for the inability of mass media to expand its geographical and topical coverage are financial and manpower shortages. As a result, the scope of news coverage has not been as broad and fair as it would have been under different financial. The problem of broad-based coverage of news across the country was also exacerbated by the chronic shortages of reporters with a journalism background. At the same time, one has to look beyond the obvious and examine whether media personnel are simply taking freedom of expression and mass media for granted and publish or broadcast anything without regard to national security or respecting the rights of individuals to privacy.

Notes

1. Guillermo O'Donnell, "Horizontal Accountability in New Democracies," in *The Self-Restraining State: Power and Accountability in New Democracies*, eds. Andreas Schedler, Larry Diamond, and Marc Plattner (Boulder, CO: Lynne Rienner Publishers, 1999), pp.29-30.

2. David Guralnik, ed., *Webster's New World Dictionary of the American Language* (Cleveland, OH: William Collins + World Publishing Co., 1976).

3. O'Donnell, "Do Economist Know Best?," *Journal of Democracy* Vol. 6, 1 (1995): 23-8.

4. Samuel Huntington, *Political Order in Changing Societies* (New Haven, CT: Yale University Press, 1968), p.28.

5. Huntington, "Democracies Third Wave," in Larry Diamond and Marc Plattner, eds., *The Global Resurgence of Democracy* (Baltimore: Johns Hopkins University Press, 1996), p.4.

6. Lijphart and Carlos Waisman, eds., *Institutional Design in New Democracies: Eastern Europe and Latin America* (New York: Westview Press, 1998), p.2.

7. Francis Fukuyama, "The Primacy of Culture," *Journal of Democracy* Vol. 6, 1 (1995): 7-14.

8. Jeffress Ramsay, *Global Studies: Africa*, 5th ed., (Guilford, CT: Dushkin Publishing Group, 1993).

9. Axel Hadenius, *Democracy and Development* (New York: Cambridge University Press, 1992), p.147.

10. Brian Smith, *Understanding Third World Politics: Theories of Political Change and Development* (Indian: Indiana University Press, 1996), pp.16-7.

11. Robert Dahl, *Democracy, Liberty, and Equality* (New York: Norwegian University Press, 1986), p.127.

12. Ibid., pp.131-5.

13. Claude Ake, *Democracy and Development in Africa* (Washington, DC: Brookings Institution, 1996), p.1.

14. Ibid., p.7.

15. Collier, Elbadawi, and Sambanis, p.15.

16. Peter Mair, "Electoral Markets and Stable States," in *The Market and the State, Studies in Interdependence*, eds. Michael Moran and Maurice Wright (New York: St. Martin's Press, 1991).

17. Paul Henze, "A Political Success Story," *Journal of Democracy*, Vol., 9, No. 4 (1998): 40-54. See also, Fasil Nahum, *Constitution for a Nation of Nations: The Ethiopian Prospect* (Asmara: Red Sea Press, 1997), p.45.

18. John Harbeson, "A Bureaucratic Authoritarian Regime," *Journal of Democracy*, Vol. 9, No. 4 (1998): 62-9.

19. Henze, 40-54.

20. Anthony Downs, *An Economic Theory of Democracy* (New York: Harper & Row Publishers, 1957), p.83. See Chapter VII of this study for further analysis of Downs conceptualization of the basic logic of voting and the types of voters.

21. Ibid., p.83.

22. Mair, p.20.

23. Robert Mattes and Amanda Gouws, "Race, Ethnicity, and Voting Behavior: Lessons from South Africa," in *Elections and Conflict Management in Africa*, eds. Timothy D. Sisk and Andrew Reynolds (Washington, DC: United States Institute of Peace Press, 1998), p.120.

24. Mattes and Gouws, pp.132-8.

25. Robert Weissberg, "The Democratic Party and the Conflict over Racial Policy," in *Do Elections Matter?*, eds. Benjamin Ginsberg and Alan Stone (New York: M. E. Sharpe, 1986), p.205.

26. Weissberg, p.207.

27. John Wiseman, *Democracy in Black Africa: Survival and Revival* (New York: Paragon House Publishers, 1990), pp.6-7.

28. Mattes and Gouws, p.124.

29. Ministry of Information, *BeEthiopia YeDemocracy Sirat Ginbata Gudayoch* (Issues of Building Democracy in Ethiopia) (Addis Ababa: Ministry of Information, 1994), p.99.

30. Lijphart, p.72.

31. Jennifer Widner, "Building Judicial Independence in Common Law Africa," in *The Self-restructuring State: Power and Accountability in New Democracies*, pp.177-8.

32. World Bank, *Building Institutions for Markets* (New York: Oxford University Press, 2002).

33. World Bank, *The State in a Changing World* (New York: Oxford University Press, 1997), pp.3-4.

34. Mhathir Mohammed, speech delivered at the Asia Pacific Economic Cooperation forum, Vancouver, Canada, November 1997.

35. Office of the United States Trade Representative, *1991 National Trade Estimate Report on Foreign Trade Barriers* (Washington, DC: US Government Printing Office, 1992), p.86.

36. Department of Justice, "Statement of Subject Matter and Appellate Jurisdiction," 8 November 1999, at <http://www.usdoj.gov/atr/cases/f1900/1947.htm>.

37. "Judge Says Microsoft Wields Monopoly Power Over Rivals," *The Washington Post*, (6 November 1999), Sec. A1.

38. Human Rights Watch, "Human Rights Curtailed in Ethiopia," 11 October 2001, at <http://www.hrw.org/press97/dec/ethiop.htm>.

39. Ibid.

40. Widner, p.178.

41. World Bank, *Building Institutions for Markets*, p.130.

42. "Ethiopian press freedom symposium held without press," 3 October 2003, at <http://www.afrol.com/News2003/eth002_press_law.htm>. See also a letter submitted to President Thabo Mbeki, President of the Republic of South Africa and Chair of the African Union, <http://www.ifjafrique.org/english/dernouvelles/200603_5.htm>.

43. "CPJ Urges African Union to Guarantee Press Freedom," 20 September 2003, at <http://www.internews.org/mra/mrm/oct02/oct02_story11.htm>.

44. "Journalists in prison – press freedom under attack," 20 September 2003, at <http://www.africaaction.org/docs98/east9804.htm>.

45. "Ethiopian press freedom symposium held without press," 3 October 2003, at <http://www.afrol.com/News2003/eth002_press_law.htm>.

46. Ibid.

Chapter IV

Socioeconomic Policies and Strategies

National or regional development policies critically assess a country's resource base and outline specific strategies with which to achieve a set or sets of clearly defined objective(s). The primary development policy objectives of most developing countries in Africa usually include improving agricultural productivity, providing better access to public goods, and increasing the contribution of the manufacturing sector to Gross Domestic Product. The priority areas of development policy objectives may differ from one country to another, but they often project positive images of the social and economic conditions of the society in the near future. Until the end of the Cold War, exogenous rather than endogenous forces generally dictated the content and essence of most African countries' development policies.

In some cases, especially when political power is gained through unconstitutional means, the policies of the previous government are discarded as faulty and inappropriate for solving such challenges as poverty, unemployment, homelessness, crime, and the like. In other cases, in an effort to impose policies favorable to the new ruling clique, the political elite fabricates social and economic classifications to break down society into hostile religious, ethnic, or economic groups. For the new elite, it seems to make little political sense to learn from the previous government's failure and success and build upon social memories and common heritage to develop policies that are more effective than the policies of the deposed regime.

Indicting the outgoing regime for the dreadful socioeconomic condition of the people has been more pronounced in Ethiopia than in most African countries. The national policy of the military government of Mengistu Haile-Mariam, which took power through a coup, has been criticized for dis-empowering the people from actively participating in the economic arena. The current national policy under the leadership of Meles Zenawi, who also came to power through unconstitutional means, is in many ways similar to its predecessor.

While the objectives of the three governments may understandably focus on industrialization, job creation, social wellbeing, and greater use of domestic resources, questions such as why some or all the objectives have not been realized received little attention. The three governments seem to have been obsessed with legitimizing a centralized or a free market economic policy than formulating a development policy that addresses the condition of the majority poor. Of course, there are a few exceptions. For instance, in 1961, the Planning Board made a compelling and visionary statement calling for the formulation of an enforceable land redistribution policy. It went even further to remark on the distribution of idle imperial land holdings to farmers that could best maintain and benefit from it.[1]

One would expect that as more experiences accumulate and data collection methods improve, Ethiopian leaders would be able to formulate a more effective and sound development policy. Yet, however sound and pragmatic the policies of the three governments appear, the result has been nothing more than a nominal expansion of educational and health service facilities which are concentrated in a few of the core regional states and scantily dispersed in the peripheral regional states.

To a large extent, policymakers of the three governments have been reluctant to take a holistic approach to development, including making genuine reforms to tackle political and cultural obstacles to development. There has been a consensus among many policymakers that the country's industrialization and economic development generally depend on speeding up agricultural productivity and efficiently utilizing scarce resources. This seemed to be a realistic approach to development, because the agricultural sector is one of the major sources of employment and foreign exchange earnings. Consequently, Ethiopian governments over the past half a century paid particular attention to the agricultural sector. For example, the government of Emperor Haile-Selassie allocated 27% of its budget during the First Five Year Plan (1956-1961) to fostering agricultural productivity and enhancing the role of agriculture as a major supplier of raw material to the industrial sector.[2]

The military government's national development policy and strategy focused on redistributing land to the tiller and regulating the price of agricultural goods. The government also directly intervened in the production and distribution of goods and services with a view to speeding up the process of industrialization based on accelerating agricultural productivity. The current government has also adopted a similar development policy. It seeks to industrialize the Ethiopian economy by investing material, financial, and human resources in the agricultural sector because the agricultural sector is believed to serve as a spring-board to industrialization.

Since the formulation and implementation of the first economic policy in the mid-1950s, the agricultural sector has been vulnerable to external forces, including internationally-induced price shocks, adverse terms of trade, deteriorating soil fertility and unfavorable environmental condition. All of these weakened the ability of Ethiopian farmers to effectively compete in regional or international trade. In the past four decades, unfavorable environmental condition, coupled with poor policy choices, have had a devastating impact on the lives of Ethiopian farmers and more generally on the Ethiopian economy. For example, Ethiopia was once hit hard by a severe drought in the early 1970s and more frequently since the early 1980s.

The number of peoples and regions falling victim to drought increased from about 1 million people in Tigray and Wollo provinces in the 1970s to over 14 million people in Affar, Amhara, Oromiya, Southern Nations and Nationalities, and Tigray regions in 2003. The drought in 2003 was so severe that the United States government had to divert emergency food aid from Iraq to Ethiopia. Moreover, due to forced resettlement and internal displacement, the frequency of social crises, including the number of school dropouts, begging, and theft grew at an alarming rate.[3] Yet, the governments of Haile-Selassie, Mengistu Haile-Mariam, and Meles Zenawi insisted that the agricultural sector is the foundation for the industrialization of Ethiopia. Clearly, there is a contradiction between the expressed interests and goals of the governments to fuel industrialization through an increase in agricultural productivity and recurring food insecurity and starvation.

The purpose of this chapter is, therefore, to analyze the social and economic policies of the three governments from the mid-1950s to the late 1990s. It also explores whether decisions on public investments in the social and economic sectors were influenced by ethnic considerations. By the time this study was completed, the government of Prime Minister Meles Zenawi was (mis)managing the economy almost arbitrarily because it formulated neither agricultural nor industrial policy which would have guided the public and the private sector in assessing and determining, for example, budget requirements, tax relief and incentives for investment in either sector.

While there are no formally instituted agricultural and industrial policies at present, some documents obtained from the Ministry of Agriculture and the Ministry of Trade and Industry are relevant for explor-

ing the economic and social policies of the present government. In
short, the main purpose of this chapter is to examine if the policies of
the previous two governments favored a few ethnic groups at the expense of socially and economically marginalizing other ethnic groups
in Ethiopia. This chapter also examines how the present government
seeks to transform the subsistence-based economy into an industry-
based market economy anchored in agriculture.

National Policies of the Haile-Selassie Government

A remarkable attempt at identifying Ethiopia's resource base and
defining the course of actions necessary to modernize the country was
set in motion in the early 1950s by the government of Emperor Haile-
Selassie. What makes it remarkable is not the scope and depth of the
policy, per se, but public officials of the time had to start from scratch
with a few individuals who had some training in public policy administration. For instance, in his memoir, *My Life and Ethiopia's Progress*,
Emperor Haile-Selassie noted that until his return from exile in May
1940, over 750,000 people were killed during the Ethio-Italian war. In
addition, at least 500,000 homes and over 2,000 churches were set on
fire and approximately 14 million cattle were killed during the war. The
post-war reconstruction efforts became even more complex and monu-
mental due to either the disappearance or killings of over 75% of the
educated youth. Five days after his return from exile, the Emperor appointed members of his cabinet to formulate a post-war reconstruction
and development policy.[4]

Therefore, except for issues that emanate from ideological differences between the outgoing and incoming administrations, the groundwork for identifying the country's resource base and perhaps the most
difficult stage in formulating public policies were undertaken by the
government of Emperor Haile-Selassie. Even if the policy of the Haile-
Selassie government was distorted, subsequent governments could certainly draw on lessons from previous experience to develop sound economic and social policies. In other words, the succeeding governments
of Ethiopia did not need to devote a significant amount of public resources, for example, to survey the hydroelectric power generating potential of the Awash or the Nile rivers.

Additionally, policymakers of the early 1960s identified the need
for greater backward and forward linkages between the agricultural and
manufacturing sectors. This groundbreaking step could have lifted the
financial and human resource burdens on the military government,
which could have allocated public funds to determine whether there is a
link between the two sectors. This is not to suggest that the policies that

dictated social and economic activities during the reign of Emperor Haile-Selassie were flawless and effective in bringing about the desired outcomes. As the following analysis reveals, the development policies of the 1960s produced mixed results.

The First Five Year Plan was formulated with the view to laying the foundation for stimulating the economy through investment in communication networks, manufacturing, agriculture, and social sectors.[5] In addition, the Plan emphasized the need for establishing manufacturing industries that utilized domestic resources and produce durable and non-durable consumer goods for domestic consumption and export. Investment in the transportation and communication sectors also constituted a major part of the Plan. The total amount of public expenditure under this Plan was 673.6 million Birr (Ethiopian currency). Of this amount 35.6% was designated for the construction and expansion of the transportation and communication networks and 20.5% for the exploration of natural resources, expansion of electric power services, and building new manufacturing industries. The government also earmarked 27% of the budget to modernize the agricultural sector and to protect and exploit the country's forest resources. Finally, 8.5% of the budget was allocated to education, health, and other social services.[6]

In the Second Five Year Plan (1962-1967), the Planning Board noted that the agricultural sector was progressing slowly in responding to the growing demands of the industrial sector. The Planning Board highlighted that in order to ensure food security and meet the demand for input in the production of manufactured goods, the agricultural sector should continue to receive budgetary support. It went on to assert that the linkage between the agricultural and industrial sector was strong enough to warrant the implementation of a development policy that emphasized import substitution and export promotion strategies, greater government intervention through financial schemes, and active participation of private investors in the agricultural sector.[7] The Second Plan also noted that peasants continued to use traditional farming techniques and maintained a land tenure system that was passed from one generation to the next. As a result, farmers did not reap any benefits from their hard work on the land. Consequently, the Plan pointed to the need for urgent land and tax reform measures not only to stimulate growth in agricultural output but also to ensure that farmers reaped the gains from their labor on the land.[8]

The policy paper also reiterated some of the accomplishments of the First Plan and noted that overall the economy was growing steadily with the doubling of industrial output and an appreciable (11%) increase in agricultural output. Gross Domestic Product (GDP) per capita

increased from 89 *Birr* ($37 at the 1960s exchange rate) at the begin-
ning of the First Plan year to 97 *Birr* (or a $2 increase at the same ex-
change rate) at the end of the First Plan year. There were, however,
some unexpected developments arising from the expansion of the
transportation networks and international trade. For instance, the government stressed the need for experimenting with import substitution
and export promotion strategies because the country was experiencing a
trade deficit largely due to the growing tendency of infant industries to
rely on imported inputs.

The Plan also suggested that the provision of health services, even
though limited to urban dwellers, improved appreciably at the end of
the First Plan. During the First Plan, new hospitals with at most 300
beds each were built in each of the provinces. In order to expand health
services throughout the country, 50 health stations and 100 clinics were
also built. The same was also true with education. Although the total
number of schools built during the First Plan was high, the number of
secondary and tertiary schools was significantly low.

Therefore, the Second Five Year Plan proposed an increase in primary school gross enrolment ratio by at least 200% compared with the
gross enrollment ratio during the First Five Year Plan. Secondary and
tertiary schools were also to expand accordingly. In addition, emphasis
was "laid on those forms and types of education and training which will
open the most efficient means for achieving the development targets set
forth in the Second Plan." One of the strategies suggested by the Ministry of Education was to develop a curriculum with particular attention
to technical education and vocational training in order to meet both the
short- and long-term development goals. Moreover, the report noted
that "Education constitutes an important component of the standard of
living and as such it is a goal in itself." The quality of education was
another area of concern that required careful assessment of the situation
with the intent to reverse the downward trend in teacher/pupils ratio.
The total number of teachers during the First Plan was, for example,
7,195, of which 1,301 were foreigners.[9]

The Second Plan also noted that no one should receive preferential
treatment and that legislation on equitable land redistribution and fair
tax systems were urgently needed. Citing the constitution of Ethiopia,
the Planning Board pointed out that the civil service was to serve the
people rather than the people serving public officials.[10] The lack of
cooperation between the Ministries was also viewed as partly responsible for the staggering inflow of foreign investment.[11]

The Third Five Year Plan (1967-1972) followed a similar approach
in analyzing the social and economic situation of the country and high-
lighting that the "central aim remains that of assuring the steady expan-

sion of the economy and improvement in the real standard of living."[12]
The Plan stated that given "the enormous predominance of agricultural
production and its basic importance for both domestic consumption and
industrial economy, as well as 90% of total export," it was evident that
a significant contribution to economic growth during the plan year must
come from increased agricultural output.[13]

The second objective of the Third Plan was to expand manufacturing output by establishing new small- and medium-scale enterprises
that could "absorb an increasing share of surplus agricultural labor."
The construction of transportation, electricity, and irrigation facilities
was also identified as a prerequisite for accelerating agricultural and
industrial outputs. The Plan indicated that the focus on the construction
of transportation networks should be on building secondary, feeder, and
farm-to-market roads, geared to meeting the transportation needs of
farmers and to stimulating economic activities at the regional and national levels.[14] Moreover, increased storage capacity, particularly at the
farm and local market level was also identified as an integral part of
reducing cost and spoilage, and ensuring a steady supply of agricultural
products to the industrial sector.[15]

The Third Plan stressed that the provision of social services should
not simply be viewed in terms of economic returns but also as a "basic
political and social imperative for any modern government." Particularly for Ethiopia, "the standards in much of the country [were] so low
as to have a direct negative effect on the level and efforts of productivity of the population." Furthermore, recognizing the apparent and persistent inequitable distribution of facilities in the social and economic
sectors that may have immediate or long-term social and economic
returns, "the government placed emphasis on the goal of sound regional
development of various types. But, this must take place within the
framework of overall national development."[16] Public participation and
understanding of the development objectives and constraints were also
perceived as key components to maximizing the effectiveness of the
policy. The Planning Board took the view that participation in the decisionmaking process should not be limited to a selected few regions but
"to all citizens of the Empire."[17]

The education policies of the previous years were carefully evaluated in the Third Plan as well. The Third Plan highlighted that the
country's education system was largely irrelevant to the rural population of Ethiopia and remained highly concentrated in a few regions.[18]
Therefore, the Plan signaled "the need to broaden the primary education stream and assure a more adequate flow of students to secondary
levels." In addition, the Plan emphasized that there should be "a more
equitable regional spread of school investment and teacher allocation,

especially to the poorer less-advantaged provinces and *awrajas* of Ethiopia, of mainly rural character."[19]

For the first time since the First Plan, the Third Plan raised a critical issue with regard to the scope and quality of the health sector. The Plan emphasized the need to go beyond mere infrastructural expansion of hospitals and clinics. Instead, it proposed that the health policy of the country should be geared to preventive health services "with stress on malaria eradication, mass vaccination campaign, and on the provision of pure water supplies, sewage disposal and other sanitary works, both for urban and rural populations."[20]

The Fourth Five Year Plan (1973-1978)[21] built upon previous policies and strategies and continued along the same line of development objectives and priority areas as the previous ones. It suggested that while agriculture remained the leading sector of the economy, production in this sector needed to be accelerated through an emphasis on training and education of agronomists. Diversifying and improving the quality of agricultural products, encouraging the development and use of technologies that were tailored to Ethiopia's dependency on agriculture, and at the same time engaging in labor intensive production possibilities were to be the focus of agricultural research programs. It was also hoped that a new irrigation system would open employment opportunities and diversification as well as increase agricultural productivity. The need for a new sector-specific policy framework was also highlighted to initiate the expansion of small-scale irrigation methods and to divert water resources to "less-endowed areas such as the northern highlands,"[22] thereby narrowing the gap in regional income distribution.

The statement by the Planning Board also recognized new developments such as the growing rate of population displacement and its effect on agricultural productivity, soil erosion, and the diminishing of water and forest resources. Therefore, the Fourth Plan included a priority area in devising a strategy to protect the country's "dwindling forest resources." The statement highlighted the need for streamlining the agricultural and education policy in training technical staff and sound management of land use, especially in the northern highlands, with the adoption of a curriculum geared towards averting soil erosion and deforestation. It noted that coordinating the two sectors' activities was as much necessary for meeting the nutritional needs of the people and ensuring food security as they were for speeding up the process of economic growth.

As in the previous development plans, it was hoped that the manufacturing sector would create employment opportunities far greater than the prevailing employment rate, which was estimated at 1% of total employment in all sectors. Moreover, "the basic strategy for the sector for the Fourth Five Year Plan center[ed] around [the] desire to sustain a high rate of growth of output, but in ways which pays considerable attention to questions of employment, of economic efficiency, and of regional distribution."[23] Some of the industries established during the Third Plan were increasingly based on imported raw materials. Therefore, the Fourth Plan stressed the promotion of import substitution and export promotion strategies to improve the country's foreign currency reserves and utilization of domestic resources.

In short, the socioeconomic policies and strategies of the government of Haile-Selassie generally recognized the absence of an equitable distribution of schools and teachers, hospitals and medical personnel, transportation networks, and manufacturing industries between regions. However, regional development planning required a detailed and reliable, sector-oriented, and specific statistical data on each region's natural resources, manpower, level of income, infrastructure, health and education. The lack of reliable data on these areas made regional planning difficult and perhaps even unrealistic. Financial constraints also exacerbated the problem of formulating an effective regional development policy. Nonetheless, the primary interest of the government of Haile-Selassie remained the formulation of a policy framework to ensure a just and equitable distribution of industries, expansion of transport systems, and educational opportunities and health services.

Even though the development plans of the Haile-Selassie government targeted the agricultural sector as the basis for the industrialization of the Ethiopian economy, they had little or no impact on producing tangible results for the majority of Ethiopians. Indeed, the number of drought victims soared just before the Fourth Year Development Plan took effect in 1973. The realities on the ground and the conditions of the drought victims on television screens in many parts of the world stimulated the rise of a popular movement that demanded immediate measures to reduce the number of victims. Many in the Ethiopian academic community (students, teachers, and administrative staffs) urged the government to search for a lasting solution to the catastrophic consequences of soil erosion, deforestation, gasoline and food price hikes, and the depressing social and economic situation. Unable to cope and respond positively to these and other demands, the government of Haile-Selassie was brought down by a military coup.

Development Policies of the Mengistu Government

The government of President Mengistu came to power in 1974 after a violent demonstration by high school and university students, taxi

drivers, and teachers against Emperor Haile-Selassie and his government. These and other social groups demanded an immediate response
to the early 1970s starvation in the province of Tigray and Wollo. Subsequently, they raised their demands from provincial to national issues,
including the implementation of a major land reform policy and the
resignation of cabinet and members of parliamentary of the government
of Haile-Selassie. The spontaneous movement that sought a significant
improvement in social and economic conditions was quickly hijacked
by a group of military officers who appointed themselves as the Transitional Military Government of Ethiopia.

The military government inherited a largely stagnant economy,
structurally and functionally deficient institutions and a generation of
politically conscious social, economic, and political groups. The
chronic structural problems that persisted in the country required radical policy measures. One of the most important steps undertaken by the
military government was to subscribe to socialist ideology, in general,
and a centralized economic policy, in particular, with the objective of
dismantling the oppressive and exploitative production relations. The
centralized economic policy dictated the country's direction towards
development through the management, control, and regulation as well
as production and distribution of goods and services by the socialist
government. Initially, the incoming regime appeared to engage the public in a concerted effort at social justice, economic growth, and political
freedom.

To that end, the government transferred the means of production to
"public" ownership. A few months after the establishment of the transitional military government in 1974, proclamations were issued to legal-
ize public ownership and control of the means of production, including
the mining and manufacturing industries and communications, electricity, insurance and banking services. While some strategically insignificant and underdeveloped industries were designated for joint ownership
between the government and foreign investors, small-scale manufacturing, retail trade, transportation, import and export trade, and hotel and
tourism activities were reserved for domestic private investors. Even
when joint activities were undertaken between the government and
foreign investors, the government retained at least 51% of the share in
the joint venture.[24]

In a country like Ethiopia, a person's economic wellbeing and social standing is deeply ingrained and reflected in the person's relations
with the land. However, according to the military regime, "several
thousand *gashas* of land have been grabbed from the masses by an insignificant number of feudal lords and their families as a result of
which the Ethiopian masses have been forced to live under conditions

of serfdom." Thus, recognizing the misappropriation of land as one of the most important factors behind the overthrow of the Emperor and to empower the masses with a sense of ownership of both land and its fruits, the military government passed a decree in 1975 to confiscate rural lands. The proclamation that provided for the collective ownership of land was ultimately intended to increase rural income and "lay the basis for the expansion of industry and the growth of the economy by providing for the participation of the peasantry in the national market."[25]

Peasant Associations were established at the local, *woreda*, and district levels with various functions and administrative responsibilities. These functions and responsibilities included redistribution and conservation of land and cultivating the "holdings of persons who, by reason of old age, youth or illness, or in the case of women, by reason of her husband's death, cannot cultivate their holdings." Peasant Associations were also granted authority and responsibility to establish marketing and credit cooperatives, schools, clinics, and other social service institutions necessary for improving the lives people. The Peasant Association was also given a mandate to establish judicial tribunals and resolve land disputes arising within the jurisdictions of the Association.[26]

The military government also perceived the majority of urban dwellers as "mere instruments for the furtherance of the comfort and luxury of the ruling class." To abolish the exploitative and oppressive landlord/tenant relations, the government passed a proclamation for public ownership of urban lands and extra-urban houses. Under this proclamation, a tenant was set free from any obligation of debt or rent to the landowner. Additionally, the government took steps to significantly reduce monthly rents of urban dwellings and business houses that were between 25 and 300 *Birr*. They were reduced by 50% to 15%, progressively. For the purpose of executing and enforcing the proclamation, the government established Cooperative Societies of Urban Dwellers (CSUD) with similar functions and responsibilities as those of Peasant Associations. Apart from resolving disputes between urban dwellers and managing and maintaining urban lands and houses, the CSUD was responsible for collecting rents and government subsidies and reinvesting proceeds in the community, including building affordable houses and other activities that improved the quality of life.[27]

Politically, it sought to equip the society with a Marxist-Leninist ideology by taking radical measures to create new education systems and introduce politically inclined curricula and programs. The strategies included compulsory elementary education for all children, mandatory participation of high school graduates, university students, and teachers in the Campaign Against Illiteracy program, and the retraining

of teachers through extension programs in accordance with the new
socialist education system. The government envisioned a gradual reduction of the rate of unemployment, poverty, and prostitution through
cultural and educational programs.[28]

The military government also sought to streamline the agricultural
and the industrial sectors and disentangle the country from feudalist
and imperialist production relations. Increased productivity of the agricultural sector was believed to stimulate the rise in the rate of employment in the industrial sectors as well. The government emphasized the
need for taking simultaneous steps to promote the establishment of and
support for small- and medium-scale industries. As part of the strategies to invigorate agricultural production, the government established
cooperative and resettlement programs, expanded state farms, encouraged the role of women in the economy, regulated the price of agricultural products, and increased the use of fertilizer by farmers and cooperative groups.

Particular attention was paid to industry as the second most important sector to advance the country from a largely feudal to a socialist
economy. The concentration of industrial establishments in a few of the
regions was identified as a factor that widened the gap in the standard
of living, in general, and income distribution, in particular, between
peoples of the different regions. For example, out of the 197 industries
confiscated by the military government, a total of 174 were located in
Shoa, Eritrea, and Harar. The remaining 23 publicly-owned industries
were scattered in Kaffa, Sidamo, Tigray, Wollo, Gonder, Arusi, and
Gojjam provinces. There were 79,791 employees working in the 197
industries, of which 90% were from the first three regions indicated
above.[29] Therefore, to narrow the gap in income disparities, the government sought to establish manufacturing industries in the neglected
regions of the country.

To reverse the trend in the disproportional distribution of industries
and income, the Ten Year Plan proposed a number of key objectives,
including the production of manufacturing goods for domestic consumption and expansion of small-scale industries and handicraft enterprises across regions based on economic viability. The need to insure
availability of the necessary equipment for road and transportation construction and opening employment opportunities for the masses were
some of the main objectives stated in the socialist development plan.
Finally, the socialist regime highlighted greater improvement in the
country's foreign currency reserve through export promotion
schemes.[30]

The extent to which the military government's redistributive and
economic development policies were effective in achieving their objec-

tives are issues that will be tackled in chapter five. From the point of view of policy analysis, however, it can be inferred that the military government appeared to have responded to popular demands by taking swift and radical measures to dismantle the exploitative production relations. Unfortunately, its development strategies dictated what was best for the people. For example, the military government introduced a resettlement program known as *Sefera*, which was similar to the *Ujamma* villages of Tanzania, to promote collective social and political consciousness and to foster self-reliance and industrialization. It did so without any input from the people that were directly affected by the resettlement programs.

Even though the *Sefera* program may have appealed to the socialist regime and to some people in the drought-stricken provinces of Wollo and Tigray, participation in this program was not based on the consent of the people. Indeed, most of the people who traveled from the rural to the urban centers for shopping were abducted and resettled miles away from their villages. What the *Sefera* program did to the psyche of the families in a traditional society is not difficult to imagine. Moreover, the forced resettlement program to boost agricultural productivity and reduce the number of drought victims had harmful economic consequences. Most of the captives, perhaps because they felt that there was little or no incentive for them to participate in the collective farming scheme and that it was better to die in dignity than be treated as a commodity, escaped from the resettlement areas to rejoin their families. Obviously, this was a significant disruption of their lives as well as the productivity of individual farmers and the *Sefera* program.

The same was true of the transformation of the political system. With the exception of the formation of grass-root organizations such as the CSUD and Peasant Associations and a few other professional groups, the military government had no interest in entertaining alternative political views. Indeed, the formation of these seemingly grass-root organizations was orchestrated by political cadres of the military regime. As such, their purpose was to gather intelligence on the organizational hierarchy and activities of opposition political parties. In some cases, the *Tibeka Guadoch* (Security Comrades), who were recruited from members of the local people, took arbitrary and extrajudicial measures against suspected members of opposition political groups. Thus, even though the creation of these associations was designed to link the leadership to the general public, they were terrorizing the youth and were agents of political repression.

Furthermore, the military government was preoccupied with militarily defeating nationalist and secessionist political groups that waged urban and rural guerrilla warfare against government forces and politi-

cal leaders. It was unable to diplomatically settle the border dispute
with Somalia and, as a result, it fought wars against Somalia in the late
1970s which had a significant impact on the country's human and material resources. Nationalist as well as secessionist groups put up major
obstacles to the government's attempt to construct feeder-roads and
expand social services to the rural community. The military government in its efforts to subdue rival groups such as the Ethiopian Peoples
Revolutionary Party, the Ethiopian Democratic Union, the Oromo Liberation Front, and the Tigray Peoples Liberation Front had to divert
resources from the provision of public goods (excluding national security) to purchasing arms. In 1980, the military government spent 35.5%
on defense and only 19.6% on social services.[31]

In short, the military government not only failed to address the socio-cultural components of development, but it also undermined the
role of opposition groups in the economic and political development of
the country. As a result, it left a legacy of mistrust between socio-
cultural groups and helped secessionist movement leaders and nationalist groups to start up armed struggles. It was against this backdrop that
the current government came to power and liberalized the economic
and political marketplaces to avoid history repeating itself.

Development Policy of the Meles Government

There is a widespread belief among contemporary policymakers in
Ethiopia that policies are nothing but eloquent statements. Policymakers of the new federal system of Ethiopia assert that policies are merely
descriptive statements to help chart the path that the government wishes
to follow in its efforts to achieve a certain set of objectives. Cynically,
some policymakers argue that what matters is not whether a government has a national policy, but how effectively the government mobi-
lizes human, material, and natural resources to translate economic
growth into economic development or to transform an inequitable into
an equitable distribution of social benefits. Such arguments currently
circulate among high-ranking members of the Ministry of Trade and
Industry and the Ministry of Agriculture of the government of Prime
Minister Meles Zenawi. The argument is nothing more than a sign of
resignation towards taking a concerted effort at conceiving policies to
help lift the country out of its economic backwardness.

A policy is one of the instruments of restraint. As an explicit government plan of action, it holds the policy executing and enforcing
arms of the government accountable for their action or inaction. In the
absence of a policy framework, it would be extremely difficult to assess
whether or not public funds were improperly allocated or the extent to

which progress has been made to rectify distortions in the regional distribution of public investment. The importance of formulating policy under the current government is also compelling because of the government's ideological shift from a centralized to a decentralized politico-economic system.

Sadly, however, interviews with senior members of the policy divisions of the Ministry of Agriculture and the Ministry of Trade and Industry reveal that the government has been unable to live up to the expectations of the people. At present, it appears that "there is no human scapegoat in sight" and the responsibility of guiding the country's economy towards development is handed over to "the invisible but ubiquitous Devil" of the market economy, which is a misnomer as it relates to Ethiopia's economic realities.[32]

Nonetheless, the government of Meles Zenawi is confronted with endogenous and exogenous forces of change, which may be in a direct collision course with the aims and goals of the government. For example, Joseph Stiglitz argued that "he [Meles] and his government were generally committed to a process of decentralization, bringing government closer to the people and ensuring that the center did not lose touch with the separate regions."[33] However, the International Monetary Fund (IMF) remains the strongest multilateral financial institution, even though the institution seem to have outlived its original purpose of promoting free trade and discouraging protectionist paths to development.

According to Stiglitz, the IMF attempted to impose the liberalization of the Ethiopian financial sector as one of the conditionalities for the reimbursement of $127 million loan which was approved under the Enhanced Structural Adjustment Facility lending program. In spite of the fact that the market does not have built-in mechanisms to avoid negative externalities, the IMF told Meles either to privatize the Ethiopian financial sector or lose the country's borrowing "privileges."[34] Given the country's dwindling resources, the Meles government had little or no choice but to engage in a series of negotiations with the financial giant for the release of the loan.

Whether the continued existence of the IMF contradicts the conventional belief that the market has a self-correcting mechanism or its policy prescriptions are inconsistent with the economic and political realities of Ethiopia is beyond the scope of this study. However, suffice it to say that while endogenous and exogenous elements may differ in the degree to which they influence changes in the economic and political systems, the present government of Ethiopia needs to ensure that its development and redistribution strategies are not significantly compromised by the distorted policies of the IMF.

Among the few comprehensive documents that are used as reference texts among mid- and high-ranking public officials is the "Rural
Development Policies and Strategies [RDPS]." According to the government, previous governments designed and implemented inappropriate national policies that hindered Ethiopia's economic development
and exposed it to structural problems. This document stated that the
present government has drafted prudent economic programs that reflect
the social and economic realities of Ethiopia.[35]

The economic policy of the present government is based on the
principles of a market economy, anchored in the agricultural sector and
geared towards facilitating rapid and sustainable economic development. The focus is to utilize scarce resources efficiently, to make use of
the country's abundant resources (land and labor), and to create a political environment for public participation in the decisionmaking process. The document states that a clearer vision and dedication of public
officials is also essential to execute the development policy.[36]

In the RDPS document, emphasis is placed on the need to enhance
the productive capacities of farmers through basic education and training programs on farming techniques. The document stresses that the
quality of education is as important as the expansion of education for
rural communities. In addition, the government asserts that courses
offered, particularly in primary schools, should focus on convincing the
younger generation to engage in farming and cottage industry activities.
It seeks to sensitize the growing number of school attendees to accept
the reality that the completion of primary and secondary education,
perhaps even tertiary education, will not automatically lead to employment in the urban and civil service sectors. In other words, the cultural
transformation of the younger generation is viewed as essential to
bringing about positive attitudinal changes towards low-level and non-
civil sector employment.

Furthermore, the RDPS notes that a healthy population is a productive population. Given the shortage of financial resources and human
capital in Ethiopia, it would be difficult to deliver health services to the
rural community. The health situation in Ethiopia is that the majority of
the people are suffering from preventable diseases that account for almost 80% of the total number of patients treated. Thus, the document
highlights that instead of building structurally appealing hospitals,
which are mainly erected in major cities, the government should speed
up the establishment of health centers for every 2,500 residents as a
practical approach to improving the delivery of health services to the
people.

The document further states that the expansion of trade and industry should be accompanied by an increased absorption of domestic re-

sources such as agricultural raw material and labor as well as creating employment opportunities for the urban labor force. In the absence of reliable and transportation services, adopting a market-driven economic policy would be an ineffective policy instrument to bring about rapid and sustainable development. In this case, both the Federal and Regional governments share the responsibility for maintaining and constructing main and feeder roads.

The overriding objective of the government is not merely to ensure the construction of roads on an equitable basis, measured by the length of roads in each region, but to integrate one region with another, and the nation with the outside world through a network of transportation systems. Regional governments are entrusted with the responsibility of linking feeder roads with highways and other main roads that are built by the Federal government based on economic viability. On the other hand, if the development of an area has the potential to cause a ripple effect in the development of the region and other sectors of the regional and national economy, the Federal government is expected to play a leading role in building feeder or main roads.[37]

Agriculture-Development Led Industrialization Policy

The Agriculture-Development Led Industrialization (ADLI) scheme was formulated soon after the present government came to power in 1991. The ADLI approach reflects the country's prevailing realities of an acute shortage of capital as well as surplus labor endowment and potentially cultivable land in most parts of Ethiopia. The government envisioned that for "agriculture to continue serving as an engine of growth," the long-term development strategy needed to emphasize labor-intensive and land-enhancing technologies "such as fertilizer and improved seeds and other cultural practices."[38] The strategy sought to encourage the active and direct participation of the rural community, which necessitated the need for empowering farmers with a sense of ownership of land and building their skills and capital. The government asserted that subsequent to "the removal of the monarchy and the dissolution of feudalism in Ethiopia, there is no landlessness as all farmers have landholdings" and that the necessary skills and capital are acquired through extension programs and credit schemes.[39]

However, according to a study conducted by the World Bank, until 1998, the current government discouraged (though not explicitly prohibiting) the redistribution of land, which ultimately worked as an exogenous disincentive factor for investment in the land. The study noted that local administrators are often influenced by political pressures to determine who gets how many hectares of land and where. A household survey in Amhara, Oromiya, Southern Nations and Nationalities Region (S.N.N.R), and Tigray regional states suggests regional variations in the expectation of losing or gaining land because of administrative redistribution measures. The World Bank report concluded: "Large inter-regional differences in the expectation of future redistribution (ranging from 20% in Amhara to 2% in Tigray) suggest that policy decisions affecting these issues are indeed taken at the regional rather than national level."[40] More importantly, although there may be variations across regions, "land rights in Ethiopia are highly insecure" and "higher tenure security and transferability could enhance investment and agricultural productivity."[41]

Implicit in building a political and economic community of states within the framework of a federal system is the awareness that the greater the probability of losing or gaining land through redistribution, the lesser the propensity for farmers to invest and to maintain their land. Therefore, ensuring "producers tenure security could have a large pay-off in terms of rural productivity and poverty reduction."[42] In addition, such measures could have important implications for reducing environmental degradation and managing conflict between neighboring farmers and ethnic groups.

On the other hand, regional differences in tenure security and transfer rights may also undermine poverty alleviation and rural-centered development strategies, thereby instilling a sense of marginalization between ethnic groups in the various regions. Having said that, however, with more intensive farming and better use of farming technologies, the ratio of exportable agricultural output is likely to increase proportional to the decline in the ratio of production for the domestic market.[43] The assumption of the Ministry of Finance and Economic Development is that the production of exportable agricultural commodities is inversely related to the production of agricultural commodities for the domestic market. "But the extremely small ratio urbanization of the country could well raise market outlet as a critical issue due to inadequacy of domestic demand, thereby making exports a necessity."[44]

Thus, the expectation for a proportional rise and decline in the production of agricultural goods for export and own-consumption is undermined not only by the domestic market size but also by the weak purchasing power of urban dwellers. Consequently, an effective execution of ADLI strategy must necessarily and sufficiently address the ways in which domestic market outlets and urban dwellers' purchasing power could improve. In addition, tariff and non-tariff barriers to trade need to be included in the economic policy equation.

Although Ethiopia is one of the beneficiaries of the African Growth and Opportunity Act and the European Union preferential treatment legislation, these seemingly appealing opportunities for opening markets of the developed nations to developing countries' commodities are conditional on reciprocal market access to developed nations' goods and services. The effect of reciprocal response by developing nations on the growth of their infant industries may even be more harmful to their economies than eliminating traditional tariff barriers to trade. A progressive or dramatic removal of tariff barriers to trade is simply the tip of the iceberg in the international trade arena. As Maria Norrfalk, Director-General of the Swedish International Development Cooperation Agency, noted, the total amount of aid to developing nations is about $54 billion annually, which is the same amount of grants that the United States government annually gives to its farmers. Thus, the current policy of the developed world is that it "takes away with one hand what it gives with the other."[45]

Qualitative requirements for accessing United States and European Union markets are obviously difficult to quantify and are inherently subjective and left to the discretion of customs and international trade officials' decisions on whether or not such commodities meet the health, safety, and environmental regulations of the client nation. Meeting these tariff and non-tariff barriers to trade may warrant the issuance of a license; even so, an exporting country such as Ethiopia still needs to acquire the financial and human resources that enable it to stimulate the appetite of consumers in a client nation to purchase its products. That is, social and cultural barriers are also factors that condition consumers' preference in the client nation. Such subjective barriers to trade could reduce the gains from preferential treatments.

Furthermore, given the historical and current rate of productivity of the agricultural sector in Ethiopia, ADLI seems to be more of an abstract construction than a prudent development strategy. For instance, conflict over grazing land and the sporadic and sometimes persistent drought followed by a sharp decline in agricultural productivity and tremendous loss of lives characterizes the Horn of African countries, especially Ethiopia. The recurring and devastating consequences of drought and conflict are precisely the reasons for setting up the Early Warning System by the governments of the Horn of Africa in cooperation with international development agencies. This institutional arrangement has been established to predict potential threats to human lives, either as a result of drought or inter-ethnic and intra-state conflict in the region. The plan emanates from the belief that it may not be entirely possible to stop drought immediately but the Early Warning System can help prepare governments and non-governmental organizations to mitigate the catastrophic consequences of drought and war.

According to *The Reporter*, in late 2002, there were over 30 million people in need of emergency food aid in Southern and Eastern Africa, and almost 50% of them were in Ethiopia. In 2000, the need for food aid in Ethiopia may not have been as urgent as it was in late 2002. Nevertheless, it was serious enough for some Ethiopians in North America and Western Europe to raise funds and make donations to the government agency responsible for delivering and distributing food to the affected regions. Other international organizations such as the United States Agency for International Development (USAID) and the European Union (EU) have done their part to offset the catastrophic consequences of drought by donating thousands of metric tons of rice, wheat, and cooking oil. In the past five years alone, Ethiopia has received 3.3 million metric tons of food aid from international donors. The country has grown more dependent on foreign food aid than it was in the 1980s. "The volume of food aid in response to emergency needs … had increased by 2.3 percent per annum since 1980, which marks a growth of more than 60 percent over the period."[46]

Financially, the EU allocated 25 million *Euros*, of which 9 million *Euros* have already been disbursed, to finance the implementation of the government's food security programs in the most vulnerable regions to drought in Amhara, Oromiya, and Tigray Regional States. The balance, 16 million *Euros*, was to be disbursed sometime during the 2004 fiscal year.[47] The World Bank has also signed a $60 million grant agreement with the government of Ethiopia that was earmarked for assisting the government "to respond to the [drought] emergency and help affected families to survive the emergency, regain productive assets and also develop sustainable livelihood."[48]

As the data in Table 4.1 shows, with the exception of Benishangul/Gumuz region, which has less than 1 million people, no region has escaped the immediate and direct impact of the drought in Ethiopia. While the magnitude and scope of the impact of the drought transcend the rural areas, one would expect that the resources generated from various sources would significantly reduce the number of drought victims. For example, on May 25, 2003, the former spokesperson of the government, Selome Tadesse, and a number of other individuals organized a fund raising event in Addis Ababa under the slogan "A *Birr* for A Compatriot."

The event was held in two places, the Sheraton Hotel and *Meskel Adebabay*, which is a promenade designated for citizens and public officers gathering during a national holiday. The promenade was fenced off so that the ordinary citizens of the city had to pay a cover charge of at least one *Birr* as part of the fund raising efforts. At the Sheraton Hotel, there were foreign dignitaries as well as officials, including the President, Minister of Education, and Commissioner of the Emergency Preparedness and Response Commission of the government of Ethiopia. Obviously, they gathered for the same purpose, but one needs to be wary of the potential impact of the physical distancing and the level of commitment between public official and citizens on the formation of a united front to waging a war against drought. The very fact that the fund raising event was held in two different places suggests that public officials did not seem to take the opportunity to live up to the expectation of the government of "bringing government closer to the people."[49]

Table 4.1: Regions Affected by Drought, 2002-2003

Region	In Need of Urgent Food Aid	Number of People Affected	Required Food Aid (in metric tons)
Affar	786,2000	1,093,400	130,726
Amhara	3,296,200	3,958,000	374,192
Ben/Gumuz	-	-	-
Dire Dawa	73,500	98,500	12,222
Gambella	58,400	69,600	8,017
Harari	20,000	38,000	2,220
Oromiya	3,110,900	4,150,100	407,353
S.N.N.P	1,114,700	1,586,500	116,748
Somali	1,028,900	1,147,100	124,515
Tigray	1,831,600	2,131,900	265,149
Total	**11,320,400**	**14,273,600**	**1,441,142**

Source: Dawit Kelemework, "How serious is the drought," *Reporter* (16 December 2002), p.5, col.1.

Nevertheless, at the end of the event, the total pledges from individuals and government and private institutions amounted to over 11 million *Birr*, which is approximately 1.3 million dollars at the current exchange rate. This is in addition to the millions of dollars that have been raised for drought victims from the EU, United States government, the World Bank, and many international organizations since the government of Ethiopia announced its preliminary assessment and prediction of food insecurity in 2000. Given the generous donations by Ethiopians and the international community, it is reasonable to expect that the number of drought victims would significantly decline. Instead, the number of people affected by the drought does not seem to have diminished. To be sure, relief aid has been distributed to some areas, for example, Alamata district, Southern Zone of the Tigray State. A total of 49,000 drought-affected people in the district have received more than 6,000 quintals of relief grain, which is approximately 13 kg per person per month.[50]

By mid-2002, the government begun to engage in what appears to be an expeditious response to the crisis in resettling farmers in the most affected regions of Amhara, Tigray, and Oromiya in fertile areas within the same region. In some cases, the farmers have been "voluntarily" resettled, with some leaving their children and wives outside the ethnic boundaries imposed by the government. Following reports by *Doctors Without Border*[51] and Ethiopian newspaper staff reporters on the disastrous situation of the resettlement areas, the United States Ambassador to Ethiopia and other Ethiopian government representatives paid a visit to the resettlement areas in the three regions.

Ethiopian Television reporters that accompanied the delegates conducted interviews with some of the settlers. In all cases, the interviewees complained about the absence of medical services, water, schools, farming tools and oxen. Some of them courageously and forthrightly stated that they were in a worse situation now than they were before. Irritated by such responses, the Minister of Rural Development and Deputy Prime Minster, Addisu Legesse, told Ethiopian Television that farmers, especially when they see foreigners and government officials, believe that their miserable situation will go away and that foreigners always come with charities and immediate solutions to their plight. He went on to suggest that such complaints are not uncommon and that they reflect tactics often used by farmers with dependent tendencies and habits.[52]

Indeed, according to *Doctors Without Border*, the reality is that settlers started arriving "in Shawe camp 10 months ago as a result of migration from Hararghe due to land pressure . . . [and that] their health status had already deteriorated." *Doctors Without Border* further commented that: "The recent resettlement in Bidre took place in a rushed attempt because of the anticipated rains."[53] Furthermore, in a desperate attempt to survive and because of a lack of systematic and organized settlement programs, farmers took the initiative to migrate to and settle in what may be potentially conflict-ridden settlement areas. The possibility of inter-ethnic conflict is not far-fetched, particularly given the government-imposed "ethnic" boundaries and lack of preemptive studies on the capacity of the settlement areas. The total number of displaced families or "resettled families," as they are conveniently termed, was estimated at 140,000, which was expected rise before the end of the 2003 farming season.

There is an even more disturbing reason why drought and starvation and their consequences such as mass displacement, food insecurity, wrecking of social and family lives, and death revisit Ethiopia time and again, even though a significant amount of relief aid reaches the country. On the containers of donated food supplies, particularly those from the USAID, notices are printed in bold marks which read: "This product is neither for sale nor for exchange." Despite the warning, one finds these items on sale in the shops and street markets in some of the major cities in the country. This takes place at a time when almost 15 million or 25% of the population look to their government and the international community for salvation.

The discovery of donated items at the local markets in many cities in Ethiopia demonstrates the lack of accountability and transparency of the Emergency Preparedness and Response Commission and its disregard for the agonies and suffering of drought victims. One wonders if the millions of dollars contributed by Ethiopians and the international community reach those in dire need of salvation. If these officials found it difficult to investigate why donated food items are on the market rather than in the homes of the drought-stricken families, then it is even more difficult to account whether relief funds from the World Bank, EU, and others are appropriately utilized. That is, it would be even more difficult to account whether the relief funds were appropriately utilized to help reverse the destitute conditions of drought victims.

Equally alarming is that the government has no sector-specific policy for agriculture and industry in spite of the fact that it claims to pay special attention to the needs of the rural community and build an industrial economy anchored in agriculture. Through state-controlled media outlets, the government expounds the notion of transforming the subsistence into a market economy by creating the necessary conditions for domestic and foreign investment in commercial agriculture. While this may suggest a far-sighted approach to development, it is, however, disconcerting to realize the absence of a policy framework to guide investments in the agricultural sector. Why the government is determined to bring about industrialization based on the agricultural sector is theoretically and practically reprehensible. Dwindling soil nutrients and fertility as well as fluctuating prices and unpredictable and, often, declining agricultural productivity have often caused the country to be dependent on foreign food aid. No sector is more vulnerable to a host of domestically and internationally rooted currents of price shocks and diminishing rate of productivity than the agricultural sector of developing countries, especially Ethiopia. These are precisely some the reasons why the industrialized nations heavily subsidize their own agricultural sector, which adversely affects and penalizes developing countries' farmers.[54]

Nevertheless, in the absence of a policy, domestic and foreign investors would have no way of knowing the exact terms, conditions, liabilities, or incentives for investment in the agricultural sector. The result is often investors' anxiety, a heightened sense of uncertainty, and confusion, which worsens if some officials undertake arbitrary decisions in granting or rejecting, for example, a request for a plat of farmland. A sense of uncertainty and confusion among investors and the general public usually provide breeding ground for corrupt practices and nepotism. Because, in a policy there would have been a clear statement of what is expected of investors and what they should expect from the government. When the rules of the game are blurred, it widely opens the door for decisionmakers, individuals, and corporations to bend the rules in a direction that brings the most desirable outcome.

To be sure, there were discussions and workshops on the draft agricultural policy in 2001 and 2002, which were held primarily in Addis Ababa. If presented to the Council of Ministers, the draft policy would have automatically been approved for further debate and approval by the legislative body. In turn, the proposed policy could have faced little or no opposition by members of the legislature—the House of Peoples Representatives—principally because one party dominates the decisionmaking process. Nevertheless, while the absence of an agricultural policy clearly results in a short-term disincentive for investment in this sector, the government continues on pursuing an Agriculture-Development Led Industrialization policy for three main reasons.

First, it is a political calculation to claim gearing national policies toward addressing the needs and desires of the agricultural community because they are the majority electors and major contributors to government revenue and Gross Domestic Product. Second, agriculture is labor-intensive and requires little or no skilled manpower and capital. Since Ethiopia is endowed with surplus labor and abundant water resources and fertile land, which are suitable for agriculture, it seems to make economic sense to concentrate efforts and resources on the sector which provides greater comparative advantage vis-à-vis other sectors of the economy. Third, unlike the economic policies of the previous governments, the present government seeks, at least in principle, to make land a truly public property where individuals have constitutionally and legally protected property ownership rights. While rhetoric is quite different practice, owning a piece of farm and/or residential land has always comforted and created a sense of pride in the minds of Ethiopians.

To be sure, the three governments of the past half-century have had similar visions, but the strategies were distinct from one another. For example, the government of Haile-Selassie envisioned industrializing Ethiopia's economy by promoting agricultural productivity and drawing on resources from that sector to build industrial complexes in and around Addis Ababa and Asmara. Much of the country's accessible and suitable land for commercial farming was also in the hands of members of the royal family, a few landlords, and the church, which discouraged domestic and foreign investment in commercial farming. To a large extent, land holdings by the aristocracy were kept idle mainly due to the aristocrats' perception and attitudes towards farming as a profession of the lowest class of the Ethiopian society. Looking down on farming as an ascriptive role for the lowest social and economic classes has certainly been an anti-development cultural problem. Consequently, the successive regimes launched an attack on anti-development cultural practices and perceptions.

Comparatively, one of the first major steps taken by the military government was outlawing private ownership of land and recognizing the *Arso-Ader* (farmers) as the backbone of the Ethiopian economy and inseparable ally of the proletariat. It then went on transferring private farms into state farms, establishing *Sefera* programs, and creating marketing boards to control the price of food. In the early years of the socialist movement, one of the military government's main objectives was also to culturally transform the society, including celebrating and recognizing the role of farmers and farming, *Arso-Ader* and *Gibrena*, in the Ethiopian economy. Empowering farmers with a sense of leading the socialist revolution in partnership with the proletariat may have paid off. There were signs of revival in agricultural productivity, even though total agricultural output did not meet the target to enable industrial growth and expansion.

Cooperative farms were widely recognized as a significant contributor to the revival of agricultural productivity, but the management of marketing boards, administration of price mechanisms, and mismanagement of state-owned farms depressed the contribution of the agricultural sector to the economy, in general, and to industrial growth, in particular. In this regard, an alternative argument holds that with visionary leadership and efficient management, private investment in the agricultural sector could have led to industrialization. Opening the agriculture-based economy for domestic and foreign investment could also relieve the public sector from the responsibility of purchasing equipment for medium and large-scale mechanized farming. The private sector is known for its management efficiency and utilization of resources to maximize profit and, as a result, land would not remain idle as it happened during Haile-Selassie's government.

Given past experiences and practices, the problem with the Ethiopian economy cannot be resolved by merely formulating policies and strategies. This is because the previous governments of Ethiopia had generally a coherent policy framework, but they failed to achieve their development objectives for the apparent reason that the country has remained one of the poorest in the world. For decades, the contribution of each sector of the economy (agriculture, industry, manufacturing, and services) to GDP remained almost constant. The contribution of agriculture, industry, manufacturing, and services as percentage of Gross Domestic Product in 1965 were 58%, 14%, 7%, and 28%, respectively. By 1989, agriculture as percentage of GDP declined considerably to 40%, with significant increase in the contribution of the services sector (42%), and a slight increment in the contribution of industry and manufacturing (16% and 11%) to GDP.[55] Almost five years later, in 1995, after the coming to power of the Meles government, agriculture, industry, and services as percentage of GDP were 57%, 10%, and 33%, respectively.[56]

To say that employment generated by any of the sectors is, except for agriculture, in the single digits of the total percentage of employment is not surprising. Foreign exchange earnings from the export of semi-finished manufacturing goods would be remarkable small as well. Exports of hides and skins constitute a significant proportion of primary and semi-processed leather products which undergo a second and final phase of production in foreign industries. Some of these finished manufactured leather products are imported back into Ethiopia. Few Ethiopian industries have limited productive capacities to manufacture these goods domestically either for export or to meet domestic demands for manufactured leather products. This happens because Ethiopia lacks the human and physical capital which are essential to making industrialists and manufacturers in Ethiopia effectively compete in the global economy. For private investors, the availability of cheap labor may be one essential component that stimulates their appetite for investment. But, labor is cheap in Ethiopia because it is unskilled and industry demands, at a minimum, semi-skilled labor.

For a country facing structural problems, having a trade and industrial policy cannot be sufficient to realize the long-held yearning for industrialization. A policy for one sector of the economy has to be harmonized and coordinated with the policies of other sectors. Moreover, land—which has been a source of conflict and a political platform and ideology that helped the elites to rise to power—has been transferred from State ownership to public ownership, which are essentially two sides of the same coin. It is dumbfounding to note that while almost everything in Ethiopia is auctioned, the question of land reform is now considered a "dead issue." This will not only frustrate potential foreign investors, but it will soon have devastating long-term environmental consequences and serves as a breeding ground for social crises.

Ethiopia lacks able and visionary leadership, and perhaps a benevolent authoritarian government. It is interesting to note that the government of Meles, like the military regime, is expending scarce financial resources and exhausting limited human capital to turn the theory of free market economy into practice, a theory divorced from Ethiopian realities. Contextually, the military regime was ardent in making socialism a reality and sacrificed not merely computable material and financial resources but also immeasurable human lives. Clearly, Ethiopia could benefit enormously from producing skilled manpower and formulating a national development policy that takes a hard look at the internal and external dynamics of development. Even designing a subsector policy requires leadership that takes lessons from the past, critically assesses the present environment, and makes projection for future.

Summary and Conclusion

The three governments placed an unwarranted emphasis on the agricultural sector, which is ironically the most vulnerable sector of the economy. From Haile-Selassie to Meles Zenawi, Ethiopian policymakers remain exceedingly preoccupied, perhaps even obsessed, with the notion that agriculture should fuel and propel the process of industrialization and help bring about rapid and sustainable development. Agricultural productivity in Ethiopia has been declining since the 1973 drought. Yet, three successive governments have insisted on relying on an agricultural sector that cannot meet the growing domestic demand for food.

If the purpose of a policy is to reflect reality, then the realities in Ethiopia do not justify the prescription of Agriculture-Development Led Industrialization or, generally, the wholesale adoption of a market-economic policy. Therefore, the apparent paradox between relying on the most vulnerable sector of the economy and reaching an industrial stage or achieving economic development seems to be justified by the importance of land as a tool for political legitimization. Nevertheless, the fact remains that without a policy framework, it is impossible to harmonize one sector with another, strengthen backward and forward linkages, reevaluate achievements and failures, and take the necessary reform measures.

The policies and strategies of the previous two regimes sought to identify the ways in which land, as the country's main resource, could be the foundation for industrialization. Land was one of the main sources of revenue and continues to be the case. The granting of large hectares of land to a selected few with or without the capacity to increase industrial or non-industrial agricultural products was not primarily based on economic feasibility but served as a political instrument to appease real or potential dissidents against imperial rule. The military government issued a proclamation to eliminate private land holdings, whether they were idle or not, as well as extra urban houses. Unlike the Haile-Selassie government, the military government took steps so that the country's main and essential resource—land—was no longer a political instrument at the cost of under-utilization and over-aggrandizement by unproductive segments of society.

The government of Prime Minister Meles seems to have drawn some important lessons from its predecessors. On the one hand, it views land as the country's main resource for generating revenue and leading the country to industrialization and food self-sufficiency. On the other hand, making land public property and distributing it based on family size inculcates in the minds of Ethiopian farmers a sense of dependency on the government. The effort to incorporate both lessons and harmonize the economics and politics of land will have a long-term environmental side effect and political consequences. The question of land redistribution remains contentious and one of the main political instruments that creates a sense of public dependency on the will of the government. To the extent that this issue remains unresolved, the expansion of industrial establishments will not stimulate agricultural productivity of farmers, especially in the regions where there is a higher degree of uncertainty about tenure security and transferability.

Furthermore, an executable land redistribution policy that empowers farmers with a sense of ownership of property is as urgent an issue for increasing agricultural output as it is for political stability. To increase industrial productivity and to enhance the delivery of social services, electric power generation and its equitable distribution are also critical. If one takes the example cited by Legesse, the huge profits of Muger Cement Factory are partly derived from the labor power expended in the production of cement as well as from the denial of social services by diverting electric power from residential services to industries such as Muger.

In Addis Ababa, it would be difficult to imagine that electric power distribution to residential areas, retail traders, and small business firms is disrupted frequently. The supply of electric power to these areas is on a weekly ration basis to meet the demand for electric power by a few industries with little or no social returns or contribution to reducing the level of poverty in any meaningful way. With the exception of a few residential areas occupied by high-level government officials and some industrial establishments, the rest of the capital city experiences frequent power outages. In such instances, a responsible government would have taken fiscal and monetary policy measures to compensate loses that may have incurred to small business and inconveniences to households due to the diversion of electric power services. Such policies not only reflect the government's commitment to social and economic justice but also strengthen consumers' purchasing power and buttress the production and consumption of domestic products.

Notes

1. The Imperial Government of Ethiopia, *Yehuletegnaw Amist Amet Yelemat Ekid, 1955-1960* (The Second Five Year Development Plan, 1962-1967) (Addis Ababa: Berhanena Selam Printing Press, 1962).

2. Ibid.

3. Abebe Tadesse, "Drought imposes social crisis, number of severely affected drought victims increases," *The Reporter* (14 May 2003), p.1. See also, "United States announces additional food contribution," *Reporter* (14 May 2003), p.3; Emrakeb Assefa, "US diverts food aid from Iraq to Ethiopia," *Reporter* (14 May 2003), p.1.

4. Emperor Haile-Selassie, *Hewotiena YeEthiopia Ermja, II Tiraz,* (My Life and Ethiopia's Progress, Vol. II) (Addis Ababa: Berhanena Selam Printing Press, 1941), p.325.

5. The Imperial Government of Ethiopia, *Yehuletegnaw Amist Amet Yelemat Ekid, 1955-1960,* p.40.

6. Ibid.

7. Ibid., p.84.

8. Ibid., p.148.

9. The Ministry of Education and Fine Arts, "The Second Five Year Development Plan, 1962-1967," (Addis Ababa: Ministry of Education Archive, n.d), Chapter 17, p.12.

10. Ibid.

11. Ibid., p.61.

12. The Ministry of Education, "National Development Goals, Priorities, and Policies for the Third Five Year Plan, 1967-1972," (Addis Ababa: Ministry of Education Archive, n.d), p.10.

13. Ibid.

14. Ibid., p.15.

15. Ibid., p.7.

16. Ibid., p.24.

17. Ibid., p.3.

18. Ibid., p.17.

19. Ibid., p.42.

20. Ibid.

21. Office of the Planning Commission, "Strategies Outline for the Fourth Five Year Plan, 1973-1978," (Addis Ababa: Ministry of Education Archive, n.d).

22. The Ministry of Education, "National Development Goals, Priorities, and Policies for the Third Five Year Plan," (Addis Ababa: Ministry of Education Archive, n.d), Chapter 3, p.6.

23. Ibid., p.11.

24. The Transitional Military Government of Ethiopia, "Government Ownership and Control of the Means of Production," *Negarit Gazeta*, Proclamation No. 26/1975 (Addis Ababa: Berhanena Selam Printing Press, 11 March 1975).

25. The Transitional Military Government of Ethiopia, "Public Ownership of Rural Lands," *Negarit Gazeta*, Proclamation No. 31/1975 (Addis Ababa: Berhanena Selam Printing Press, 29 April 1975).

26. Ibid.

27. The Transitional Military Government of Ethiopia, "Government Ownership of Urban Lands and Extra Houses," *Negarit Gazeta*, Proclamation No. 47/1975 (Addis Ababa: Berhanena Selam Printing Press, 26 July 1975).

28. The Transitional Military Government of Ethiopia, "*Yebeheyrawi Abiyotawi Yemirt Zemecha Yemejemeria Amet Ikid, 1971*" (National Revolutionary Production Campaign: First Year Plan, 1978," (Addis Ababa: Ministry of Education Archive, 1978), p.5.

29. The Transitional Military Government of Ethiopia, "*YeIndustry Kifle Economy YeAser Amet Meri Ikid (Rekik), Meskerem 1975*" (A Ten Year Industrial Policy Principal Plan) (Addis Ababa: Ministry of Education Archive, September 1984), p.2.

30. Ibid.

31. World Bank, *The State in a Changing World* (New York: Oxford University Press, 1997), p.240.

32. Gelase Mutahaba and Jide Balogun, *Enhancing Policy Management Capacity in Africa* (West Hartford: Connecticut, Cumarian Press, 1992), p.24.

33. Joseph Stiglitz, *Globalization and Its Discontents* (New York: W.W. Norton & Company, 2002), p.25-7.

34. Stiglitz, p.27.

35. The Federal Democratic Republic of Ethiopia, *Yegeter Lemat Policiwoch Strategewochina Seltoch* (Rural Development Policies and Strategies) (Addis Ababa: Ministry of Information and Culture, November 2001).

36. Ibid., p.3.

37. Ibid., p.221.

38. The Ministry of Finance and Economic Development, The Federal Democratic Republic of Ethiopia, "Ethiopia, Sustainable Development and Poverty Reduction Program," unpublished report prepared for the World Bank (Addis Ababa), July 2002.

39. The Federal Democratic Republic of Ethiopia, "Ethiopia: Interim Poverty Reduction Strategy Paper 2000/01-2002/03," unpublished report prepared for the World Bank (Addis Ababa), November 2000.

40. Mulat Demeke and others, "Market and non-market transfers of land in Ethiopia: Implications for efficiency, equity, and non-farm development," unpublished study conducted for the World Bank (Washington, DC), January 2003.

41. Berhanu Nega and others, "Tenure Security and Land-Related Investment: Evidence from Ethiopia," unpublished study conducted for the World Bank (Washington, DC), 2001.

42. Ibid.

43. The Ministry of Finance and Economic Development, "Ethiopia, Sustainable Development and Poverty Reduction Program."

44. The Federal Democratic Republic of Ethiopia, "Ethiopia: Interim Poverty Reduction Strategy Paper 2000-2002."

45. "What the US gives its farmers each year is equivalent to total annual global assistance," *Ethiopian Herald* (22 May 2003), p.3, col. 3.

46. Melaku Demissie, "Ethiopia becomes world's 15th largest food aid recipient," *The Reporter* (21 May 2003), p.1, col. 4.

47. "The European Union granted 9 million *Euros* for the implementation of the food security program," *Addis Zemen* (31 May 2003), p.1, col.1.

48. "World Bank grant," *Ethiopian Herald* (13 May 2003), p.3, col.1.

49. Stiglitz, p.25.

50. "Relief distributed among 49,000 needy," *Ethiopian Herald,* (22 May 2003), p.1, col.1.

51. See, for example, "Inadequate Planning of Resettlement Leads to Unnecessary Suffering," *Addis Tribune* (16 May 2003), p.1, col. 3

52. Ethiopian Television, news broadcast, 10 p.m., (27 May 2003).

53. "Inadequate Planning of Resettlement Leads to Unnecessary Suffering," *Addis Tribune* (16 May 2003).

54. Michael Todaro, *Economic Development*, 5th ed., (White Plains, NY: Longman, 1994), p.355.

55. World Bank, *World Development Report 1991* (New York: Oxford University Press, 1991), p.208.

56. United Nations Development Programme, *Human Development Report 1998* (New York: Oxford University Press, 1998), p.183.

Chapter V

Inequity in the Distribution of Socioeconomic Resources

The previous chapter critically examined the development policies and strategies of the three successive governments of Ethiopia (Emperor Haile-Selassie, President Mengistu Haile-Mariam, and Prime Minister Meles Zenawi). This chapter reflects on the outcome of the development policies and strategies of the three governments by examining statistical data on revenue and expenditure, agriculture, manufacturing industries, health, education, and transportation.[1] Ultimately, the various statistical data analyzed in this chapter should give the reader an in-depth understanding of how socioeconomic resources were distributed under the three governments of differing and, often, antagonistic political persuasions and objectives.

Data on each sector are presented and analyzed separately according to three successive eras: the era of aristocratic, militaristic, and civilian rule. The policies of the various sectors of the Ethiopian economy—or the economy of any country for that matter—are ideally designed to reinforce one another. Thus, one should not rush to conclusion that the people in a particular region or province were denied of access to social opportunities simply because the number of schools, for example, happened to be less than the number of schools in other regions or provinces. This is because regional and national development requires alignment and realignment of sector-specific policies and harmonization of each sector in line with national development objectives. One sector of the economy may be a priority area of investment at some point in time, depending on how policymakers chose to protect and advance the interests of the ruling elites or the public at large.

    More often than not, previous studies on Ethiopia identify very
few sectors to make generalizations about the extent of resource maldistribution in that country. Comparatively, the data presented in this
chapter are broad enough to give the reader a clearer and a holistic
perspective on the scope, depth, and variations of socioeconomic maldistribution in Ethiopia. In particular, the data analyzed in this chapter
include the contribution of the agricultural, industrial, and service sectors to the Gross Domestic Product (GDP). Data on revenue and expenditure, by province, are presented as contributions to the growing
debate on whether there were diversions of resources from one province to another or from provinces dominated by subordinate ethnic
groups to the development of the alleged super-ordinate ethnic group.
Data on the distribution of manufacturing industries, number of employees, and wages and salaries, by province and region, are examined
with the view to explore the depth of regional variations in economic
growth, employment, and income.
    Furthermore, in light of the three governments' preoccupation
with utilizing domestic resources, data on the dependency ratio of the
manufacturing sector are presented to assess the degree to which
backward and forward linkages have been strengthened. Given greater
linkages between the agricultural and manufacturing sectors, the latter
may fuel the productivity of other sectors of the economy. Once the
multiplier effect is felt by other sectors of the economy, such as the
service and trade sectors, they in turn propel an increase and improvement in the delivery of social services. Notwithstanding the order in
which the ripple effect takes place, the manufacturing sector is important both as a part of the engine of growth and to examine the pattern
in the distribution of industries, employment, and wages and salaries
among the provinces or regions. The social sector (health and education) data analysis is concerned with the quantitative and qualitative
distribution of services.
    One final area of interest is exploring the maintenance and expan-
sion of primary, secondary, and feeder-roads. The provision and expansion of reliable roads is as critical to economic growth as it is to
narrowing the income differentials among the regions. Conversely,
limited access and poor road networks would mean a decline in productivity and an exacerbation of income differentials between the regions or ethnic groups. Data on road density is, therefore, analyzed as
an integral part of the holistic approach to economic growth and as a
necessary public goods to ensuring equitable regional growth and distribution of socioeconomic resources.
    Since population index is useful for placing the distribution of re-
sources into perspective, data on the population of each province or

region is provided in Appendix E and F. These regions or provinces, however they are demarcated, are ethnically heterogeneous and, therefore, any reference to a particular region or province should not be misconstrued as if the region/province is ethnically homogenous. For instance, in the Benishangul/Gumuz Regional State, the main ethnic groups are Berta (26.7%), Gumuz (23.4%), Amhara (22.2%), Oromo (12.8%), Shinasha (6.9%), and others make up 8% of the population of the region.[2]

The Harari Regional State is another example where there are diverse ethnic groups, which include the Oromo, Amhara, Harari, and Guragie ethnic groups constituting 52.3%, 32.6%, 7.1%, and 3.2% of the population of the region, respectively. Yet, the region is named after one of the minority ethnic groups, the Harari. Interestingly, even though the Oromos are a majority in Harari, they had very little interest, if any, in incorporating the region within the Oromiya State.[3] In other regional states, ethnic group A, for example, may be demographically more dominant than ethnic groups B, C, D, and so on, but the fact remains that it is erroneous to assume homogeneity in any of the newly demarcated administrative regions.[4] The redrawing of boundaries has obviously changed the geographical and demographic landscapes. For example, the province of Hararghe, which had one of the largest populations in the pre-Meles era, is now the Regional State of Harari with the lowest population (0.2%) in the country and is entirely surrounded by the Oromiya Regional State.

Having made these clarifications about the kind of data used and the ethnic heterogeneity of each region, we can now proceed with background discussions to highlight some of the internal and external forces that may have inhibited the governments' attempt at promoting equitable regional development. This discussion is followed by three consecutive sections of data analysis. The three sections comprise analysis of statistical data, presented in the form of figures (line graphs) and contingency tables. The figures and contingency tables are designed to help the reader capture the main points and patterns in the distribution of resources between provinces or regions. The last section of this chapter is devoted to summary and concluding remarks.

Background

In evaluating the success and setbacks of the Second Five Year Plan (1962-1966), the government of Emperor Haile-Selassie recognized the need for formulating a more prudent development policy that is anchored in the realities of Ethiopians. Indeed, one of the most important points revealed during the evaluation process of the Second

Five Year Plan and the contributions of the government of Haile-Selassie to succeeding governments is that it readily accepted the growing regional development variations and its lopsided national development policy. Even so, such actions as redistributing land to tillers and promoting equitable growth among the fourteen provinces had to fit conformably with the interests and aspirations of mid- and upper-tier civil servants.

In the absence of organized and dynamic grass-root organizations, a few potential losers of the policy reform within the output structure of the social system would be able to exert formidable influence in favor of maintaining the status quo. Alternatively, in countries such as Ethiopia where distributable goods are ever so deteriorating, even the most ardent and vigorous exponents of social justice could face stiff resistance from potential losers. In addition, the effectiveness of an equitable redistribution policy could be undermined by the fear of short-term losses or by the absence of politically astute and courageous members of the legislature.

Policies tend to be a paper exercise when civic groups are restricted from participating indirectly in the decisionmaking process, contribute to shaping policy agenda, or in the absence of organized constituents in support of new policy measures. The Ethiopian experience clearly demonstrates that dis-empowering ordinary citizens with the right to collectively express their views leads to a rise in the number of discontented groups and to a devastating political and economic consequences. In ways that was almost impossible to predict, the urban and rural masses spontaneously rose up against the ruling class, demanding an equitable distribution of land and expansion as well as delivery of such basic social services as potable water, primary health care, and education. However, the 1973/74 uprising was spontaneous and significantly deficient in civilian leadership. As a result, the demand for correcting maldistribution in socioeconomic resources took a violent turn and eclipsed one of the most celebrated and revered imperial rulers in Africa.

Subsequently and almost overnight, the armed force transformed itself from the Imperial State's instrument of coercion into a vanguard of the popular movement. In hindsight, the structural transformation did not turn out as beautifully as the transformation of a caterpillar into a butterfly. More by default and coercive power than by legitimacy, the armed force elevated itself to political power and, as a matter of urgency, sought to reconstitute internal law and order. The preconditions that contributed to the rise of the military government to the apex of political power will be further examined in chapter six. Suffix to say, however, the military government was, irrespective of its precarious rise onto the saddle of power, cognizant of the fact that inequity provides a fertile ground for political instability and economic deterioration. While searching for an appropriate ideological route, the military government of Mengistu Haile-Mariam took some notable measures to abolish the exploitative and oppressive production relations. It enacted such laws as the transfer of extra lands and houses to public ownership, expansion of social services to the most neglected regions of the country, and reduction of rents on residential and commercial housing.

To be sure, there were internal and external forces that worked against the aspirations of the majority poor and the efforts of the military government at abolishing the unproductive relationships. Internally, there were secessionist and irredentist groups and nationalist parties with pro-Western or Marxist inclinations that sabotaged the military government's efforts at cultural and economic transformations. However misguided and reformist the government may have been, these internal "reactionary" forces embarked on a strategy to irritate the regime like flees on an elephant skin. As such, they demanded the government's constant attention and diverted its energies away from tackling the most urgent and degenerating socioeconomic conditions of the majority. In 1980, for example, almost 36% of the government's expenditure were on defense and only 19.6% on social services.[5]

Externally, the former Soviet Union and its satellite states in Eastern Europe were busy supplying military advisors and arms, which had nothing to do with achieving the primary goal of culturally and economically transforming the country. Of all the socialist governments that either supported the military government or opposition groups in Ethiopia, only Cuba was involved both in strengthening the military capability of the government and in providing public health services. Western Europe treated Ethiopian secessionist and irredentist groups and opposition political parties as their counterbalancing forces against the spread of socialism in the Horn of Africa. Nevertheless, it is important to recall that, unlike the popular uprising that dismantled the Haile-Selassie government, the collapse of the military government was decisively influenced by the growing pubic discontent and the decline of its surrogate regimes in Eastern Europe.

While the magnitude of the forces unleashed by competing groups with varying ideologies and grievances on the effectiveness of the government's development plans cannot be underestimated, the military government was able to make some progress in setting the stage for equitable redistribution of socioeconomic resources among the provinces. To what extent the military government's development plans materialized and whether the government actually perfected the notions of super-ordinate/subordinate inter-ethnic relationships is the crux of the statistical data analysis in the subsequent section.

When the current government of Prime Meles Zenawi came to power, it inherited an economic system that appeared beyond reconstruction, ranging from an economic condition characterized by rising unemployment rate and deteriorating communication and transportation infrastructure. Socially and politically, the people were highly disempowered and had little or no confidence towards the new political elite. The military government's centralized system of economic management and political leadership also wrecked the intellectual and social foundations necessary for the new elites to experiment with a market-driven economic policy and a multiparty political system. In addition to these interlocking forces of underdevelopment, the present government had to reconcile conflicting demands that have been generated by internally and externally induced perceptions of marginalization.

Myth is a probability game in which its likelihood of becoming a reality improves with persistent and repeated trials. That is to say, for almost four decades many scholars firmly asserted the prevalence of a dominant/dependent inter-ethnic relationship in Ethiopia and elsewhere in Africa, thereby inspiring a growing number of domestic and foreign sympathizers of secessionist movements. By adopting a narrow theoretical framework, they explained almost every misfortune and tragic incidences to nothing more than ethnic conflict characterized by savagery and essentialist perception of one ethnic group against another. Of course, secessionist group leaders had to embrace such presumptuous, politically motivated, and ideologically contaminated rhetoric to elevate themselves to political power and agitate the already discontented public. It is unfortunate that some academics and Western-based development agencies such as the United States Agency for International Development legitimized, consciously or otherwise, the politically tainted, divisive, dichotomization of super-ordinate/subordinate relationship. They did so by applying an overly simplified theoretical framework to isolate, for example, language as evidence of supremacy and through their allocation of funds that favored one group or region over others. Given the discussion presented in chapter one and two, the role of some academics and development agencies in translating myths into realities is not surprising. What is really fascinating is that most members of the alleged super-ordinate group are convinced of their commanding position in the Ethiopian socio-cultural, economic, and political hierarchy.

The Tigray Peoples Liberation Front, the epicenter of political power and winner of the collapse of the military government which was brought about by its internal contradictions and the changing

global political landscape, had to recast its ideological tenet from secession to national unity. At the same time, it had to negotiate with
secessionist claimants and appease those with nationalist aspirations.
While creating a delicate balance between these contending forces was
no easy task for the incoming elite, they had to formulate a national
policy that addresses the burning desires of people for distributive justice as well.

All said and done, empowering citizens with the means to economic ends is contingent on mobilizing social and political forces and
economic resources. Collective and integrated mobilization of resources stimulates economic growth not only within each region but
also across regional boundaries. As indicated in chapter four, the government's economic reconstruction and development policies are cen-
tered round creating backward and forward linkages between the agricultural and manufacturing sectors. Therefore, one of the main prerequisites to accomplish agriculture-led industrialization in Ethiopia could
be by empowering farmers with a real sense of ownership of land.

A real sense of ownership of land increases the rate of private
capital investment and the number of hours farming household devote
to maintaining the land, thereby stimulating diversified agricultural
activity and improving the quality and quantity of agricultural products. However, empowering a largely agrarian society with ownership
of land is essentially the tip of the iceberg in laying the foundation for
an agriculture-led industrial economy in Ethiopia. The nature of agricultural activities and products make the Ethiopian economy vulnerable to a host of unpredictable shocks that affect the level of productivity and incomes of Ethiopian farmers.

Agricultural products are often perishable and susceptible to
changes in weather conditions and, therefore, their timely delivery depends on the existence of efficient and reliable road networks. While
expanding and upgrading road networks is generally left to the state
and is considered public goods, the benefits that accrue to each farming
household and to the national economy from accessing reliable roads
cannot be overemphasized. Reversing the pattern of resource maldistribution among the regions or ethnic groups also depends not merely
on adopting a free-market economic policy and leaving indigenous
enterprises to their own devices but also on the provision of public
goods and creation of a fertile ground for increasing household incomes, including through the provision of farm-to-market outlets.

A national policy that is designed to accelerate economic growth
based on one of the most susceptible sectors of the economy is certainly detached from reality. Alternatively, to the extent that policy
experts make the necessary fine-tuning, the reintroduction of the agri-

culture-centered industrialization policy may indeed be justified. Given the accumulation of experience and skills in traditional farming techniques and extreme imbalance between domestic demand and supply of agricultural goods, the government's renewed commitment to accelerate the productivity of the agricultural sector and, consequently, making this sector the basis for industrialization seems pragmatic. Although Ethiopia's small-scale farming communities are as industrious as they could be, their marginal productivity has diminished due to natural and man-made forces for which they have little or no control. Accepting the proposition that any genuine, practical, and visionary Ethiopian leader would find the wholesale adoption of free-market economic principle unrealistic and distorted, a principle which is not practiced even in the most advanced nations of the West, one still has to contend with such issues as re-stimulating the propensity to consume "homegrown" products and developing domestic market outlets.

Perhaps the most important difference that distinguishes the current government from its predecessors is its recognition that civic and political groups could contribute to the policymaking process. Such rhetoric stimulated many civic and political groups to flourish, seeking to contribute, even marginally, to the setting of the country's development agenda and policy. Whether or not the public is meaningfully participating in the decisionmaking process is a subject that deserves in-depth analysis. Thus, the extent of public participation in the decisionmaking process, directly or indirectly, will be addressed in subsequent chapters. Meanwhile, it can be argued that regression from democratic principles and practices would have implications not only on the country's economic development potential but it would also undermine the very objective of the present government; namely equitable redistribution of socioeconomic resources among the various regions or ethic groups.

Myths of Historical Distortions

The overarching principle that guided the economic policy of the government of Haile-Selassie was the growing conviction among policymakers of the time that a developing country such as Ethiopia has comparative advantage in the production of agricultural goods. The economic policy of the Haile-Selassie government was designed to ensure food security and, at the same time, encourage the production and continuous supply of raw material to the manufacturing sector. Its long-term goal was to leapfrog from agrarian to industrial economy.

As shown in Appendix A, the average rate of agricultural productivity, in 1962, at the end of the First Five Year Plan, was less than a quarter of quintal per hectare of land.[6] By the late 1960s, the average rate of productivity increased dramatically to more than a quarter of a quintal per hectare of land. Retrospectively, this was a significant accomplishment in terms of raising the level of incomes of farmers, utilizing domestic resources, and establishing and enhancing backward and forward linkages between the agricultural and manufacturing industries of the food processing, beverage, and textile sub-industries.

According to *Menen* (a journal named after Empress *Etege Menen*), in the 1950s and mid-1960s, at least 25 new industries were established annually. Most of these industries were food, textile, and beverage industries, in that order of significance in generating public revenue and to the national economy. The food and textile industries also tended to be more labor-intensive than other industries in the country,[7] thereby opening employment opportunities to urban dwellers and attracting labor from the rural sector.

However, the trickling down of benefits from the establishment and expansion of industries were limited to very few cities. This is because, for whatever their worth, much of the economic and social sector activities were concentrated in and around the politically and strategically significant provinces and cities. For instance, in December 1971, of the total number of manufacturing industries in Ethiopia, 64% were in Addis Ababa (including Debre Zeit and Nazrett), 28% in Asmara, and 5% in Dire Dawa and Harar. In other words, approximately 92% of the manufacturing industries were concentrated in and around Addis Ababa and Asmara, whereas twelve out of the fourteen provinces had practically no industries.[8] Thus, throughout the Haile-Selassie era, industrial activities continued to benefit members of the "prominent families both as partners to the expatriates' enterprises and from the sale or rent of land and buildings."[9]

Moreover, although the demand for agricultural raw material may have increased due to the establishment of new food processing and textile industries, by the end of the Third Year Plan, agricultural productivity declined along with the average area of cultivated land. Yet, the average yield per hectare of land was almost the same as that of the end of the Second Five Year Plan.[10] The increase in the average rate of productivity per hectare of land, despite a decline in the percentage of cultivated areas, seem to be correlated with investment in research and development, favorable whether conditions, and usage of fertilizers and modern farming techniques.

For instance, seven new agricultural research centers were created in the late 1960s in different regions of the country; namely Holeta (Shoa province), Melka Worera (Harar province), Bako (Wollega province), Jimma (Kaffa province), Nazrett, Gambella (formerly in

Wollega province), and Gode (presently in Somali region). These research centers were established mostly in central and southern Ethiopia, which were identified as regions suitable for agricultural research and development.[11]

Despite the government's efforts at stimulating agricultural productivity, total agricultural output deteriorated from 433 metric tons in 1962 to 333 metric tons in 1973. The apparent decline in average output by 100 metric tons in ten years seems statistically insignificant. But, within that decade, there was also population growth at annual rate between 2.5 to 3.0 percent which makes the extent of imbalance between the demand for and supply of food more pronounced and magnified. Taking population growth into the production and consumption equation, the total agricultural output could not have possibly met the manufacturing industries' demand for agricultural raw material while satisfying the domestic demand for food products.

Obviously, farmers were not necessarily reaping the gains from the increase in productivity or that their income has improved substantially. One of the main reasons could be lack of expansion of road networks to facilitate the shipment and timely delivery of agricultural products from producers to consumers. Although rapid expansion and construction of roads was one of the aims of the government, as outlined in the Third Five Year Plan, there were little or no expansion of road networks that linked producers with consumers.

The data on government expenditure (see Appendix B) clearly demonstrate which social and economic areas were actually given priority.[12] From the table in Appendix B, it is evident that the government allocated a significant amount of its annual budget to "General Service," particularly to national defence and internal law and order. Comparatively, public investment in economic and social services were below the total amount of budget earmarked for General Service. Among the categories in "Economic Services," public works and communication received a higher percentage of the total amount of annual budget. This was perhaps intended to reassert the conviction that meeting one of the preconditions for increasing public and private investment, laying the infrastructural foundations for economic and social development, is indeed inescapable.

In 1966, the Planning Board made a compelling statement concerning the need for urgent legislative response to the widening socioeconomic gaps between the rural and urban community. Consequently, there was a tremendous increase in annual budget (almost 400% in 1966 when compared with the previous years) earmarked for formulating and implementing agriculture and land reform policies. Even so, between 1965 and 1969, with the exception of the 36.1 million *Birr* budget for agriculture and land reform of the 1966 fiscal year, there seemed to be little emphasis on providing direct budgetary support to farmers through credits and low interest loan schemes. However, after this remarkable budget increase, government expenditure for the same purpose plummeted from 36 million to about 10 million *Birr* during the subsequent years.

In comparison with other sectors, excluding "General Service," the government of Haile-Sellasie certainly paid attention to building the human capital through expansion of education and health services in most of the provinces. Yet, the fact that the annual budget for education and health remained largely constant throughout the 1960s ignores the increasing demand for access to education and health services. These demands may partly arise due to population growth and partly as a result of increased public awareness of the correlation between education and health, on the one hand, and standard of living, on the other. To counterbalance shortages of schools and teachers, the interests of the public would have been best served not only by increasing annual budget but more importantly by efficiently utilizing available resources.

Table 5.1: Percentage of Students in Different Type of Schools, 1965

Province	Government	Missionary	Private	Church
Arussi	88.4	8.6	0.0	3.0
Bale	87.2	12.8	0.0	0.0
Gonder	94.9	5.1	0.0	0.0
Eritrea	58.8	11.6	23.9	5.7
Gamu Goffa	85.6	10.3	0.0	4.1
Gojjam	95.5	0.6	0.0	3.9
Hararghe	75.5	11.8	10.3	2.4
Illubabor	91.9	0.9	5.8	1.4
Kaffa	82.9	12.5	1.4	3.1
Shoa	86.0	8.6	3.5	1.8
Addis Ababa	70.5	9.7	17.8	2.0
Sidamo	74.4	17.4	3.4	4.8
Tigray	74.8	7.4	1.6	16.2
Wollega	65.2	15.1	13.6	6.1
Wollo	91.9	2.9	3.0	2.2

Source: Central Statistical Office (CSO), "Statistical Abstract 1967 and 1968," (Addis Ababa: CSO, n.d.), p.200.

Consider the data in Table 5.1, where the government was clearly the single most important provider of educational opportunities for the majority of school-age children across the country. Until the mid-1960s, the ratio of pupils-to-schools, pupils-to-teachers, and pupils-to-classrooms was lower in private, missionary, and church schools than in government schools.[13]

Given the country's economic backwardness and deficiency in the number of teachers and administrative staff, it can be argued that those students in private, missionary, and church schools received quality of education and better training than those students enrolled in government schools. Therefore, there were proportionally higher percentage of students receiving quality education, coupled with varying degrees of choices, in regions of what are now largely within the Oromiya State (Bale, Keffa, and Wollega), Eritrea, and Hararghe (now the Regional State of Harari). The children in most of the other provinces were enrolled mainly in government schools. Matching the role of the state with its capability would have improved the quality of education and opened greater access to educational opportunities in many other provinces.[14]

Figure 5.1: Revenue and Expenditure, 1965 and 1971

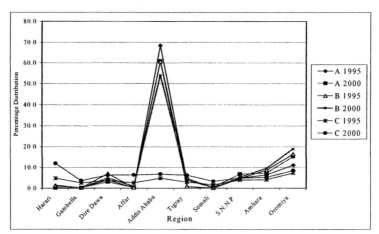

Source: Central Statistical Office, "Statistical Abstract 1967 and 1968," (Addis Ababa: CSO, n.d.), p.146. See also, CSO, "Statistical Abstract 1975," (Addis Ababa: CSO, December 1975), pp.153-4. For population figures, see "Statistical Abstract 1964," (Addis Ababa: CSO, 1970), p.1.

Figure 5.1 above indicates that the largest revenues in 1965 and 1971 were from the city of Addis Ababa and approximately an equal amount of funds were transferred back into the city. On the other hand, in 1965, revenues were generated from the rest of the provinces somewhere in the order of 1 million *Birr*. Indeed, except for Hararghe, Shoa, and Addis Ababa, trends in revenue and expenditure in each of the province were closer to the horizontal line, indicating that both revenue and expenditure were at their lowest level. The figure clearly shows not only the amount and sources of revenue but also the corresponding public expenditure to each province. That is, Addis Ababa, Hararghe, and Eritrea (particularly in 1971) were the primary sources of revenue and the focal points for public expenditure, while each of the remaining provinces contributed little in the way of revenue. In turn, with the exception of Gojjam province where the gap between revenue and expenditure was wider, government expenditure across provinces was generally negligible.

The gap between revenue and expenditure for Gojjam province, which is insignificant, to begin with, does not necessarily suggest that there were ethnically-driven policies to divert resources in the development of this province. This is because the people of that province constitute only a marginal percentage of the population of the supposed "ruling ethnic group." Thus, it would be grossly erroneous to make a blanket statement that the Amhara reaped the benefits from the diversion of revenues away from investment in other provinces. Indeed, the majority Amhara lived under destitute socioeconomic conditions as most other ethnic groups throughout the country. If anything, the relatively higher expenditure in the province of Gojjam, during the 1965 and 1971 fiscal years, must have been intended by the Haile-Selassie government to deliberately undermine further civil unrest by admirers of Belay Zeleke, Mengistu and Germame Neway, Workneh Gebeyehu, and Bitwoded Negash Bezabih of Amhara descent.[15]

Nevertheless, alternative explanations to conventional beliefs which holds that the distribution of socioeconomic resources reflected a super-ordinate/subordinate inter-ethnic relationships requires more evidence than has been presented so far. Because, apart from education, improving the conditions of the Amhara that were allegedly disenfranchizing all other ethnic groups during the imperial and, subsequently, the military government could have been achieved through the expansion of industrial establishments, roads, health facilities, and increase in the number of health personnel. The data in Figure 5.2 is, therefore, presented to examine whether some regions or ethnic groups were dis-enfranchized from receiving health services during the Haile-Selassie government. The data is self-explanatory in the sense that the number of hospitals, clinics, and health centers increased exponentially, although this exponential growth occurred in very few provinces. The construction of health facilities is merely one aspect of the provision of health services. Measured in terms of the number of doctors, there existed considerable qualitative differences between Addis Ababa, Eritrea, Hararghe, and Shoa, on the one hand, and the remaining provinces, on the other hand.

Throughout the Haile-Selassie era, there were essentially two main medical colleges: *Tikur Ambesa* in Addis Ababa and Gonder Medical Science College. Most of the medical doctors, laboratory technicians, and nurses were trained at the Addis Ababa *Tikur Ambesa* Hospital and Gonder Medical Science College, but the majority graduates either preferred to stay in or relocate to Addis Ababa. This is perhaps one of the main reasons why the total number of doctors in Addis Ababa, in 1966, far exceeded the number of doctors in Eritrea, Hararghe, Gonder, Shoa, Kaffa, Wollo, Gojjam, Wollega, and Arussi combined.

Figure 5.2: Distribution of Health Facilities and Personnel, 1966 and 1970

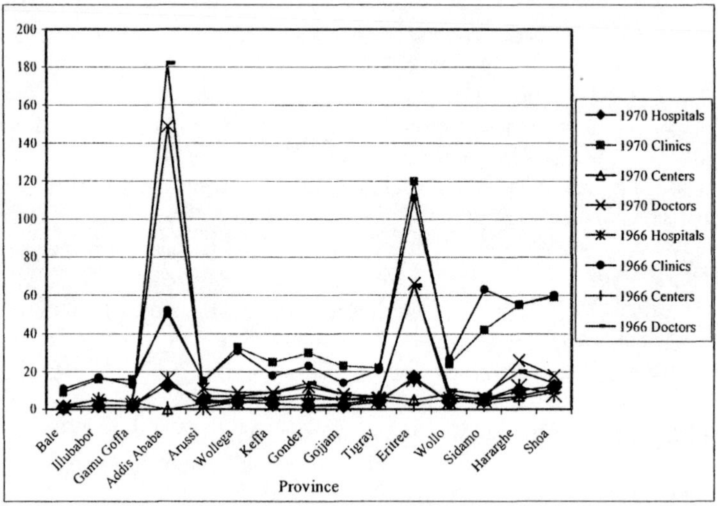

Source: Central Statistical Office, "Statistical Abstract 1968," (Addis Ababa: CSO, 1970), p.184. See also, "Statistical Abstract 1971," (Addis Ababa: CSO, 1972), p.181.

Five years later, in 1970, the total number of doctors in Addis Ababa declined slightly while the number of doctors in Hararghe and Arussi increased by about 30% and 57%, respectively. From the data in Figure 5.2, it can also be discerned that in many of the provinces there were some fluctuation in the number of hospitals, doctors, clinics, and health centers between 1966 and 1970. However, these fluctuations in the number of health personnel and facilities were not due to transfers and relocations caused by the desire to improve the delivery of health services to the supposed provinces of the "ruling ethnic group".

Therefore, based on the statistical data analyzed so far, it would be a distortion or facts and realities to see the distribution of resources through the prisms of ethnicity. That is, it is impossible to support the assertion that the social and economic development policies of the government of Haile-Selassie were biased in favor of one ethnic group while all other ethnic groups were denied access to social opportunities. As the data on revenue and expenditure clearly indicate, it is patently erroneous to suggest that public resources were deliberately diverted to provide access to the means of improving the socioeconomic wellbeing of the people of Gonder, Gojjam, and Wollo provinces.

One of the most vivid illustrations of marginalization in access to economic opportunities is the establishment of industries, however insubstantial, in cities in and around Addis Ababa and Eritrea. The most important common feature of these cities was not their ethnic makeup, but it was rather their political and strategic importance to the nation and the ruling elites of the Imperial Government. The fact that Eritrea is inhabited by nine nationalities in which the Tigray is demographically dominant and that Addis Ababa is the convergence point for almost all ethnic groups in Ethiopia should have signaled that the opening up of social and economic opportunities were not dictated by ethnicity.

Redistribution of Resources

Except in the city of Addis Ababa and the province of Shoa and Hararghe, the government of Haile-Selassie was able to extract an insignificant amount of revenue from the rest of the provinces (refer to Figure 5.1). A decade after the downfall of the government of Haile-Selassie, that seemed to have changed significantly. When the military government came to power in 1974, it transformed the Internal Revenue Authority, as it did to all other public institutions, into a more aggressive and effective arms of the government and was able to collect at least 1 million *Birr* from each province.

As Figure 5.3 demonstrates, with the exception of Gamu Gofa, the military government successfully generated revenue and, correspondingly, increased the amount of annual expenditure for each province by more than two-fold. In particular, the provinces of Sidamo, Kaffa, and Gojjam were the largest sources of revenue for the military government. Although data on revenue and expenditure in 1985 are not available for Addis Ababa, it can safely be assumed that the city was, as it was during the aristocratic reign, one of the main sources of revenue throughout the military government's rule. The figure also indicates that the province of Gonder was as much an important source of revenue as Gojjam, Kaffa, and Sidamo provinces.

Figure 5.3: Revenue and Expenditure, 1980 and 1985

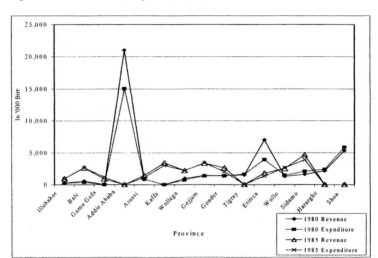

Source: Central Statistical Authority (CSA), "Statistical Abstract 1990," (Addis Ababa: CSA, 1993), pp.205-8.

The variances in the amount of revenue generated from Eritrea, Gonder, and Sidamo and expenditure to these provinces appear to be statistically insignificant. But, given that Eritrea had the second largest manufacturing industries and was the main import/export outlet of the country, its contribution was significantly smaller than other provinces. This is especially disappointing because some of the largest revenues were collected from the provinces of Kaffa and Sidamo, which rely on the production and exportation of coffee beans, and Gonder and Gojjam that essentially produce cereals, oil seeds, and pulses for the domestic market.

According to the data in Figure 5.4, over 60% of manufacturing establishments and employment were in the province of Shoa, including Addis Ababa. Eritrea also claimed its lion share of manufacturing establishments, which also opened employment opportunities to the people of that province. Although there were some signs in the overall expansion of manufacturing industries and increase in the total number of employees nationally (from 77,895 in 1979 to 91,141 in 1985), the percentage distribution of employment among the provinces remained essentially constant. The percentage of employment in "other regions," which accounted for less than 10 % of the total employment created by the manufacturing sector is trifling.[16]

Figure 5.4: Distribution of Manufacturing Industries and Employment

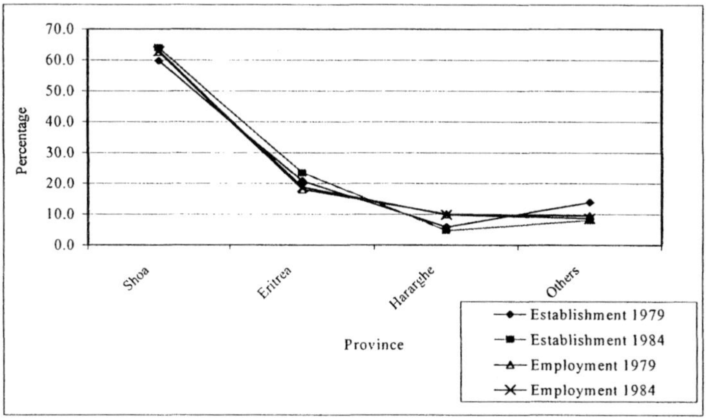

Source: Central Statistical Office, "Results of the Survey of Manufacturing Industries 1979," (Addis Ababa: CSO, 1982), pp.22-8. See also, "Results of the Survey of Manufacturing and Electricity Industries, 1985," (Addis Ababa: CSO, 1989), pp.49-61.

In "other regions" or provinces, the percentage of manufacturing establishments was indeed higher in 1979 than in 1985. However, both the percentage of manufacturing establishments and employment were negligible when compared with those in Eritrea and Shoa. The relative deprivation in the distribution of manufacturing industries and their attendant benefits becomes even more startling when compared from the standpoint of the total population of the two provinces against the population of the other provinces. This is because, of the total population of Ethiopia in 1985 (43.5 million), Shoa, Eritrea, and Hararghe accounted for 35% (or 15.3 million). Therefore, manufacturing industries and concomitant benefits such as lucrative retail trades and profits, training, and possibly better transportation and communication systems were disproportionately concentrated in the three provinces.

Generally, the data in Figure 5.4 suggests that approximately 85% of the industries and employment were located in the three provinces with 35% of the total population of Ethiopia. In comparison, approximately 15% of the industries and employment were distributed sparsely among the "other provinces" that constituted 65% of the

population of Ethiopia. The low percentage of employment opportunities in "other regions" reveals an important point regarding the nature
of distribution of resources in Ethiopia. Because, these "other regions"
are inhabited by various ethnic groups, including Affar, Amhara,
Gambella, Somali, and Tigray as well as the diverse ethnic groups in
what is presently known as the Southern Nations and Nationalities
Region (S.N.N.R). Within the 65% of the population of the "other regions" are the people of the province of Gojjam, Gonder, and Wollo,
which accounted for about 23% of the total population of Ethiopia and
are predominantly Amhara.[17] The data above also underscores the fact
that the concentration of manufacturing enterprises in a few of the
provinces must have been achieved at the expense of socio-
economically dis-empowering the various ethnic groups residing in the
other provinces, including Arussi, Bale, Gonder, Gojjam, and so on.

Clearly, if provincial boundaries were redrawn to reflect as nearly
as possible the ethnic composition of the provinces, then a significant
number of industries and employment were in Shoa, which has largely
been occupied by the Oromos. The implication is that under the present
regional demarcation, except for the city of Addis Ababa, much of the
territories of Shoa, along with all the industries, fall within the jurisdiction of the Oromiya Regional State. This presents quite a different picture than what has been depicted by many scholars and leaders of
southern secessionist groups and ethnogogues. Moreover, although the
Oromos are the largest group in the Harari Regional State, the Oromiya
Regional State is guaranteed special privilege to utilize the resources in
Addis Ababa, but not in Harari. In this connection, it is beyond anyone's comprehension why the capital city of the Oromiya Regional
State is Addis Ababa.

Consider also the case of Eritrea, where the proposition that the
people of that province were disenfranchized and repressed by the supposed ruling ethnic group was plausible enough, though politically
divisive, to assert Eritrean elites' claim for secession. Yet, when Eritrea was one of the provinces of Ethiopia, it was the second major
beneficiary from public and private investments in the manufacturing,
health, education, and transportation sectors. This alone partly demonstrates that relative deprivation existed not between ethnic groups, as
many have contended, but among provinces which are now divided
haphazardly as administrative regions.

If the redistribution of resources in Eritrea were to be placed in the
context of the dominant/dependent paradigm, then before one makes
any generalization one has to investigate how resources were distributed among the nine nationalities or between the northern highlanders
and southern lowlanders. Two main points can be derived from the

ethnic diversity and the presence of a significant number of manufacturing industries in Addis Ababa and Eritrea, which happen to be ethnically diverse. While the nature of public goods makes the discussion
on the distribution of resources more complicate, the concentration of
manufacturing industries and greater employment opportunities created
in Addis Ababa and Eritrea is indisputable. To be sure, there may not
have be substantial expansions of manufacturing industries and creation of jobs in that sector, but there were notable expansions and
growth of health facilities and an increase in the number of health professionals during the government of Mengistu Haile-Mariam.

Figure 5.5 below indicates that the total number of doctors in 1981
and 1986 almost doubled from what it was in the 1970s (refer to Figure
5.2). In addition, the number of clinics and health centers in most of
the provinces was higher in 1981 than in any previous years. This is to
be expected in such a government committed to the ideal of socialism.
The rate of expansion of health services throughout the country, shown
by the parallel upward shift, was indeed impressive. Yet, the pattern
suggests that the military government was unable to reverse regional
disparities in access to health services.

Figure 5.5: Health Facilities and Personnel, 1981 and 1986

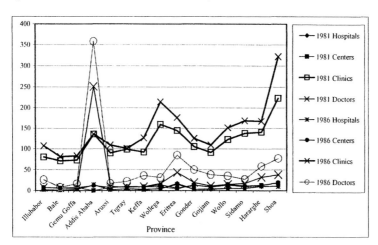

Source: Central Statistical Office, "Statistical Abstract 1982" (Addis Ababa:
CSO, 1984), p.235. See also, "Statistical Abstract 1986," (Addis Ababa: CSO,
1990), p.267.

To get the depth of perpetual maldistribution in health services
among the provinces, one only needs to take the per capita distribution

of hospitals, heath centers, clinics, and doctors into consideration. For example, the population of Wollega and Tigray in 1985 was 2.5 million each. The population of Illubabor, Gonder, and Wollo for the same year was one million, 2.5 million, and 2.5 million, respectively.[18] In Illubabor, which had the smallest population, there were 26 doctors while Tigray, with more than twice the population of Illubabor, had only 22 doctors. In Wollo, on the other hand, there were only 35 doctors providing health services to one of the largest populations in the country, while there were 15 more doctors in Gonder. Even more extreme is the per capita distribution of doctors between provinces (Addis Ababa, Eritrea, and Hararghe), on the one hand, and the rest of the provinces, on the other hand.

Therefore, inequity in the distribution of health facilities and personnel not only existed between provinces inhabited by different ethnic groups but also between provinces largely dominated by members of the same ethnic group. Stated differently, disproportional distributions of health facilities and personnel were as extreme between Illubabor and Wollega (now parts of the Oromiya region) as it was between Gonder and Wollo.[19]

Another important area of interest lies in analyzing the extent to which the military government was able to transform the Ethiopian economy from food dependency to self-sufficiency. The data on the sectoral contribution of agriculture, industry, trade, and service sectors suggest that the percentage contribution of each sector to the Gross Domestic Product (shown in Appendix D) essentially remained constant between 1974 and 1979. Between 1979 and 1980, the highest contribution to the GDP came from the agricultural sector which remained almost constant during the following two years.

In 1982, however, agricultural productivity and its contribution to the GDP was disappointingly low because Ethiopia was once again suffering from drought and insufficient rainfall. The downward curb in productivity also occurred at a time when the government was aggressively pursuing its villagization programs, which disrupted the lives and economic activities of small holder farmers. By 1984, agricultural productivity revived and, between 1985 and 1990, it gained its momentum as a major contributor to the GDP.

The contribution of the service sector to the economy grew slowly, but steadily from 1974 until 1985, and accelerated from less than 2 billion in 1985 to almost 3 billion *Birr* in 1990. The data also show a similar pattern of growth in the industrial and trade sectors of the economy. Even though until 1985 the industrial sector's contribution to the GDP was less impressive, its contribution declined significantly in the subsequent five years (1985-1990), while the percentage contribution of the agricultural and service sectors increased notably. It appears that the military government, in light of its economic policy of breaking away from agricultural dependency towards industrialization, was unable to speed up the process of industrialization throughout its entire seventeen years of rule.

In short, the data examined above suggest that there were indeed inequalities in the distribution of socioeconomic resources. However, such disequilibrium in social and economic opportunities was not between ethnic groups, but it was generally between provinces. Although there may be instances where some ethnic groups in some provinces were demographically more dominant than other ethnic groups, each of the province was inhabited by multiple ethnic groups. Therefore, the assertion that the military government perfected the super-ordinate/subordinate inter-ethnic relationships is simply an oversimplification of the causes of the conflict, economic stagnation, and political instability in Ethiopia.

Overall, based on the data presented above, one can easily reach at a more objective view and understanding of the ways in which resources were distributed during the previous governments. Lest we deliberately avoid dealing with facts and scientific methods of investigation, the evidence conclusively supports the position that no single ethnic group reaped the benefits from the national or regional development policies of either the Haile-Selassie or the Mengistu government. It also goes without saying that the claim that the Amharas are hampering the current government's democratization and development processes, presumably because they lost their hegemonic status, is a logical fallacy. If anything, such claims and assertions are phases in the process of instilling myths with the hope of causing havoc in the lives of ordinary Ethiopians.

Rectifying Historical Distortions?

The presumption that isolating each ethnic group minimizes the incidence of ethnic conflict and helps to achieve equity in the distribution of resources emanate from the belief that, historically, the distribution of resources favored one minority ethnic group over others. That is, the overriding conviction among contemporary policymakers is that the problem of inequality was not between provinces, but it was correlated with where one falls in the dichotomized intra-ethnic structural hierarchy. This is a classic case of deductive fallacy with detrimental implication on formulating a nationalist development agenda and harmonizing trans-ethnic relationships.

The data examined so far suggest the need for innovative approaches to achieve fair and equitable distribution of socioeconomic resources. Thus, one of the questions to be addressed is whether the present government narrowed, sustained, or exacerbated the gap in the distribution of resources. In order to evaluate these and related successes or setbacks, we need to examine, as we have done in the previous sections, the distribution of social services and opening up of economic opportunities under the present government. Thus, the data analyzed in the subsequent sections include Gross Enrollment Ratio (GER) in primary and secondary schools, in 1992 and 2000, and the distribution of health facilities and personnel, in 1995 and 1999. Also included are data on the percentage contribution of the four sectors of the economy to the GDP, the ratio of imported to total raw material consumed by the various branches of industry, and the distribution of manufacturing industries and employment opportunities in the manufacturing sector. Data on revenue and expenditure were not available for the current government; nevertheless, we should be able to gain a deeper understanding of what has been taking in the past fifteen years.

The data below refers to the year immediately after the downfall of the military government in 1991. Clearly, the disparity among the regions is caused by the policies and actions of the previous government. Still, from Table 5.2, it can easily be discerned that there were profound imbalances between regions in access to education. The data also reveals the degree to which myths could distort realities even when the data point towards a different conclusion. In a funding proposal for the implementation of the education overhaul program, designed by the United States Agency for International Development (USAID) and submitted to the transitional government for approval, the agency asserted that lack of equity, quality, and quantity are major shortcomings of the Ethiopian educational system. It then justified its intervention in overhauling the basic education system in Ethiopia.[20] Two regions, Tigray and the S.N.N.R, were selected as the target regions of the education system overhaul program and, arguably, received $80 million to finance pilot projects in both regions.

However, the evidence produced by the agency (refer to Table 5.2) does not justify the expressed interests of either the government or the USAID. At best, the data is inconsistent with the historical and contemporary realities of Ethiopia and, at worse, it reflects profound insincerity and indifference on the part of the Agency and the host government. Because, it is obvious enough that the disenfranchized regions were not Tigray and the Southern Nations and Nationalities Region. To the contrary, the lowest Gross Enrollment Ratio was in

Benishangul/Gumuz, followed by Somalia, Amhara, and Dire Dawa, in that order of degree of exclusion from access to education.

Table 5.2: Primary School Enrollment, 1992

Region	School Age Population	Enrollment	GER
Addis Ababa	480	253,183	53
Affar	176	42,491	24
Amhara	2,406	320,058	13
Ben/Gumuz	103	7,313	7
Dire Awa	94	17,268	18
Gambella	35	6,865	20
Harari	13	10,511	81
Oromiya	3,235	698,111	22
Somali	245	27,545	11
S.N.N.R	1,931	386,980	20
Tigray	542	261,269	48
Total	**9,260**	**2,031,694**	

Note: School Age Population is in thousands. GER = Gross Enrollment Ratio.

Source: World Bank, *Education Sector Public Expenditure Review 1993*, quoted in USAID, "Basic Education System Overhaul Program Assistance and Project Paper," (Addis Ababa: USAID/Ethiopia, September 1994), p.11. Unpublished document.

The purpose of intervening in the educational affairs of the country may not necessarily be driven by the desire to ensure equity because the Agency's policy rhetoric and the data it presented are inconsistent with its actions. The underlining concerns of the Agency are to maintain leverage and meaningful political influence on the government. Whether the desire to gain political influence overshadowed the ways in which the Agency interpreted its data is an issue beyond the focus of this study. In any case, the data on GER fall short of confirming the classical assumptions and conclusions on the prevalence of a superordinate/subordinate relationship between ethnic groups.

Before examining the GER data for 2000, a few explanatory statements may be appropriate. At the beginning of this chapter, we noted some of the problems associated with the incompatibility of dividing a country with more than fifty ethnic groups into only nine regional states and two administrative councils. Thus, as we have shown previously, when we talk of the regional distribution of Gross Enroll-

ment Ratio, there should not be any misconception that these regions
are ethnically homogeneous.

Below are multivariate data of an increasing function where the
population of Harari and Oromiya are the lowest and highest values in
the interval. Thus, the independent variable becomes the population
index of each regional state, whereas the dependent variables are the
GER, number of health facilities and personnel, and percentage of
manufacturing industries, employment, and wages and salaries.

Figure 5.6: Gross Enrollment Ratio, 2000

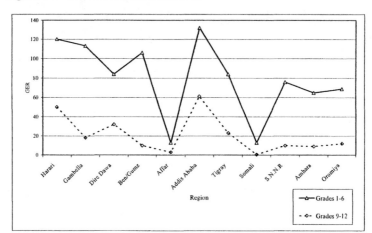

Source: Ministry of Education, "Education Statistics Annual Abstract
2000/01," (Addis Ababa: Ministry of Education, 2001).

The pattern lines in Figure 5.6 suggest at least two main points:
inequity at the national level and an extreme low rate of GER in Somali and Affar Regional States, both in the primary and secondary
schools. Generally, the lines form an erratic pattern and seem to be the
graph of a decreasing function or the inverse of what is supposed to
have taken place if there were progress towards equity. With the exception of Somali and Affar where the ratio of population and GER
were approximately equal, the ratio of population to GER for other
regions tended to be inversely related. Particularly, the three regions,
Tigray, Addis Ababa, and Harari had a higher GER in 1992 and maintained their dominant position in 2000 as well.

Furthermore, suppose that the distance between two coordinate
points of a given region's elementary and secondary school GER is a
measure of drop out rates. Thus, the drop out rate seems to be even
greater in the S.N.N.R, Benishangul/Gumuz and Gambella than in

other regions. However, unlike Affar, Somali, Amhara, and Oromiya, the high drop out rate in Benishangul/Gumuz and Gambella may be compensated by the enrollment of students in primary school ages of above 12 years old.

The implication of high drop out rates on the economic and social wellbeing of the people in those regions is far-reaching. For instance, to the extent that political appointment is dictated by ethnic considerations, the regions with the highest drop out rate between grades 9 to 12 would be less endowed with the necessary human, intellectual, capital that enables them to take up leadership positions at the regional or national level. Since students drop out of school before they gain the necessary skills for entrepreneurship or at least to earn a decent income to support themselves, they add to the soaring unemployment rate and exacerbate the economic problems that has been strangling the country for almost fifty years. Although there were improvements in opening access to education for most school-age children in many of the regions, inequity in access to education persisted in 2000 as it did in the past decades.

In Figure 5.7, except for the exponential increase in the number of clinics in Oromiya in 1999 (excluding doctors in Addis Ababa), the pattern lines tend to form a curve of an increasing function between the intervals. In particular, the horizontal line is almost asymptotic to the curves formed by the coordinates of the number of hospitals in 1995 and 1999 in each region. That means, despite significant population differentials among the regions, there were not corresponding increase in the number of hospitals. The same is true for the number of health centers in 1995. However, in 1999, the number of health centers in the S.N.N.R region almost quadrupled and approximately equaled the number of health centers in Oromiya.

Instead of increasing proportionally so as to reflect the rate of population growth in the Amhara, S.N.N.R, and Tigray regions, in particular, and in Ethiopia, in general, the number of doctors in these regions decreased notably from 1995 to 1999. This imbalance was also exacerbated by the concentration of doctors in a few regions where the second less populated administrative region in the country, Addis Ababa, had as much doctors as the second most populated region in the country—the Amhara Regional State. Similarly, there were more doctors and clinics in Tigray than there were in Somali. If progress towards equity was to be made, the per capita distribution of doctors should have been in reverse order so that the pattern lines formed by the coordinate points are graphs of an increasing function.

Figure 5.7: Health Facilities and Personnel, 1995 and 1999

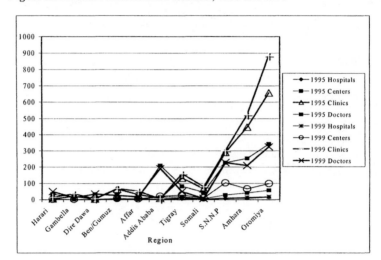

Source: Central Statistical Authority, "Statistical Abstract 1997," (Addis Ababa: CSA, 1998), pp.317-8. See also "Statistical Abstract 2000," (Addis Ababa: CSA, 2001), pp.322-5.

The pattern line formed by the coordinate points of the number of clinics appears to look like a graph of an increasing function until it reaches the coordinate points that correspond to the population of the Southern Nations and Nationalities Regional State. From that point on, it dives down towards the point that corresponds to the population of the Somali Regional State and rises up to more than 150 clinics at the coordinate points of the Regional State of Tigray. Finally, like the number of doctors, the number of clinics in 1999 declined in the Oromiya and Amhara Regional States. Another point to note is the steady growth in the number of clinics in Tigray and Affar from 1995 to 1999. One should also note that there were more clinics in Tigray than there were in Somali, Affar, and Dire Dawa combined.

Another area with a direct implication on the economic welfare of Ethiopians may be measured in terms of the sectoral contribution of the different sectors of the economy to the GDP. The present government, in the tradition of its predecessors, has been preoccupied with ensuring food security and harmonizing the link between the agricultural and manufacturing sectors. However, in much of the 1990s, all sectors of the economy have shown little or no changes in their percentage contribution to the GDP.

Joseph Stiglitz and others maintained that the present government had a sound rural development strategy with a focus on alleviating poverty,[21] but it has been unable to realize its objectives due to financial constraints and the intervention of the IMF in the economic decisionmaking process of the present government. While this may partly explain the sluggishness of the Ethiopian economy and lack of harmony among the sectors, the present government is also faced with enormous challenges that had little to do with the IMF's centralized imposition of prescription that often harm rather than cure the ailing Ethiopian economy. The institutional behavior of the IMF, which may be characterized as authoritarian of the first order, should no longer be a scapegoat, because rising above obstructive intrusion is part and parcel of the equation that defines effectiveness and vision in leadership.

Figure 5.8: Sectoral Contribution to GDP, 1991-1999

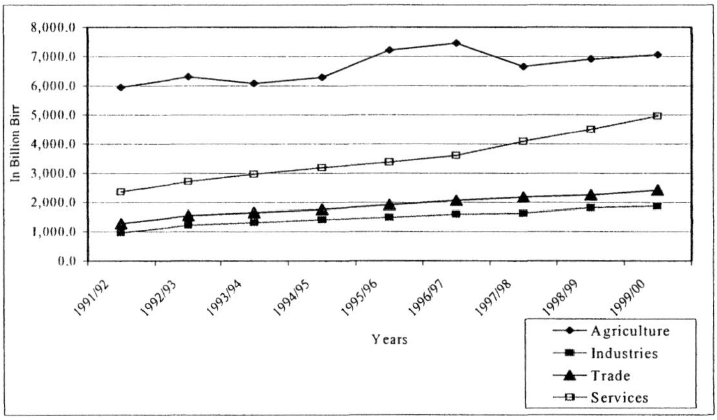

Note: Values are at constant factor cost, 1980.

Source: Central Statistical Authority, "Statistical Abstract 1995," (Addis Ababa: CSA, 1996), p.217. See also, "Statistical Abstract 2001," (Addis Ababa: CSA, 2002), p.254.

Whatever theoretical tool one adopts to examine and explain the state of the Ethiopian economy, the fact remains that the contribution of the agricultural sector to the economy has long been characterized by volatility. Against the development aims of the Ethiopian government—strengthening inter-sectoral interdependencies between the agricultural and manufacturing sectors—Figure 5.8 depicts the degree to which the economy is guided by a prudent policy framework. The

rapid rise in the contribution of the service sector to the GDP, especially from 1996/97 onwards, suggests that the economy is not behav-
ing in accordance with the industrialization policy of the government.

Additionally, the pattern lines for the industrial and trade sectors
of the economy travel largely along a parallel path and closer to the
horizontal line. For most of the early 1990s, the contribution of trade to
the GDP remained below two billion *Birr* and grew slowly from 1996
until 1999. The industrial sector appears to be more depressed
throughout the decade than the trade sector of the economy. The figure
also reveals that the present government failed to ensure food security,
foster industrial growth, or enhance the contribution of the agricultural
sector to the economy. Indeed, since the First Five Year Plan of the
government of Haile-Selassie, the number of manufacturing industries
and their contribution to the economy has not risen according to the
expectations of the government or any optimistic observer. To the contrary, the sector's mid-level position between the service and trade
sectors seems to have been lost to the steady and remarkable growth of
the service sector. Therefore, if the economic policy of the present
government is to be effective in transforming the agrarian into indus-
try-based economy, the trend line for the agricultural sector should
have been at least closer to or, even better, above the pattern lines of
the service sector.

What does the adverse consequences and outcomes of the policy
mean to equitable growth among the regions? It means that those regions with the infrastructural and human capital bases are more likely
to reap the gains from the expansion of the service sector than other
regions with a low road density, low Gross Enrollment Ratio, and high
drop out rates. It also means the widening of the gaps in income and
standard of living between the majority of the rural population, on the
one hand, and minority urban dwellers, on the other hand. In effect, the
Ethiopian economic policy is haphazardly coordinated and that there is
little or no trickle down of benefits that may accrue to the rural poor as
a result of the rise in the income of service providers.

This interpretation is further demonstrated by the data on the ratio
of imported to total raw material costs, the distribution of manufacturing industries, employment, and wages and salaries, and by the density
of roads between maintenance districts. The extent to which the different sectors of the economy form interdependent relationships may be
explained by examining the ratio of imported to total raw material
costs. The economy is said to be dependent on the agricultural sector
and, as a result, the three consecutive governments placed special emphasis on stimulating the agricultural sectors to respond to the raw material demand of other sectors. From this assumption, it is reasonable to

expect a decline in the rate of dependency of the manufacturing sector on imported raw materials. Interesting enough, except for the manufacturing of basic iron and steel, fabricated metal, and assembly of vehicles, trailers, and semi-trailers the dependency ratio of the other sub-sectors on imported raw materials fluctuated from a minimum of less than 15% in 1982 to a maximum of 82% in 1986.

Figure 5.9: Ratio of Imported to Total Raw Material Cost, 1982-1999

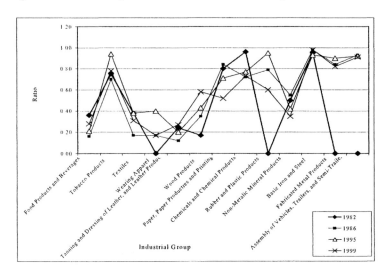

Note: Data for some of the industrial sub-sectors for the 1982 fiscal year are not available.

Source: Central Statistical Authority, "Results of the Survey of Manufacturing and Electricity Industries 1986/87," (Addis Ababa: CSA, 1990), pp.62-93. See also, "Report on Large and Medium Scale Manufacturing and Electricity Industries Survey, 1998," pp.179-80; "Reports on Large and Medium Scale Manufacturing and Electricity Industries Survey, 2000," pp.143-6.

As shown in Figure 5.9, between 1982 and 1999, out of the thirteen industrial sub-sectors, four of them had a dependency ratio of less than 40%. The remaining sub-sectors were highly dependent on imported raw materials. Indeed, there seems to be little or no value added in the manufacturing of tobacco, paper, chemical, rubber and plastic, basic iron, fabricated metal, and assembly of vehicles and trailers. Perhaps because of the early 1980s drought, the food and beverage industrial sub-sectors were more dependent on imported materials, in 1982, than in 1986, 1995, or 1999. Furthermore, instead of a gradual or even

better a robust increase in the use of domestic products for the processing of food and beverage products, their dependency on imported materials continued to rise from 1986 onwards. The same is true for the
manufacturing of tobacco and wood products.

On average, in the past two decades, the Ethiopian industrial sector has been highly dependent on imported raw materials. Any dependency on imported raw material, particularly agricultural raw material,
is not only strategically risky, but it may negatively affect the social
and economic welfare of farming households. It is equally risky to
gear the economy, in general, and the manufacturing sector, in particular, towards excessive reliance on the agricultural sector, a sector that
has failed to meet the growing domestic demands for food. Additionally, if demand for agricultural raw material does not increase, then the
level of income of farmers is likely to decline, which, in turn, affects
the demand for domestically produced durable and perishable manufactured goods.

Sector-specific policies, especially of the manufacturing and agricultural sectors, may be designed not only to harmonize cross-sectoral
relations between the two but also produce a multiplier effect on other
sectors of the economy. For example, if the manufacturing of leather
products for which the Ethiopian cattle breeders become major suppli-
ers, then at a minimum and due to the possible reduction of the cost of
transportation for importing finished leather products, there would be
savings to domestic producers and consumers. Consequently, the tendency for cattle ranchers to specialize in cattle breeding and the demand for foodstuffs and textile products may increase in response to
the rising income of farmers.[22]

Under a similar scenario, the productivity and level of income of
cotton growers, cereals, and the like will also rise. Furthermore, since
85% of the rural population is engaged in agricultural activities, raising
their level of income would also mean stimulating the demand for domestically produced manufactured items. To the extent that the government executes its policy of greater harmonization and integration
between the agricultural and manufacturing sectors, Ethiopian manufacturing industrial entrepreneurs will expend less resources in accessing foreign market outlets for their manufactured commodities. Whatever economic model the government chooses to adopt, domestic market development is critical for food security and industrialization.

Having made a few remarks on the importance of cross-sectoral
policy harmonization and coordination, we now return to our analysis
of whether the present government made any notable inroads in rectifying inequity in the distribution of resources. Accordingly, Figure
5.10 is designed to analyze the regional distribution of manufacturing

industries, employment, and wages and salaries. In line with what has been said at the beginning of this section, resources are said to be distributed equitably when the percentage of establishments, employment as well as wages and salaries rise along with the percentage of population in each region. In a situation where there exists a fairly balanced distribution of resources among the regions, each of the trend lines would form a curve of an increasing function bounded between two intervals. Broadening while sharpening our analytical lenses, what is stated here holds true if each region is placed on equal footing in terms of access to education, health services, and employment opportunities as well as access to reliable roads.

Figure 5.10: A, B, and C Distribution, 1995 and 2000

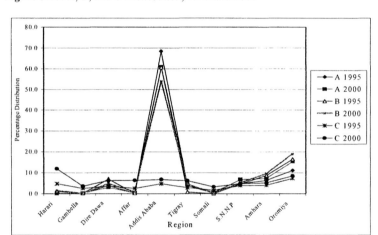

Source: Central Statistical Authority, "Report on Large and Medium Scale Manufacturing and Electricity Industries Survey, 1997," (Addis Ababa: CSA, 1997), pp.135-6. See also, "Report on Large and Medium Scale Manufacturing and Electricity Industries, 2001," (Addis Ababa: CSA, 2002), pp.122-3.

Key: A = % of establishment, B = % of employees, C = % of wages and salaries.

Contextually, it is possible to focus on the manufacturing sector alone and still make some observations concerning whether the present government has been successful in rectifying intra-regional or intra-ethnic maldistribution of resources. Tracing the pattern lines of the three regions, reading from right to left, Figure 5.10 depicts what appears to be a reorientation in the direction of equity in the distribution of manufacturing industries, employment, and wages and salaries.

Starting from the coordinate points of the S.N.N.P and moving to the left, the graph becomes erratic with sharp jump at the coordinate point of Addis Ababa. Furthermore, the figure shows that, in 1995, the percentage of employees and wages and salaries in the manufacturing sector in the Amhara, Somali, and Tigray regions were the lowest in the nation. It should also be noted that, in 1995, there were approximately equal numbers of manufacturing establishments in Tigray as there were in the S.N.N.R. By 2000, there were little public and private investments in the Regional States of Somali, Affar, and Gambella.

The Regional State of Tigray, on the other hand, appears to have created the preconditions, such as reliable infrastructure, tax holidays and other incentives, and the human capital to increase its percentage share of manufacturing industries, employment, and wages and salaries. In sharp contrast with the State of Tigray and others is the State of Benishangul/Gumuz where there were no manufacturing industries and, therefore, no employment opportunities in the manufacturing sector. Obviously, the Addis Ababa Administrative Region had the highest number of manufacturing establishments; and the number of employees and the percentage of wages and salaries were comparatively higher in Addis Ababa than in other regions. However, in 2000, the number of establishments, employment, and wages and salaries in Addis Ababa diminished remarkably. The Administrative Council of Dire Dawa, which had the third lowest population in the country, ranked high in the three main variables discussed here. Like the Addis Ababa Regional Administration, there was a decline in manufacturing establishments, employment, and wages and salaries in the Dire Dawa Administrative Council, in 2000, as well.

In 2000, there were slight increment in the percentage of manufacturing establishments in the Amhara and S.N.N.R States. However, the corresponding points to the 1995 and 2000 percentage of employees and wages and salaries in both regions overlap with that of the coordinate points of the percentage of manufacturing industries. This suggests that manufacturing industries in the two regions were capital-intensive and employee earnings were not competitive with the earnings of employees in other cities. Comparatively, in the Oromiya Regional State, there was a steady growth in the number of manufacturing industries, job opportunities, and wages and salaries.

Leveling the Playing field through Expansion of Roads

Differences in the number of manufacturing industries among the regions emerge for a number of dynamically interacting reasons. Tax incentive, adequate supply of skilled manpower, natural resources, and dependable road networks could affect the type and magnitude of private investment. In particular, the cost and efficiency of transportation is a critical factor in private investment decisions, which is often driven by short-term profit maximization.

The rate of profits is inversely correlated with the cost and efficiency of transportation and, therefore, the flow of private capital tends to gravitate in regions where there are dependable transportation systems. In other words, regions with reliable road networks are more likely to attract foreign and inter-regional private investment than regions with dilapidated roads. Constructing, upgrading, and maintaining roads is, in and of itself, one aspect of leveling the playing field among the provinces or regions. It also enables the expansion and efficient delivery of social services, which in turn contribute to reducing the inter-regional gap in private investment, employment opportunities, and wages and salaries.

One of the main objectives of the three governments was expanding primary, secondary, and tertiary (feeder) roads to accelerate agricultural productivity, ensure food self-sufficiency, and reduce the cost and dependency of the manufacturing sector on imported raw material. Thus, we need to examine whether the three successive governments made inroads toward facilitating the infrastructural basis for a sustainable supply of raw material to the manufacturing sector and to close the inter-regional development gaps.

In the early 1960s, a total of eight maintenance districts, excluding Asmara, were created to construct and expand roads throughout the country. Each of the maintenance districts were ideally located in the major cities of each province in order to expand and maintain roads in and around the vicinity where the maintenance districts were located. The locations were strategically chosen so that each maintenance district could carry out construction works by branching out from the core (maintenance district) up to the provincial boundaries, thereby forming a web-like road system.

In practice, there were political and budgetary constraints that affected the expansion and construction of roads during the three governments under consideration. While budgetary constraint may be a common impediment to linking the rural with the urban center, the unfavorable political atmosphere for achieving such an objective was more pronounced during the military government than either during the Haile-Selassie or the Meles government. Having noted the constraints to the expansion of roads, some comparative analysis could be made concerning the expansion of road networks among the provinces.

Analyzing data on road density (length of gravel and asphalt roads) among provinces will shed some light, for example, on whether farmers were provided with reliable farm-to-market road networks and increase their level of income. As Paul Krugman argued, if industries were established further away from the market, goods shipped to the political center would "simply melt away" before they reach their destination. The process by which goods "melt away in transit ... [may] take place at a constant rate per distance covered."[23] Therefore, the greater the length of roads per region, the greater the region's access to market outlets, industrial centers, and the more favorable it becomes for public and private investment.

From the figure in Appendix G, it can be observed that in 1967 there were essentially no asphalt roads in Gonder (Begemder province), Debre Markos (Gojjam province), and Jimma (Kaffa province). In the city of Dire Dawa and in the province of Tigray (Adigrat maintenance district) there were at least 50 km asphalt roads in and around these maintenance districts. In the province of Shao (Alemgena maintenance district), Wollo (Kombolcha maintenance district), and Sidamo (Shashemene maintenance district), there were significant expansions of asphalt roads, ranging from a minimum of 200 km to a maximum of 650 km.

When one compares the density of gravel roads in 1967 and 1974, one finds that there was no notable road construction or expansion projects carried out by the Dire Dawa, Gonder, and Debre Markos maintenance districts. The Alemgena and Shashemene maintenance districts expanded gravel roads by more than 350 km in 1974, compared to the 1967 level. Perhaps due to lack of maintenance, gravel roads in the province of Kaffa and Tigray deteriorated from over 600 km in 1967 to about 500 km in 1974. In the 1980s (refer to Appendix H) asphalt roads in Alemgena, Kombolcha, and Shashemene maintenance districts more than doubled from the previous decade. There was also expansion of asphalt roads in Jimma, while there were no measurable asphalt roads constructed by the Gonder, Debre Markos, and Adigrat maintenance districts.

Furthermore, with the exception of Kombolcha, Shashemene, and Jimma, the density of asphalt roads in other maintenance districts in 1990 remained almost the same as it was a decade before. The density of gravel roads was generally enhanced from a minimum of 500 km in 1980 to a maximum of 900 km 1990 in Gojjam and from a minimum of 1,500 km in 1980 to a maximum of 1,900 km in 1990 in the province of Shoa. The construction of new gravel roads in other provinces also increased slightly. An exception was that gravel roads in the province of Wollo deteriorated significantly from over 650 km in 1967 to approximately 400 km in 1990. Additionally, there were essentially no constructions of gravel roads in the province of Begemder and Tigray from 1980 to 1990. Equally disappointing is the deterioration of gravel roads in Sidamo and Dire Dawa between 1980 and 1990 for there were no corresponding transformation of gravel into asphalt roads or the expansion of existing primary or secondary roads.

Under the current government (see Appendix I), the only province with less than 25 km of asphalt roads is Begemder, which was also known as Gonder province. Except in Gonder, asphalt roads in other provinces expanded from a minimum of 96 km to a maximum of 1,200 km in Gojjam and Shoa province, respectively. However, throughout the 1990s, in the majority of the regions, the need for expanding or upgrading roads seemed to have been placed in the back burners of national development agenda. Indeed, gravel roads in Sidamo deteriorated from over 2,800 km in 1995 to about 1,700 km in 2000. This is not due to the transformation of gravel into asphalt roads, because asphalt roads in that province also deteriorated from over 700 km in 1995 to about 400 km in 2000.

In short, formulating a policy to strengthen inter-regional and rural-urban communication through networks of infrastructure is perhaps one area that may not be directly inspired by ideological calculations. In other words, expanding road networks is as essential for achieving development through a centralized economic management as it is for a market-oriented development policy. Comparatively, the construction and expansion of asphalt and gravel roads, including rural roads, was a remarkable achievement by the government of Haile-Selassie. Since the groundwork has already been laid, one would expect that subsequent governments would have the benefit of building and expanding on what has already been started.

The data in Appendix H reflect the military government's dismal failure in narrowing the regional and rural-urban gap in access to one of the most basic requirements of development. Given the current political climate and given the growing realization of the importance of transportation, the Meles government would have been more attentive to facilitating the infrastructural basis for economic advancement. Unfortunately, except for some negligible improvements in a few provinces, there has not been expansion of both gravel and asphalt roads since the early 1990s.

Without maintaining, upgrading, and expansion of communication networks, it would be difficult to achieve economic and social development at the regional and national levels. It would also be inconceivable to integrate the rural with the urban community, producers with consumers, and to deliver health and educational services to the rural community. The lack of greater integration of the community through the expansion of main and feeder roads also hampers the public from participating in the political process. One may even extend the conversation to suggest that failing to meet this basic requirement would have a ripple effect on the ability of the mass media, for example, to report on events such as drought and internal migration on a timely fashion.

Summary and Concluding Remarks

The concentration of manufacturing industries in a few cities has been misconstrued as a deliberate policy of advancing the social and economic interests of the "ruling ethnic group"—the Amhara. The data presented in this chapter clearly demonstrate that any assertion that correlates distribution of resources with ethnicity is overly simplified and theoretically misguided, at best, and politically divisive, at worse.

To understand why socioeconomic resources have been unevenly distributed among the provinces, both from historical and contemporary viewpoints, one has to look beyond the simplistic frame of reference that correlates resource distributions with ethnicity. Until the separation of Eritrea from Ethiopia, a significant percentage of manufacturing industries were concentrated in and around the capital city, Addis Ababa, and Eritrea (or Asmara to be specific). Although the percentage distribution of manufacturing industries as well as health and education services varied over time, the pattern of distributive injustice continued under the present government as it did during the Haile-Selassie or Mengistu government.

If ethnicity has anything to do with the distribution of socioeconomic resources, then one has to explain the reasons why Eritrea had a share in the monopoly of manufacturing industries, health and education services, and road networks, even though the Tigray ethnic group, not the Amhara, predominantly inhabited the province. The fact that the State of Oromiya is granted exclusive and special rights to utilize the resources in Addis Ababa also dispels the myth that developmental resource allocations were aligned with ethnic calculations. Sadly, those unqualified and dogmatic assertions found their expressions in the elitist movements of the 1970s and 1980s and became useful political tools to advance a secessionist and separatist political agenda.

Most of the earlier researches ignored or deliberately failed to consider if there were other factors that may be responsible for the convergence of social and economic activities in very few provinces or regions. This is partly due to the use of narrow theoretical lenses and partly due to erroneous assumption or deductive fallacies, which excluded the ways in which some components of the social system interact to produce fundamental changes or adapt to new phenomenon. Exploring and explaining Ethiopia's social, economic, and political phenomena through the prisms of ethnicity is patently inaccurate and does not reflect the realities on the ground.

Indeed, socioeconomic resources and activities gravitated toward cities that were strategically and politically important to the ruling class. Moreover, it needs to be noted that the political and strategic centers, Addis Ababa and its neighboring cities as well as Asmara, had the highest percentage of enrollment ratio and a transportation system that is comparatively more reliable and efficient than other cities in the country. This also means that the potential for localized market development and market access is greater in these cities than in others. If local manufacturing industries are to generate some profits or remain operational, even with little or no profits, the selection of sites for the establishment of industries takes on such variables as market potential, cost and availability of production input, distance, and purchasing power. This dynamic interaction between the political and economic components of the social system also has implications on worsening the conditions of the people of the peripheral regions.

The tendency to establish and expand health and education services, infrastructure, and manufacturing industries to meet the needs of the political elites may lead to a marginal improvement in the standard of living of the local population. The ripple effect generated and fueled by such social and economic current leads to further increase in the establishment of more industries and expansion of health and education services, leading to a further marginalization of the peoples of other provinces. Thus, the framework within which the policy of correcting historical distortions in the distribution of socioeconomic resources should be fine-tuned so that it takes account of the concentration of resources in very few cities at the expense of marginalizing the majority of the people in Ethiopia. Such a policy of distributive justice should reject the notion that ethnicity was a determinant factor in the distribution of resources.

Notes

1. Data on revenue and expenditure are only for the previous two governments. Since the early 1990s these data are excluded from the Central Statistical Office annual report.

2. "The Regions of the Federal Democratic Republic of Ethiopia," 4 December 1999, at <http://www.ethiospokes.net/Backgrnd/b0311981.htm>.

3. One could argue that if there were extractable resources in Harari, the Oromiya State would have possibly insisted on incorporating this region as it has the city of Addis Ababa.

4. See "The Regions of the Federal Democratic Republic of Ethiopia."

5. World Bank, *The State in a Changing World* (New York: Oxford University Press, 1997), p.240.

6. Central Statistical Office (CSO), "Statistical Abstract 1964," (Addis Ababa: CSO, 1970), p.7.

7. See *Menen*, 13th year, No.8, (Addis Ababa: Commercial Printing Press, May 1967), p.15.

8. And Alem Mulaw, "The Role of Development Planning and International Assistance in Post-World War II Ethiopia, 1941-1988: A Comparative Analysis" (Ph.D. Diss., Howard University, 1990), p.290.

9. Ibid., p.290.

10. CSO, "Statistical Abstract 1969," (Addis Ababa: CSO, n.d.), pp.42-3. See also, "Statistical Abstract 1975," (Addis Ababa: CSO, 1975), p.48.

11. *Menen*, 16th year, No.5, (Addis Ababa: Berhanena Selam Printing Press, February 1971), p.21.

12. CSO, "Statistical Abstract 1967 and 1968," (Addis Ababa: CSO, n.d.), p.138. See also, "Statistical Abstract 1972," (Addis Ababa: CSO, n.d.), p.131.

13. CSO, "Statistical Abstract 1967 and 1968," (Addis Ababa: CSO, n.d.), p.192. See also, "Statistical Abstract 1975," (Addis Ababa: CSO, 1975), p.209. See also, "Statistical Abstract 1982," (Addis Ababa: CSO, 1984), p.244.

14. World Bank, p.25.

15. Ayhun Alemseged, *Fana Wogi* (Addis Ababa: Bole Printing Organization, 1991).

16. CSO, "Results of the Survey of Manufacturing Industries 1979," (Addis Ababa: CSO, 1982), pp.22-8. See also, "Results of the Survey of Manufacturing and Electricity Industries 1985," (Addis Ababa: CSO, 1989), pp.49-61.

17. CSO, "Statistical Abstract 1986," (Addis Ababa: CSO, 1988), p.26.

18. Ibid.

19. According to the new division of administrative regions, some parts of the former two provinces are sparsely scattered as parts of Gambella, Benishangu/Gumuz, Southern Nations and Nationalities Region, or Oromiya Regional States. Most parts of Gonder and Wollo are parts of the Amhara Regional State, while some parts of Gonder and Wollo and all of Tigray provinces form the Tigray Regional State.

20. USAID, "Basic Education System Overhaul Program Assistance Approval Document and Project Paper" (Addis Ababa, Ethiopia: USAID/Ethiopia, September 1994), p.21. Unpublished document.

21. Joseph Stiglitz, *Globalization and Its Discontents* (New York: W.W. Norton & Company, Inc., 2000), pp.28-31.

22. Wilfred David, *The Conversation of Economic Development: Historical Voices, Interpretations, and Reality* (New York: M.E. Sharpe, 1997), p.107.

23. Paul Krugman, "Space: The Final Frontier," *Journal of Economic Perspectives*, Vol.12, 2 (Spring 1998): 161-74.

Chapter VI

Sinking Ethnic Cleavages
and Promoting Political Loyalty

The statistical data analyzed in chapter five strongly suggest that there was indeed extreme maldistribution of socioeconomic resources among the various provinces in Ethiopia. The data also demonstrate that ethnicity played very little, if any, role in the allocation of socio-economic resources during the governments of Emperor Haile-Selassie and President Mengistu Haile-Mariam. Inequity in the distribution of socioeconomic resources continues to manifest under the current government of Prime Minister Meles Zenawi as well. Like its predecessors, the present government has been unable to rectify distortions in the distribution of socioeconomic resources among the provinces, let alone among the diverse ethnic groups in Ethiopia.

In terms of the distribution of political power, the previous governments made no claim that the electorate would participate in a political process that pays considerable attention to the will of the people in deciding the outcome of elections. The present government is, therefore, accurate in claiming that the need for rectifying distributive injustice in political power is long overdue. It is, however, erroneous and divisive to assume that the consolidation of political power in the hands of a few ethnic group representatives also translated into the domination of socioeconomic resources by the alleged ruling ethnic group.

To the extent that members of a single ethnic group dominated the political system, their political domination did not have a positive impact on the social and economic well-being of the majority members of the supposed super-ordinate ethnic group. Conversely, socioeconomic marginalization of the majority by the few does not necessarily imply the political servitude of the former by the latter. That is, the monopoly of political power may not have had a positive ripple socioeconomic effect on the rest of the group whose members may, for the purpose of argument, have played a dominant role in the decision making process. Generally, the fact that the majority of a particular ethnic group is as economically marginalized as other ethnic groups in the country does not necessarily mean that "one nationality group" could not have dominated the political space or controlled machineries of the state.

The question now becomes, to what extent the alleged "super-ordinate" ethnic group dominated the Ethiopian political space at the expense of repressing and excluding the "subordinate ethnic groups" from meaningful participation in the political process? For the purpose of this study, "Amhara" is loosely defined as a super-ordinate ethnic group that, according to some policymakers and scholars, is responsible for Ethiopia's poor economic performance, which transformed into ethnic tensions and conflict. Similarly, subordinate groups are those ethnic groups that have been politically repressed and economically marginalized by the super-ordinate ethnic group.

Thus, to examine the validity of conventional assumptions and conclusions regarding the dominant/dependent political power relation-ships, we begin by analyzing the 1957, 1961, and 1965 parliamentary elections. Subsequently, we explore the sources of resistance to and appointment in high-ranking public posts during the aristocratic rule of Emperor Haile-Selassie. This chapter also includes analyses of the so-cial and economic conditions that created a fertile environment for the rise of an opportunist military junta during the 1974 popular uprising. Its composition and characteristics are also important areas of investi-gation that may provide a greater sense of understanding of the diverse ethnic groups that made up the military government.

If biographic data on members of the Standing Committee and Ministers of the military government were available, it would have been useful to examine the extent to which political power was domi-nated by members of a particular ethnic group. However, since writing on the biographies of leading personalities was either politically risky or uncustomary, there is a chronic shortage of such information. There-fore, biographies of only a few of the most important political leaders have been identified (see Appendix J) and are presented here to show their ethnic diversity. A list of names and official ranks of individuals that were executed by the military government is included in Appendix K. The data in Appendix J and K are presented as supplementary to the historical and analytical data and encourage further research on the subject. A research that identifies the ethnic backgrounds of prominent leaders during the government of Haile-Selassie would be extremely useful to our understanding of Ethiopian politics.

Resistance to and Political Appointment in the Imperial Government

The coronation of Teferi Mekonen as Emperor Haile-Selassie in November 1930 and the promulgation of the first constitution in 1931 were intended to consolidate the power of the monarch and symbolize the progressive nature of the state.[1] These measures were undertaken as declarative statements to undermine the resurgence of potential rivals to the throne. The Emperor drew lessons from the experience through which He came to power by eliminating Lij Iyasu,[2] heir to the throne, who was next in line following his deceased grandfather, Menelik II. Nevertheless, the government of Haile-Selassie continued to experience sporadic and, sometimes, persistent opposition until the eruption of a violent mass demonstration in 1974.

Generally, there are two opposing views on the sources of political resistance to imperial rule. Some are of the view that the few isolated resistance movements since the death of Emperor Menelik II in December 1913 until the overthrow of Emperor Haile-Selassie in 1974 were essentially internal struggles for political power between the Amhara nobles and elites.[3] The proposition that the struggle for power was between members of the same ethnic group implies that the distribution of political power during Haile-Selassie's rule was biased in favor of the Amharas. Aaron Tesfaye, for example, insisted that expansion of the provincial bureaucracies was designed to absorb an increasing number of Amhara into the civil service. Its expansion was often disguised under the "ambitious objectives in local development," which "led to increased employment, often in the form of patronage." Furthermore, he asserted that past policies discriminated against the Oromo, Tigray, Benishangul/Gumuz, Gambella, and other ethnic groups.[4]

There is also the view that resistance to aristocratic rule, especially the first attempted coup of 1960, was prompted by the deplorable social and economic conditions and the suppression of political freedom of the majority of Ethiopians. Some of the uprisings against the ruling class were partly successful in exerting pressure on the imperial regime to shift from a closed and authoritarian system towards a more open and tolerant political system. Irrespective of whether the demands were fulfilled or not, the driving force for subverting the ruling class was fueled by the burning desire for equality and greater access to quality education and health services.[5]

To be sure, over the years the totalitarian characteristics of the Haile-Selassie government became more visible and irritant in the eyes of the public. Totalitarian and authoritarian regimes are structurally organized in such a way to suffocate the voices of the majority, deny the political and human rights of citizens, and dictate economic and social policy from above. In a functioning democratic system, however, the right to participate in the decisionmaking process is constitutionally guaranteed and the exercise of such a right is facilitated through regularly held elections of representatives. The very process of elections partially symbolizes the protection of constitutional rights of *all*, and actually participating in elections constitutes, symbolically or practically, the decentralization of the decisionmaking process and the delegation of political power.

If a democratic system is inherently transparent and elected and appointed officials are accountable to the public, directly or indirectly, then non-democratic systems must by definition lack transparency and accountability. A violation of the political rights of the people and the absence of opportunities for social mobility often leads to violence and armed insurrection against the government. On the other hand, if elections of representatives are conducted with little or no transgression by an incumbent party that wishes to influence the outcome of elections, then the political process enhances the possibility of working out differences and resolving grievances through democratic rather than violent means.

Equality before the Law

The constitution of Ethiopia clearly provided for the equal treatment of citizens before the law. It consistently asserted that no one, including members of the Emperor's cabinet, but excluding the Emperor himself, was above the law.[6] The first constitution of Ethiopia, promulgated on July 16, 1931, was primarily designed to ensure "the Emperor's ultimate power to delegate authority to other institutions such as the two-house parliament." The revised constitution of 1955 reasserted the supremacy of the Emperor by tracing the dynastic line to Menelik I, the son of Makeda, queen of Ethiopia, and King Solomon" of Israel.[7] Thus, the authoritarian characteristics of the Haile-Selassie government demystifies the notion that the distribution of political power was partial to the ethnic group to which the Emperor belonged, because the authoritarian government in Ethiopia made no distinction about the treatment of its citizens based on ethnicity.

The Emperor surrounded himself with the people loyal to the throne and proponents of the continuation of aristocratic rule. The power of the Emperor was incontestable and his rulings on legal matters, constitutional, and socioeconomic affairs were indisputably final. Indeed, the first and revised constitution of Ethiopia provided for the rights and obligations of citizens, carrots and sticks, but there were more of the latter than the former.

For instance, using the constitution as an instrument of repression, the Emperor moved against "an outstanding anachronism, Abba Jifar II of Jima," demoting him to a position of "titular ruler" of Jima, on charges of "developing an army to challenge his authority." As his replacement, the Emperor elevated Ras Desta Damtew as governor of Jima and steadfastly moved against Ras Hailu of Gojjam. Although Ras Hailu was granted administrative autonomy and "made a great success of the national economy," he was brought to the capital city for detention on charges of treason. Ras Hailu was allegedly cooperating with the Italians in the late 1920s and, as a result, was considered a threat to national security.[8]

Interestingly, three years before the first coup attempt in 1957, the government of Haile-Selassie took an unprecedented measure to introduce a parliamentary system through which representatives were elected from all the provinces. Such measures may be perceived as a courageous step towards political progress and openness and to resolving conflict through institutional and legal avenues. However, its significance in delegating power and as a true measure of political openness is questionable on various grounds.

The data in Table 6.1 is directly relevant to explore the nature of political openness and the scope of regional and ethnic representation in Haile-Selassie's parliament. In the table, it is apparent that, except for Bale, the 1957, 1961, and 1965 parliamentary elections were held in *all* the provinces.[9] No evidence exists to indicate that these elections were conducted unfairly or excluded certain groups from exercising their political rights.

Indeed, ethnic and religious affiliations were not differentiating factors between candidates running for parliamentary seats. Some candidates simply capitalized on their popularity as active participants or leaders in community affairs or invited local electors to a party to solicit their votes. Each candidate identified himself with some recognizable and locally and nationally meaningful images of animals such as a pigeon to represent peace, a lion for its prowess to defend its territories and interests, and a tiger for its stamina and hunting skills. Candidates for parliamentary posts did not organize themselves along political party lines, and the parliament was essentially set up as a forum for consultative groups.

Nonetheless, during the first parliamentary elections ever held, the average voting turnouts, given the low level of political activism and poor communication infrastructure, indeed suggest a growing interest of the electorate to participate in the political process. The increase in the percentage of voting in the second parliamentary elections also confirms that interest, perhaps even improvement in the organization and conducting of elections, mass political education, and delivery of the necessary pre-election materials to polling stations.

Table 6.1: Voters Registered, Voting, and Percentage of Voting, by Province

	1957			1961			1965		
Province	Reg. ('000)	Voting ('000)	% voting	Reg. ('000)	Voting ('000)	% voting	Reg. ('000)	Voting ('000)	% voting
Arussi	196.1	145.8	74.3	96.5	89.9	93.2	87.9	60.0	68.3
Bale	-	-	-	25.9	23.0	88.8	50.3	27.4	54.5
Gonder	300.2	214.0	71.3	515.2	395.3	76.7	536.0	366.4	68.4
Eritrea	203.9	190.7	93.5	308.4	242.9	78.8	254.5	197.6	77.6
Gamu Gofa	79.7	26.2	32.9	48.5	38.5	79.4	113.8	81.4	71.5
Gojjam	239.6	195.3	81.5	226.0	179.6	79.5	409.6	252.0	61.5
Hararghe	298.3	196.5	65.9	122.1	64.1	52.5	457.5	275.6	60.2
Illubabor	117.8	110.8	94.1	151.3	109.0	72.0	161.3	99.6	61.7
Kaffa	141.4	73.0	51.6	173.3	109.7	63.3	330.7	269.2	81.4
Shoa	541.0	292.0	54.0	555.6	473.2	85.2	698.0	459.5	65.8
A.A	128.1	45.4	35.4	119.4	34.0	28.5	128.2	33.2	25.9
Sidamo	237.8	224.7	94.5	286.4	205.1	71.6	495.4	208.7	42.1
Tigray	459.6	331.4	72.1	373.8	305.7	81.8	444.7	283.5	63.8
Wollega	337.3	290.3	86.1	327.1	238.7	73.0	465.3	228.4	49.1
Wollo	463.3	296.4	64.0	367.2	341.3	92.9	504.0	360.3	71.5
Total	**3,744.1**	**2,632.5**	**70.3**	**3,696.7**	**2,850.0**	**77.1**	**5,137.2**	**3,203.1**	**62.4**

Note: Bale was a sub-province of Hararghe until 1961 when it became a separate province.

Source: Central Statistical Office, "Statistical Abstract 1966," (Addis Ababa: CSO, 1966), p.35.

On the other hand, with the exception of Gamu Gofa, Kaffa, Shoa, and Wollo provinces, there were declines in the percentages of people voting; some were marginal while others were significant. The most significant declines occurred in the province of Gojjam, Illubabor, Sidamo, and Wollega from 81.5% to 61.5%, from 94.1% to 61.7%, from 94.5% to 42.1%, and from 86.1% to 49.1% in 1957 and 1965, respectively. One of the highest voter turnouts was in Arussi (93.2%) in 1961, which declined appreciably to 68.3% in 1965. In all cases, the decline in the percentage of voter turnouts during the 1965 parliamentary elections was partly caused by the growing realization that the presence of representatives in parliament was symbolic as far as the social and economic interests of the electorate were concerned. It may have also been an expression of apathy, disenchantment, or voluntarily withdrawing participation in the electoral process.

The 1957, 1961, and 1965 parliamentary elections were practically designed to draw consultative groups from among sympathizers of and loyalists to the absolutist regime on matters of a provincial nature to mask the authoritarian characteristics of the regime. Practically, the aristocracy did not tolerate social or political opposition groups or permit elite circulation without the "seal of approval" of the King.

The absence of opposition groups and, more bluntly, the approval or removal of ministers and other political appointees by the Emperor and the Emperor alone made the government of Haile-Selassie absolutely totalitarian. Indeed, the 1931 constitution and the establishment of the parliament seemed to suggest a fundamental departure from an absolutist aristocratic rule to a constitutional monarchy. However, the "fifty-five articles enshrined the rule of law while acknowledging the Emperor's ultimate power to delegate authority to other institutions," including the parliament.[10] The data in Table 6.1 also suggest that there were no preferential treatment such as restrictions or accommodations of where elections should or should not be conducted and whose political rights and civil liberties were exercised through participation in parliamentary elections. It is unfortunate that most scholars who claimed to be experts in Ethiopian affairs ignored whether these elections, however meaningless, suggest the extent to which political power was dominated by one nationality group.

Linguistic and Cultural Necessities

When one gains insight into the meaning of the term "Amhara," from which the language Amharic is derived, one finds that it has been a social construct without distinctive subjective and objective attributes of ethnicity. Until recently, the term "Amhara" was not understood as an ethnic marker, but it had a religious connotation to distinguish Christians from Muslims. In other words, when one identifies oneself as Amhara, the person is not espousing ethnic identity, explicitly or implicitly, but expressing his/her religious identity.

Until the politicization of language and ethnicity in recent years, a person of Gurage, Gambella, Affar, Tigray, or other ethnic origin could be an Amhara, Muslim, or a believer in a traditional faith. In fact, for members of the Arisi ethnic group who became subjected to Emperor

Menelik's expansionist policy, the Oromo and the Amhara are simply "Sidamas" or an immigrant community in the eyes of "sons of the soil," the Arisi.[11] For the Arisi, therefore, the Oromos are no less occupying forces than the Amharas who migrated southward during the Oromo expansion that was spearheaded by one of their leaders, Emperor Menelik II.

As a social construct, however, some contemporary political entrepreneurs perceive the term "Amhara" as the name of a distinct ethnic group. Encouragement of the use of Amharic as the national and official language of the country has also been misconstrued as a vicious policy of cultural domination and systematic erosion of a vital form of identity of non-Amharic speaking nationalities. It is also believed that the Amhara claimed a disproportionate number of political offices and, therefore, derive tangible benefits from their direct role in the decisionmaking processes. The promotion and celebration of the language, tradition, and culture of the "super-ordinate" group as a national emblem, a common identity, and means of communication among Ethiopians was never to undermine the development of traditions, cultures, and languages of other ethnic groups. It was rather motivated by nationalist aspirations of the government and peoples of Ethiopia and by the pan-African movement that captured the attention of leaders of the struggle for independence and unification of the continent.

Emperor Haile-Selassie was politically astute to undermine the language of the Ethiopian Coptic Church, *Geez,* and face a similar fate as Emperor Tewodros (1855-1866) who committed suicide when confronted with the British expeditionary force in 1866. Emperor Haile-Selassie inherited the northern part of Ethiopia that was linguistically and politically advanced and economically resourceful and, therefore, it would have been self-destructive to upset the northern nobility. On the other hand, there is no plausible evidence to indicate that the government of Haile-Selassie showed ill-will towards the growth and development of other cultures and languages. Indeed, it can be argued that the government took a liberal stance towards the development of other ethnic groups' languages, customs, and the like, making it possible for Ethiopia to be a mosaic of diverse cultures and languages.

Even if the assumption that the government was liberal in allowing other languages and cultures to flourish or decay naturally is faulty, any alternative to adopting Amharic as the national and official language would have been an economic miscalculation. The reason is that there are no scripts other than *Ge'ez*, from which *Amarigna* is derived, that reached an advanced level of legibility to warrant their adoption as a national and official language of Ethiopia. For instance, before the introduction of a modern and formal education system to Ethiopia, many governors, judges, and administrators obtained basic education from the informal education sector of Orthodox churches and missionary schools, using the only advanced local languages, *Ge'ez* and *Amarigna,* available to them.[12]

By historical rights as opposed to wrongs, the script and the language of Amharic developed to a level that is incomparable with any of the other languages in the country. Thus, the development of new ones or borrowing scripts from other languages, just as the State of Oromiya has done in recent years, is nothing more than an utterance of disdain and hostility to the national language. To be sure, the borrowing of the Roman script for written communication in the State of Oromiya has its own repercussions as well as paradoxes. It leads to inefficient utilization of scarce resources and manifests in a growing pedagogical confusion among school children and teachers.

Additionally and ironically, it shifts the focus of *script dependency* from *Ge'ez* to English, merely because the national language is associated with the supposed repressive ethnic group. Beyond some tainted perception of why the Amharic language is advanced to a level that is incomparable with others, it has also served as a frame of reference for the sources of ethnic conflict and a convenient political tool of political elites. Certainly, another source of grievance against the supposed "ruling ethnic group" is that most of the leaders acted and behaved as, what has become known as, "Amhara." As a result, many confuse Emperor Haile-Selassie's ethnic identity as purely Amharan. And, this is not just the Emperor but also Menelik II and Atse Fasiledes (an Oromo) (1632-1667) who raided the northwestern part of Ethiopia and established his capital city in the predominantly Amhara province of Gonder.[13] Interestingly, many Amharas in Ethiopia, North America, and Europe embrace Emperors Fasiledes, Menelik II, and Haile-Selassie as their ethnic kin and often hang their pictures and paintings of Fasiledes' Castle in their houses and restaurants.

Deconstructing the lineage of Ethiopian Emperors, Kings, and other important political figures of pre-1974 is a time consuming, if not impossible, task. It is even difficult to construct the biographies of those who were executed by the military regime as recently as mid-1970s. However, based on the biographies of a few leading personalities that ruled Ethiopia for more than a century, it is patently erroneous and misleading to argue that the "super-ordinate" group continued to dominate all other groups, socially, economically, or politically.[14]

As one of Africa's skillful, visionary, charismatic, and eminent leaders, Emperor Haile-Selassie surely had a set of criteria for appointing his cabinet and other high-ranking members of the government. In some cases, there were political appointees who were affiliated with the royal family and may have been granted a position based on ascription. In most cases, the Emperor placed more emphasis on loyalty, competence, and affiliation, in that order of importance.[15]

As Bahru Zewde argued, Haile-Selassie's approach to modernizing the bureaucracy "opened an avenue for skillful and diligent commoners to rise to positions of eminence in the government hierarchy." Indeed, the modernization of the bureaucracy "had the support of a vigorous and articulate group of intellectuals" who may have, in some cases, inspired the birth not only of the bureaucracy but also of a nobility of service rather than of birth.[16] The best candidates for political and high level ranks in the government were those that combined loyalty with competence. If ethnicity was a primary factor for political appointment, then leading political figures of the previous governments would have surrounded themselves with either Oromos or Tigrays.

In May 1940, after the end of the Ethio-Italian war, the government of Haile-Selassie formed a new cabinet comprising officials from diverse ethnic backgrounds. For instance, Dejazmach (later Lij) Endal-kachew Mekonnen was appointed Minister of Interior and entrusted with the power to create and oversee the offices of the national defense force, administration and health services. Other ministerial appointments included Wolde-Giorgis Wolde-Yohannis, Minister of Pen, Lorenzo Tae'zaz, Minister of Foreign Affairs, Mekonnen Desta, Minister of Education, Ayele Gebre, Minister of Justice, Gebre-Egziabhere, Minister of Trade and Industry, and Belachew Yadete', Minister of Communication.[17] If the argument that the expansion of the bureaucracy led to "increased employment, often in the form of patronage,"[18] holds, as Tesfaye and others insisted, then the post-independent cabinet would logically reflect and be governed by the multiplier effect of the correlation between ethnicity and appointment in the civil service.

Some competent individuals in leadership and persons with a broad social base, but without personal affiliation and loyalty to the monarch, were excluded from making any meaningful contribution to the development of the country. They were kept within the purview of the royal family and the Emperor's political allies, under house arrest, surveillance, or re-appointed as governor or district judge of a distant province away from the capital city. In other instances, irrespective of their ethnicity but largely due to their competence, experience, and level of education, some were elevated to important positions in the armed forces, as governors or ministers.[19] The rise of General Aman Michael Amdon, Maj. General Mulugeta Buli, and many others to the apex of Ethiopia's armed forces are exemplary of the trans-ethnic nature of political and civil service appointments. So loyal to the Emperor, Maj. General Mulugeta was entrusted with the authority to establish and train the Royal Bodyguard.

To say that the Emperor paid greater attention to kinship and personal affiliation in his determination of political appointment is logically and analytically inconsistent with the Ethiopian reality. To argue that ethnic allegiance superseded other politically, culturally, and economically relevant criterion for leadership is to over simplify the nature of the Ethiopian political tradition. It is also to imply that there were disproportionately larges numbers of individuals belonging to the Oromo and Gurage ethnic groups that occupied the political space during the Haile-Selassie government.

Although the lineage of the Emperor has been conveniently ignored, the Emperor mainly descended from an Oromo and partly from a Gurage and an Amhara family. Hence, it makes analytical sense to question if the advancement of the interests of Oromos superseded that of the Amhara, Gurage, and other ethnic groups. An affirmative response to such a presumptive question would have found no plausible basis of argument and intellectually-driven support. Indeed, a few of the available biographic data on the political appointees of the government suggest that ethnic sentiments and affiliations were not overriding guidelines, but rather loyalty and competence were critical factors in the Emperor's appointment of his political officers.

For some scholars, the difficulty may have been that the Emperor did not seem to have crafted a uniform imperial yardstick by which to measure how individuals that were neither affiliated with him through kinship and marriage were worthy of the Emperor's blessing for political appointment. One's cultural attributes may have also been a contributing factor in the Emperor's calculation of who could and could not be trustworthy. Of course, although cultural attributes are largely implicit, there are ways in which they can be expressed explicitly to distinguish one potential leader from another. Subjective attributes of a culture that may be inculcated through riddles and stories become valuable assets in improving the possibility of an individual's rising to political power. The ways in which an individual conducted himself before others and showed allegiance and loyalty to his superiors were desirable and sought-after characteristics, because members of the political class were more committed to consolidating their power than maintaining ethnic group solidarity.

Economic Imperatives

As much as there were political and religious elements, there were also economic factors embodied in the choice of the Amharic language.

Historically, societies engaged in sedentary economic activities are more reliable sources of revenue. They are also better at recruiting troops which are essential to state formation and the administration of public affairs. Based on the recent history of the state of the Ethiopian economy, it would be meaningless and economically unjustifiable to publish textbooks in over 80 different languages and train teachers and medical personnel in the languages of the diverse ethnic groups in Ethiopia. In the absence of suitable technologies, it was also economically imprudent to support publications of teaching/learning material in the scripts of the various languages, which are still unintelligible to pioneers of computers and typing machines.

The economic conditions and the need for national unity simply did not allow the government of Haile-Selassie to excessively preoccupy itself with implementing language and education policies that resulted in fragmenting the nation-state. Furthermore, in developing countries such as Ethiopia, income, head, or "hut" taxes are more easily levied on individuals or families that are engaged in subsistence or commercial agricultural production than on the nomadic groups of eastern and southeastern Ethiopia.

Unlike nomads who travel across provincial and international boundaries in search of grazing lands, crop farmers are restrained from movement by the nature of their economic activities, which depend on a definite territorial boundary and a landscape that is suitable for sedentary farming activities. It is even difficult to conduct a census of a nomad population, let alone collect taxes from their economic activities of animal husbandry. If this is true, then it is not an over-exaggeration to state that the social and economic bases of the political system of Ethiopia emerged from the northern part of the country that is largely inhabited by sedentary farmers. It is also not surprising that most of the resistance, organized or otherwise, to the political center and coincidentally the most successful oppositions emerged from northern resistance movement leaders and groups. When the political center shifted from northern to central Ethiopia, the social and military basis of opposition movements remained, to a large extent, within the northern parts of the country such as Tigray, Gonder, and Gojjam.

Dissenters and Loyalists

Belay Zeleke is among the few leading figures in Ethiopia's history of resistance to Italian occupation and to the imperial rule of Haile-Selassie. Belay was born to an Amhara family in Gojjam province and gained fame for his unyielding resistance against Italian incursion prior to the Second World War. Suspicious of and disgusted by Belay's growing fame among the common people who were primarily and initially from the north, Emperor Haile-Selassie charged Belay and others with conspiracy against his government. Subsequently, Belay, Mamo Hailu (son of Ras Hailu Tekle-Haymanot), and seven other patriots were brought to the capital city to face "justice." A capital sentence was carried out on Belay and Mamo and their bodies remained hanging in the capital city for an entire day as a symbolic illustration of the King's almighty power. "By the order of the king, the sentence was to be executed by the then Col. Mengistu Neway"[20] who ironically faced a similar fate as Belay and Mamo for his failed coup of 1960. As Ayhun Alemseged further noted, Emperor Haile-Selassie is said to have stated that there was no one he hated as much as Lij Iyasu and feared as much as Belay Zeleke. This is precisely why Lij Iyasu and Belay Zeleke were eliminated before they became imminent threats to the throne.

Unsuccessful as it may have seemed initially, the December 1960 coup, led by two prominent leaders, Mengistu and Germame Newya, born to an Amhara family in Addis Ababa, was the first organized attempt at shaking the political foundations of aristocratic rule. Apparently, the failure of the parliamentary election as a mechanism to accommodate opposing political views and to reduce tensions may have led to violence as an alternative avenue to bring about change in the political system. Nonetheless, as Alemseged noted, the main objective of the coup was to replace the absolutist rule with a government that was just in distributing resources and allocating political power.

Another leading participant of the 1960 coup attempt against the repressive government was Lieutenant Colonel Workneh Gebeyehu who was also born to an Amhara family in Debretabor, Gonder. "If we look at the list of participants of the coup, we find that they were born to a poor family and that they were individuals wounded and irritated by the backwardness of their country and by the destitute conditions of the people."[21] The 1960 coup attempt and the subsequent struggles against the aristocratic rule of Emperor Haile-Selassie were in pursuit of economic justice and meaningful political participation. Resorting to violence to achieve these objectives is largely attributed to the absence of alternative legal and institutional means of conflict resolution.

Even though it was not as well-organized as the 1960s coup, there were movements against the imperial rule that were led by the renowned patriot and president of the judiciary, Bitwoded Negash Bezabih of Amhara descent. Bit. Negash was known for his uncompromising and relentless effort to change the absolute monarchy into a system of constitutional monarchy. Dejazmach Takle Wolde-Hawariat (a Tigray) and Yohannis Remamo (an Oromo) were also supporters of a

constitutional monarchy to correct the gross injustices committed
against the majority.[22]

Loyal to the Emperor before and during the 1960 coup were eminent leaders, including Major General Merid Mengesha and Commander of the ground force, Brigadier General Kebede Gebre. There
were others in the upper-tier of the social, religious, and political hierarchy such as Brigadier General Wolde-Selassie Bereka (a Gurage),
Brigadier General Wakjira Tola (an Oromo), Mahiteme Selassie
Wolde-Meskel, and Patriarch of the Orthodox Church, Abune Baslios,
who forged alliances with Major General Merid to counter the coup.

It needs to be noted that the division among the leaders and followers of the coup attempt and those loyal to the Emperor were not
distinctly or otherwise organized along ethnic lines. Both camps of the
struggle for political power were not driven by the desire to ensure that
one ethnic group retained a full-hand in the political game of domination. The ethnic diversity of dissenters and those loyal to aristocratic
rule also attests to the fact that the Emperor did not appear to be preoccupied with fashioning the appointment of individuals to important
posts in the armed forces and cabinet to reflect inclusion or exclusion
of members of certain ethnic groups.

The quest for social and economic justice and the sacrifices of
those who fought to bring about gradual or fundamental change in the
political system continued to captivate the thinking of individuals in the
academic community until the overthrow of the Emperor in 1974. The
Addis Ababa University students who were among the principal supporters of the coup continued to fuel the movement towards social and
economic justice and political transformation which was sparked by
courageous and charismatic leaders such as Belay Zeleke, Mengistu
and Germame Neway, Workeneh Gebeyehu, Takle Wolde-Hawariat,
and Yohannis Remamo. The 1950 and 1960 opposition movement
leaders crossed over ethnic and professional classifications. Likewise,
university and high school students who fueled and propelled the 1974
successful coup-d'etat against the Emperor came from diverse ethnic
and economic backgrounds.

University and high school students carried the torch forward, il-
luminating and exposing political decay and corruption and demanding
a remedy. They did so not because they were interested in accumulat-
ing political capital for their own instantaneous economic gains, but
because they were fulfilling moral and intellectual obligations. The
political torch passed from forerunners of social and economic justice
to students was ignited by the many strikes of the armed forces.

Members of the armed forces were initially hesitant to join the student movement, particularly in the early 1970s, largely because the

movement was perceived as nothing more than an annual demonstration of students to commemorate the death of the Neway brothers. However, the early 1970s protests were highly charged by current events such as the drought in Wollo and Tigray, which animated the student body and later members of the armed forces to demand an immediate solution to the crisis. As Harold Marcus noted,

> In 1959, a drought and famine struck Eritrea, Wollo, Haraghe, and Tigray. In fact, the conditions prefacing the abortive coup of 1960 appear remarkably similar to those before the successful coup of 1974, except that in 1959, the government admitted the famine and asked Washington and others for food relief.[23]

In short, as aristocratic and totalitarian as the Haile-Selassie government was, its executive members were largely drawn from diverse ethnic groups who were competent and committed to maintaining the status quo. The data in Table 6.1 clearly illustrates that the government of Haile-Selassie made no distinction about who should or should not express their political rights. Whether or not the elections amounted to anything substantial for the electorate can be seen from the declining voter turnouts across the country. If there were any groups excluded from participating in the political process, it was not based on deliberately disenfranchising certain ethnic, religious, or linguistic groups, precisely because elections were held throughout the country.

The failure of the struggle for broad-based social justice and the nature of parliamentary elections of 1957, 1961, and 1965, which was symbolic, created a fertile environment for the mushrooming of secessionist movements which became useful political tools for political elites aspiring to climb to political power. As much as secessionist elite were able to exploit the growing public disenchantment, members of the armed forces were able to hijack the 1974 uprising against the Haile-Selassie government.

The Military Government: Its Rise and Composition

It is generally and uncritically accepted that the military government of Col. Mengistu Haile-Mariam "allowed one nationality group, the Amharas, to largely dominate the decisionmaking process."[24] Scholars including Donald Rothchild, James Scarritt,[25] and Peter Nyong'o[26] insisted that ethnicity was an overarching and principal element in appointing individuals to key positions during the previous two governments. Ethnicity as a reference point for acquisition of political power, a hunch that has been persuasively argued by some, fomented

the emergence, since 1991, of political parties, the creation of administrative regions with ethnic emblems, and the crafting and promulgation
of a constitution that practically legalizes ethnic divisions. Nonetheless,
the assertion that ethnicity was the overriding criteria over loyalty,
competence, and experience for appointment to important public offices during the governments of Haile-Selassie and Mengistu Haile-
Mariam is built on a weak historical, analytical, and empirical foundation.

The analysis in the previous section suggests that one of the most
important criteria used by Haile-Selassie to demote or promote public
officials, especially after the 1960s attempted coup, "stem from their
personal loyalty to the emperor." By default, political appointees' loyalty to the Emperor was also paying allegiance to the aristocratic political system. Although the Emperor reshuffled his cabinets, close advisors, and generals, he retained absolute control of the government.[27]
Therefore, what the military government inherited was not an ethic-
based allocation of power; rather it was a totalitarian political system
and political culture of obedience and passivity, and not the dominance
of one nationality group.

The military government found it inescapably necessary to retain
and promote the politics of repression and exclusion based on political
outlooks. One of the reasons for maintaining a centralized political system, instead of abolishing and replacing it with a competitive political
system, was that it lacked the social, religious, and political bases on
which to build a legitimate national government. The dictatorial substance of the military government is not a matter of contention; but to
argue that the government was built around a solid foundation on or
within one nationality group implies that the majority ethnic groups
were also culturally dominated. Any such government will have to
promote and seek to exploit cultural attributes that augment the desired
political outcomes. Exploiting rule-oriented cultures that help sustain
totalitarian, dictatorial, and authoritarian systems is as common during
the initial phases of building the Ethiopian State as it was in many other
cases.

Religion, for example, was one of the instruments with which Emperor Haile-Selassie sought to distance himself from his subjects. He
claimed that his legitimacy was derived from a divine power and that
he was representing God. For Ethiopian Christians, revering the Emperor was largely equated with greater glorification of God, and salvation was to be redeemed in life after death, if not in the worldly presence of the subjects. "Africans," Robert Cummings argued, make God
"appear remote from their daily existence but ... *manifested* in natural
objects and phenomena, allowing them therefore to worship Him at any

place and at any time."[28] Specifically, Cummings' observation is also true for Ethiopians where the King was not simply a political head but the spiritual link between the earthly and other-worldly, and the divine symbol of the health and welfare of his subjects.[29]

The socialist military regime "stripped the Ethiopian Orthodox Church of most of its landholding," especially at the height of the revolution in the early 1970s, only to court "the Orthodox patriarch and the chief Muslim mullah of Addis Ababa" in the 1980s.[30] By that time, the relationship between the government and leaders of the religious establishments plummeted to an irreparable level. Indeed, as Messay Kebede argued, if Mengistu had not "dressed up a socialist ideologue for opportunistic reasons, nothing could have prevented the Church from calling him the elect of God in the traditional sense."[31]

The need for a new political direction in Ethiopia was stimulated by the people's desire for improving the welfare of society, but progress towards achieving social justice was reversed by external circumstances. Mengistu promoted an ideology that conflicted with the internal social dynamics, which undermined the role of religion in mystifying power. Since the military government diverged from social norms and confiscated Church landholdings and other amenities, the government had to rely on other cultural attributes that promoted obedience and submissiveness.

Clearly, one may be justified to assert that those most loyal to the imperial government were either members of the royal family or those groups whose interests were protected by the continuation of aristocratic rule. There were also some ethnic groups, including the Affar, Amhara, and Tigray, whose culture placed significant emphasis on respect for elders and, perhaps, obedience to the law, even if it compromised their social and economic interests and political rights. Therefore, from a sociological point of view, one would expect an authoritarian or aristocratic ruler to surround himself with individuals whose cultural practices, inculcated through the informal and formal education systems, would help sustain the system of domination. Because of voluntary assimilation and the promotion of a culture that fed into strengthening authoritarian rule, no group was in a position to claim exclusive ownership and extract benefit from the rule-oriented cultural practices.

Prominent sociologists, including Donald Levine and others have identified, particularly, Amhara children as "obedient to orders" and laws that may be authoritatively imposed from above, both from their elders and from the government.[32] It follows that since members of a few ethnic groups were likely to be absorbed into the system, by their very culture of loyalty and obedience, they in turn may have expected a reciprocal response from others within Ethiopian society. However, voluntary assimilation and the diverse ethnic composition of the military and aristocratic regimes do not lead to the assumption that there existed super-ordinate/subordinate power relationships. That is, it is too simplistic to explain the power relationships in Ethiopia by looking at ethnicity as a point of reference and to claim that one ethnic group dominated the decisionmaking process in Ethiopia. This is partly because the Amharas, the Oromos, and the Tigrays had been intermarrying across ethnic boundaries and partly because some ethnic groups assumed the cultures of the host ethnic group. For example, Harold Marcus had this to say about the Oromo expansion and adoption of the host culture:

> The pastoralist nature of Oromo life dictated a looseegalitarian society, . . . divided into exogamous moieties, the Borena and the Barettuma. [They] moved in natural response to their inhospitable homeland, pushed northwestward into Arsi, Shewa, Welega, and Gojam; and northeastward into Harerge and Wollo (traditional Amhara), stopping only where there were blocked by forest and population or by the effective mobilization of Christian or Muslim forces. . . . Tens of thousands of people came to identify with the host society, while others remained apart or selectively borrowed new methods of production, social organization, and thought. Some Oromo became Muslim, others Christian, and many retained the faith of their fathers, even if they incorporated Allah, Muhammad, Jesus, and the Virgin Mary into their rituals.[33]

If most political leaders of the pre-Meles era identified themselves as Amhara to express their ethnic affiliation, then they were essentially responding to an irrelevant social construct in which the hegemony of the Amhara culture and language was elevated to the highest level in the Ethiopian social hierarchy. In so doing, they were also contributing significantly to Amharas' self-evaluation and perception of their social position as distinct from and superior to any other ethnic group in the country. Therefore, it is highly unlikely that members of that ethnic group could reject hegemonic positions in Ethiopian society, even if it were irrelevant to their economic wellbeing. Indeed, the former rightful owners of the rule-oriented culture failed to realize that their cultural resource and heritage were exploited by political elites of diverse ethnic origins.

As elaborated above, the term "Amhara" was originally framed to distinguish Christians from Muslims and traditional believers. However, perceptions are meaningless unless they correspond to some economic returns and political influence. If the perceptions were true, then the depressingly low rates of investment in the social and economic sectors in the largely Amhara province(s) is inconsistent with and invalidates the sweeping generalizations made by interpreters of ethnic politics in Ethiopia and elsewhere. In other words, the correlation between the diversion of resources and monopoly of political power cannot be established because the majority of the "super-ordinate" groups were as repressed and exploited as members of the "subordinate" ethnic groups.

The Limits of Primordial Barriers

The scope of the spontaneous demonstration that swept all major cities in Ethiopia in 1974 and the earlier regional dissention against aristocratic rule were not confined to ethnic barriers. Both uprisings did not value the grievances of one group as legitimate and attempted to address problems that were specific to the alleged "hegemonic group." The 1974 "revolution" was a popular uprising kindled by high school and university students and embraced by members of the armed forces, civil servants, laborers, taxi drivers, teachers, and tenant farmers. There was a sense of confusion throughout the country, exacerbated by the absence of a political group that could rise to the occasion and shape the direction of the movement.

Nonetheless, demonstrators obstinately demanded the resignation of members of Haile-Selassie's cabinet and, when the government responded positively, called for a total alteration of the political terrain. Though the army initially mutinied to advance army-specific grievances such as wage and salary increases, it took an opportunistic stance to highjack the uprising by exploiting the absence of a political organization and its ability to flex its military muscle on civilians.

To be sure, the demand for a fundamental alteration of the political system was satisfied by the replacement of the aristocracy with the military government that faithfully advanced an alien ideology of Marxism-Leninism. However, except during the first year or so, after the overthrow of the monarch, the Transitional Military Government parted company with its civilian allies and the political groups that were conceived in the midst of political chaos and political vacuum.

To centralize its power, the military government outlawed the formation of opposition political parties and independent grass-root associations. In effecting its centralization scheme, the military government brutally executed over sixty-five high-ranking members of Haile-Selassie's government.[34] Here again, it is important to note that the military government was not any less lenient on the super-ordinate group or vice-versa.

After eliminating its rival elite groups, it began indiscriminately executing suspected members of opposition movements that were largely formed by and comprised of teachers and students. Most political parties went underground due to the centralization of the political marketplace by the military government. According to Kiflu Tadesse, "The formation of underground mass organizations demonstrated the different avenues and forms that the people could resort to when deprived of legal and peaceful means."[35] The military government also recruited its cadres from among the lower economic classes of the society.

Haile Fida, who was not an Amhara, was the Derg's political architect. He contributed immensely to the creation of a symbolic opposition party known as All Ethiopians Socialist Movement (AESM). For all practical purposes, the AESM was the political wing of the Derg whose members were instrumental in waging the war against opposition political groups (for example, the Ethiopian Democratic Union and the Ethiopian Peoples Revolutionary Party) and breaking down the level of "mutual trust"[36] among ordinary citizens.

As ruthless as they were, the political cadres and "Gestapo" of the military government deeply infiltrated the channels of command within opposition groups and social safety networks such as civic associations and families. The brainchild of Haile Fida terrorized the people in ways that were unprecedented in the history of the country. The depths of infiltration were so profound that there was mistrust between parents and children, spouses, and colleagues. The scope and depth of penetration was so broad and acute that the public was denied freedom of expression and assembly.

While the majority of the people were pleased by the heavy hands of the military government on members of the aristocracy, they were horrified and annoyed by the flexing of military muscle on their own immediate family members. As a result, the majority of the people throughout the country withdrew their trust and confidence in the military government. The withdrawal of trust was a notable erosion of public confidence that facilitated an easy entrance for the TPLF to literally walk into the capital city in 1991 and seize political power from the military regime.

By a political necessity, the military government perfected the European colonial art of divide and rule. It shook the historical foundation of mutual trust between individual citizens, civil servants, and public officials, both "horizontally" and "vertically."[37] Most policymakers and scholars agree that the military regime left a profound mark on the economic and political history of Ethiopia. On both counts, there is widespread consensus among scholars and policymakers alike that the government failed to deliver on its promises of economic progress and political freedom or lay the foundation for achieving these objectives.

After seventeen years of experimentation with an alien ideology, Marxism-Leninism, the economic condition of the majority poor was as unacceptable as it was during the zenith of the military regime in the late 1970s. The same was true on the political front. Rather than "enabling its subjects to do what they cannot do on their own − trust one another," the Derg engaged in an expansive coercive enforcement of allegiance to its system of domination.[38]

On the positive side, President Mengistu and company subscribed to nationalist rather than parochial sentiments, preferential treatment, or grievances built upon ethnic loyalty and sentiments. It was not the ascendancy of the elect of God but the dictatorship of the proletariat that reigned supreme in the early days of the revolution.

The Composition of the Military Government

The composition of the military government was not based on the tracing of lineage to an "extraterrestrial" dynasty or one's place in the social hierarchy. Contrary to preexisting traditions, it dismantled systems of inheritance of leadership or property. It did so by its very act of successfully overthrowing the monarch (which was believed to be incontestable), indiscriminately executing members of the royal family, cabinet and nobility, and adopting socialism as the nation's development ideology.

The military government passed proclamations to establish Peasant and Urban Dwellers Associations with administrative and judicial power and responsibilities. Regular elections were held to nominate and appoint officials of the Associations. However, the elections were not contested in a manner that was competitive, free, and fair. Rather, they were closely monitored and regulated by cadres of the military government to ensure that they resulted in the appointment of individuals who internalized the principles of socialism and were promising enough to translate Marxist-Leninist theory into practice. Such criteria penetrated the entire system, from the lowest local elections up to the highest ranks of the government, including appointments of members of the Central as well as the Standing Committees.

The fundamental criterion for the appointment of members of cabinet was also commitment to the advancement of socialist ideology, above and beyond primordial attachments, attributes and membership to the military establishment. One could not, either as a member of the military regime or as a civilian, hold an opposing political view and expect leniency and tolerance from the military regime. Likewise, the "leadership of peasants, urban, and professional associations" were not autonomous to exercise real power or entertain alternative views from concerned citizens. For all practical purposes, members of these associations were centrally nominated and "elected" for their greed, submissiveness, and brutality.[39]

The composition of the military government transcended ethnic boundaries and included junior and high-ranking military officers, numbering over one hundred twenty. To mention a few of the leading personalities, General Aman Michael Andom (a Tigray), Major Teferi Banti (an Oromo), and Major Atnafu Abate (an Amhara) were the chairmen of the Derg for a short period during the first few years of the rise to power of the military regime. These and other members of the Derg, although they came from different ethnic, social, and economic backgrounds, found their common identity in their commitment to "the dictatorship of the proletariat." Anything short of that commitment was suicidal to members of the Derg and anyone within the territorial jurisdiction of military rule. President Mengistu and his cronies eliminated most leading politicians and civil service officers for expressing alternative views on the country's political direction and dealing with domestic resistance and secessionist movements.

As stated above, the rise of the military junta to power was mainly due to the absence of a political organization with a sense of purpose and objective which, in turn, was a result of the spontaneity of the movement that engulfed the nation in the early 1970s. The solution for the country's economic stagnation was imposing dictatorial decisions to abolish private ownership of the means of production. Administratively and politically, the military government dictated the replacement of "incompetent and corrupt leaders" of the former regime with individuals who internalized socialist ideology and committed themselves to maintaining the unity of the country.

Furthermore, the military government's indiscriminate execution of former members of cabinet, opposition political groups, and those with adversarial political viewpoints within the government suggest that the government acted in the interest of political solidarity among its members and the people at large. The elimination of individuals and groups with alternative views was simultaneously accompanied by grooming a new brand of political loyalists that saw almost everything through the prism of socialist ideology. Equally important is that the military regime was bent on the task of transforming the economic and political systems from a feudal to a socialist production relation and public ownership of the means of production.

To the extent that a particular ethnic group was previously dominant and repressive, what the military government did in its adoption of a socialist ideology was to erode the primacy of that ethnic group in favor of the historically dominated and exploited ethnic groups. In the absence of evidence to reassert the notion that the dominant/dependant relationships were based solely or primarily on ethnic stratification, an alternative conclusion would have to be that the military regime did not allow one ethnic group to dictate national policies. Indeed, contrary to conventional beliefs, the Derg passionately sought to end class-based exploitation and domination between the small ruling class and the majority poor.

Moreover, the military government's sweeping measures against junior and high-ranking members of Haile-Selassie's government, which included individuals from Amhara, Gurage, Oromo, Tigray, and other ethnic groups, clearly illustrate the brutality of the regime. If some were granted amnesty, it was mainly on the grounds of a complete renunciation of their opposing political views. It had nothing to do with a person's ethnic affiliation. Indeed, *abyot lijuan tibelalech* (meaning that "the Revolution could eat its own children") was the propaganda advanced both by cadres of the military government and underground opposition parties. More specifically and importantly, the extent of ethnic diversity of the sixty-eight victims of the revolution is proof that, indeed, one of the most important factors for appointment during the Haile-Selassie government was loyalty to the throne, not ethnic sentiments and affiliations or economic status.

The foundation of the political system and members of the military regime from the rank-and-file to the highest level of leadership was built upon a common political outlook that transcended ethnic boundaries. Indeed, like its predecessor, the military government fought against secessionist movements, including ELF, TPLF, OLF, and the Western Somali Liberation Movement (WSLM). There is little or no evidence suggesting that the military government entertained the question of inequity and the demand for secession or autonomous status from the point of view of ethnicity; rather, it took radical measures to redress the gap between the minority rich and the majority poor.

Therefore, the proposition that the military government allowed one ethnic group to dominate the decisionmaking process is analytically defective. Simply because those in the decisionmaking circle exhibited Amhara culture and spoke Amharic as if it were their mother-tongue does not lead to the conclusion that the decisionmaking body was dominated by one ethnicity. It is also analytically erroneous and morally unjustifiable to argue that the "dominant" ethnic group irrationally contributed to its own demise (the Haile-Selassie government) and engaged in the extrajudicial execution of its own ethnic kinsmen.

Although there were elections of officers of the *Kebele* Associations and the like, they were regulated and controlled to ensure that individuals, cadres of the military government, won the elections. Elections were conducted as a matter of formality without institutional means for the electors to hold elected officials accountable for their acts. It is only under the current government that members of the previous government as well as "Security Comrades" are held in prison on charges of genocide and abuse of power. For example, on May 22, 2003, the Oromiya Supreme Court in Assela sentenced 63 former members of the military government to prison terms ranging between two years to life imprisonment on charges of genocide. There may be similar cases before a Supreme Court in other regions, but what is important here is that the Oromos also participated as instruments of the repressive regime as had members of other ethnic groups.[40]

Furthermore, the military government's use of force to eliminate its rivals through extrajudicial assassinations, suppression of opposition parties, and expropriation of private properties demonstrate that the Derg was nothing more than a dictatorial regime that did not compromise its socialist ideology to protect the interests of a particular ethnic group. The military regime's genocidal acts against its political opponents and its broad-based membership do not lead to the conclusion that the policies and measures of the regime were superimposed on ethnic considerations.

Concluding Remarks

There are four main points that can be inferred from the above analysis of the sources of resistance and appointment to high-ranking positions in the government of Haile-Selassie. First, the sources of resistance during Haile-Selassie's rule were lack of economic progress and social mobility. Most leaders of the rebellion movements against the totalitarian system were born primarily to poor Amhara families in Gojjam, Gonder, and Addis Ababa.

The rise of individuals, largely from Amhara families, to challenge the authoritarian rule has been misconstrued as an internal struggle of disenchanted Amharas against others of the same ethnic group. However, given their grievances, they rose to the occasion to solve a national rather than a regional socioeconomic and political problem. Indeed, they aspired to be the champions of social justice and were not restricted to a narrow regionalist and parochial sentiment or secessionist perspective of injustices.

Second, suppose Emperor Haile-Selassie and his political allies were driven by ethnic sentiments to absorb their kinsmen into the leadership circle as they were discriminatory in eliminating their rivals to the throne. Then, it would have been possible to establish a clear pattern of political domination of the ethnic group to which Haile-Selassie's family traced their ethnic lineage. And since this was clearly not the case, the essential characteristics of individuals who were not associated by kinship, marriage, or other forms of familial ties to the aristocracy in rising to political power lies in their ability to demonstrate loyalty to the Emperor and his government.

Third, the assertion that the sources of ethnic tension and conflict are rooted in the "hegemonic" or "super-ordinate" ethnic group's cultural and linguistic domination is misplaced. The adoption of Amharic as a communication channel was driven by political and economic considerations. Moreover, the prominence of the culture and language of the Amhara to "hegemonic" status is simply symbolic as far as the economic and social welfare of that ethnic group is concerned. This is evident in chapter four which dealt with the distribution of social and economic resources. To be sure, the Haile-Selassie government promoted the development of other languages and cultures to their full potential by establishing radio and television programs in languages such as *Guragegna, Oromignya, Tigrigna*. It is therefore unfortunate that scholars who attempted to trace the root causes of conflict and economic backwardness conveniently ignored the political and economic necessities of the government of Haile-Selassie.

Lastly, the riots and demonstrations that resulted in the downfall of imperial rule were not narrowly fueled by the question of based on ethnic identity. There is no evidence to argue that the sources of disenchantment and revolt by the academic community, retail traders, taxi drivers, and members of the armed forces were motivated by ethnic sentimentalism. They neither aspired nor promoted the replacement of the Haile-Selassie government with a political system organized around ethnicity nor portrayed the country's structural problems as stemming from the monopolization of political power in the hands of the Amhara, Gurage, Oromo, or Tigray ethnic group.

Even if an ethnic group were condemned and held accountable for the complex problems the country faced, historically and presently, proponents of a minimalist approach would have been up against a difficult, if not impossible, task of reconciling paradoxes. These paradoxes include, on the one hand, the alleged concentration of political power and, on the other hand, the social and economic impoverishment of the predominately Amhara regions. The rise of individuals from the Amhara group and the ethnic diversity of drought victims, which agitated many people in other parts of the country, explain that conflict, cooperation, and allegiance were not influenced by one's parochial disposition.

Perhaps one of the most far-reaching and devastating consequences of the military government's seventeen years of misrule is the erosion of mutual trust and public confidence towards the system. The struggle for political power, the demand for autonomous status or the right to self-determination, and the transformation of the economic and political systems in Ethiopia were characterized by a lack of two reinforcing and essential elements of peace and development: mutual trust and civic engagement. By a political necessity, the present government deepened trans-ethnic tensions, making it impossible for formerly marginalized regions to break away from perpetual poverty, shortages of human and physical capital.

The challenge for social groups and the present government of Ethiopia is to de-segregate segmented horizontal trust and networks in ways that can facilitate, rather than hinder, trans-ethnic cooperation, economic activity, and the transition from authoritarian to a democratic political system. To engage the public in the decisionmaking process, be it political, economic, or social in nature, is to elevate the level of public confidence toward its government and to narrow the gap between lower-level and upper-level horizontal exchanges. Conversely, multiparty elections of no substance would mean disempowering the people, leading to apathy, indignation, and mutual annihilation and suspicion as well as eroding the social bases of reconciliation and reconstruction.

Notes

1. Harold Marcus, *A History of Ethiopia* (Los Angeles: University of California Press, 1994), p.134.

2. Lij Iyasu became Emperor following his grandfather's death in December 1913. On September 27, 1916, he was accused of apostasy by the then regent Teferi Mekonnen and Empress Taitu Bitul. Subsequently, he remained a fugitive until his capture in Temben (Tigray) in late January 1920 by the forces of Ras Gugsa and Lij Desta Damtew. On May 21, 1921, Lij Iyasu was handed over to Teferi Mekonnen who kept him imprisoned in Fitche (Shoa province). Although there is no exact date or details about the circumstances of his death, Lij Iyasu was believed to be alive until Teferi Mekonnen was crowned Emperor. For detailed accounts, see Marcus, *A History of Ethiopia*, pp.111-36. See also, Marcus, *Haile-Selassie I: The Formative Years, 1892-1936* (Lawrenceville, NJ: The Red Sea Press, 1998), pp.47-8.

3. Aaron Tesfaye, *Political Power and Ethnic Federalism: The Struggle for Democracy in Ethiopia* (Lanham, MD: University Press of America, 2002), p.52.

4. Tesfaye, pp.12-3.

5. Ayhun Alemseged, *Fana Wogi* (Addis Ababa: Bole Printing Organization, 1991), p.3.

6. "The 25th Anniversary of Ethiopian Victory, 1940-1965," *Menen* (1965), p.138.

7. Marcus, p.17 and p.165.

8. Ibid., pp.135-6.

9. *Menen*, (Addis Ababa: Commercial Printing, 1960).

10. Marcus, A History of Ethiopia, p.134.

11. Katsuyoshi Fukui and John Markakis, *Ethnicity & Conflict in the Horn of Africa* (Athens, OH: Ohio University Press, 1994), p.9.

12. See Appendix J for biographic information of political appointees of the government of Haile-Selassie who were executed during the 1960s coup attempt.

13. Marcus, p.38.

14. For lineage of Empress Taytu, Menilek II, and others, see Chris Prouty, *Empress Taytu and Menilek II: Ethiopia 1883-1910* (Trenton, NJ: Red Sea Press, 1986).

15. See Appendix J for the birthplaces and official ranks who served in the Haile-Selassie government in the early 1960s.

16. Bahru Zewde, "The Problems of Institutionalization in Modern Ethiopia: A Historical Perspective," in Institutions, Resources and Development in Ethiopia, Proceedings of the Ninth Annual Conference on the Ethiopian Economy, 8-9 October 1999, eds. Alemu Mekonnen and Dejene Aredo (Addis Ababa: Addis Ababa University Press, 2000), p.14.

17. Emperor Haile-Selassie, *Hewotiena YeEthiopia Ermja*, II Tiraz, (My Life and Ethiopia's Progress, Vol. II) (Addis Ababa; Berhanena Selam Printing Press, 1941), p.323.

18. Tesfaye, p.13.

19. Bahru Zewde, *YeEthiopia Tarik, 1848-1966* (The History of Ethiopia, 1855-1973) (Addis Ababa: Addis Ababa University Press, 1996).

20. Alemseged, p.3.

21. Other participants in the coup included Majors Haile-Mariam Lencho, Kale-Kiristos Abay, Tefera Silde-Tensay, Wolde-Kiristos Abiy, Tesema Wakjira, and Kelbesa Beka and Captains Mamo Wobte-Wolde and Asrat Deferesu and Lieutenants Tamru Guda, Tesfa Wolde-Tensaye, Asfaw Jemaneh, and Bogale Wolde-Yohannis. For extensive discussion of their role in the coup, see Alemseged, *Fana Wogi*.

22. Zewde, pp.222-7.

23. Marcus, *The Politics of Empire: Ethiopia, Great Britain and the United States, 1941-1974* (Lawrenceville, NJ: Red Sea Press, 1995), p.108.

24. Donald Rothchild, *Managing Ethnic Conflict in Africa: Pressures and Incentives for Cooperation* (Washington, DC: Brookings Institution Press, 1996), p.77.

25. James Scarritt, "Communal Conflict and Contention for Power in Africa South of the Sahara," in *Minorities at Risk, A Global View of Ethnopolitical Conflict*, Ted Robert Gurr (Washington, DC: United States Institute of Peace Press, 1993), p.278.

26. Peter Nyong'o, "The Implication of Crises and Conflict in the Upper Nile Valley," in *Conflict Resolution in Africa*, eds. Francis Deng and William Zartman (Washington, DC: Brookings Institution, 1991), p.98.

27. Marcus, p.164.

28. Robert J. Cummings, "Religious Beliefs and Economic Behavior in Contemporary Africa, South of the Sahara: Linking Religion and Development," in *Religious Belief and Economic Behavior: Ancient Israel, Classical Christianity, Islam, and Judaism, and Contemporary Ireland and Africa*, ed. Jacob Neusner (Atlanta: Scholars Press, 1999), p.127.

29. John S. Mbiti, *African Religions and Philosophy* (New York: Anchor Books, Double-day and Company, 1969), p.238.

30. Jeff Haynes, *Religion and Politics in Africa* (New Jersey: Zed Books, 1996), p.90.

31. Messay Kebede, *Survival and Modernization Ethiopia's Enigmatic Present: A Philosophical Discourse* (Lawrenceville, NJ: Red Sea Press, 1999), p.354.

32. Donald Levine, "Ethiopia: Identity, Authority, and Realism," in *Political Culture and Political Development*, eds. Lucian Pye and Sidney Verba (Princeton: Princeton University Press, 1965). See also, David Knoke and Nancy Wisely, "Social Movements," in *Political Networks: The Structural Perspective*, ed. David Knoke (New York: Cambridge University Press, 1990).

33. Marcus, *A History of Ethiopia*, pp.35-7.

34. See Appendix K for a list of persons executed by the military government.

35. Kiflu Tadesse, *The Generation, Part II, Ethiopia Transformation and Conflict, The History of the Ethiopian People's Revolutionary Party* (New York: University Press of America, 1998), p.29.

36. James Coleman, *Foundations of Social Theory* (New York: Belknap Press of Harvard University, 1990), p.188.

37. Robert Putnam, Robert Leonardi, and Raffaella Nanetti, *Making Democracy Work* (Princeton, NJ: Princeton University Press, 1993), p.173.

38. Ibid., p.165.

39. Kebede, p.355.

40. "Sixty-three genocide convicts sentenced, five absolved," *The Ethiopian Herald* (22 May 2003).

Chapter VII

Democracy with or without Substance

Democratization may be perceived as democracy-in-the-making, and it is a process of political transformation in which political parties organize along issue-oriented and/or value-oriented political platform. Political parties "endow regimes with legitimacy by providing ideologies, leadership or opportunities for political participation, or a combination of all three." Political parties may also serve as a means of conflict resolution and opening opportunities for upward social mobility. In a volatile political environment, especially, they play crucial role by providing a forum for collective interest aggregation. They minimize the tendency to resort to violent means of expressing discontent and promote political integration by "drawing support from across regions to which people feel attachment greater than" the center.[1]

Democracy is a work in progress, whereby the competition for political power is regulated by a non-partisan institution that enforces the rules of multiparty elections. Other public, private, and civic agencies and organizations also play important and specialized roles in leveling the playing field and exerting pressure on political leaders to provide electors with substantive choices. Progress towards democracy takes place when, for instance, electors are able to use their ballots as sticks and carrots to reward or punish party candidates based on their performance during their term(s) in office. Holding elections every five or so years where the outcome of elections is almost always predictable is not democracy-in-the-making; rather it is a lucent sign of regression towards authoritarianism.

Electors' and candidates' understanding of ballots as currencies in a liberalized political marketplace, which can be perceived as analogous to a fairly competitive economic marketplace, is as important for the process of political transformation as the holding of elections on a regular basis. Since progress towards democracy requires more than going to polling stations every few years, examining the role of political parties in legitimizing the regime and politically integrating the nation-state is also pertinent to the discussion on democracy with or without substance.

The Ethiopian experience with multiparty democracy has so far been undermined by the formation of political parties along ethnic lines with emphasis on promoting value-oriented issues. Such political platforms by many of the regional political parties have essentially narrowed the choices available to electors. The Ethiopian political marketplace is congested and saturated with meaningless ethnic agendas and, as a result, the values of ballots continue to depreciate significantly. The opportunity for new leadership to emerge and for political parties to cast their nets in search of new membership beyond the confines of subjective criteria such as ethnicity and language were undermined due to the prevailing political condition of the early 1990s. The formation of political parties, which claim ethnic assertiveness as their overarching platform, may have legitimized the regime during the initial phases of the democratization process. However, to the extent that they provide little or no substantive platforms they are, in the long run, obliterating the opportunity for elite circulation or brining the periphery closer to the center.

To be sure, there were historical and contemporary factors responsible for the sad state of political transformation in Ethiopia. The following section briefly deals with some of the historical and contemporary factors that helped the mushrooming of political parties with ethnic emblems. In this chapter, we will analyze the structure of the Federal Government and its implication on the extent of separation of power and the types and expectation of voters as well as the values of ballots in the "liberalized" Ethiopian political marketplace.

Examining the 1995 and 2000 multiparty parliamentary election results would help us gain some perspectives on what has taken place since the downfall of the military regime in 1991. A few months before this book was scheduled for publication, new evidences came to light which demonstrate the characteristics of the ruling party, the changing political landscape, and the growing frustration among the general public over the lack of progress towards democracy and greater economic opportunities. More will be said following the sections that examine the 1995 and 2000 parliamentary election results. For now, let us explore some of the prevailing conditions that brought about the need for political liberalization and the subsequent strategies adopted by the Meles government.

Prevailing Conditions leading to Political Liberalization

The dressing up of a socialist costume by the military government of Ethiopia, characterized by its intolerance to the formation of opposition parties, extensive brutality, and "Gestapo" infiltration, created a sense of apathy, complacency, and resignation among the general public towards the military regime. The erosion of public confidence and cynicism towards the military government was also a fundamental condition that abetted the rise of the Tigray Peoples Liberation Front (TPLF) to power. The downfall of the military regime can, therefore, be attributed more to its internal contradictions than to the military muscle and political legitimacy of opposition movements.

When the TPLF came to power, it established a transitional government but had little or no internal legitimacy because the Front was widely known as a secessionist movement and for its pro-Soviet and Albanian ideological inclinations than as a representative of the rights and interests of Ethiopians as a whole. Nevertheless, many Ethiopians convinced themselves that the collapse of the military government was the end of misrule and brutality. Therefore, the question of leadership skills and competence among members of the emerging political elites within the TPLF or the grand-coalition was less politically polarizing among the general public than TPLF's secessionist and socialist rhetoric. In fact, for over a week, the TPLF leadership and other members of the grand-coalition were unable to form a government. Routine civil service and maintenance of internal law and order in the capital city and elsewhere in the country were carried out by remnants of the old regime such as the *Kebele* Association.

Even though the leadership was unable to form a government immediately after the TPLF guerrilla wing walked into the capital city, the meeting in London in late 1991 set the stage for the formation of a transitional government. There, participants formed political parties with conviction that the problem in Ethiopia was essentially one of ethnic conflict. Consequently, they came to the consensus that this problem could be resolved by dividing the country into ethnic enclaves and establishing a government that embraced ethnic federalism. Among these present was the Oromo Liberation Front (OLF) that sought the right to self-determination up to secession. Herman Cohen had this to say about the OLF's demand: the OLF's "objective was understandable, as the Oromos experienced linguistic, educational and social discrimination from the more powerful Amhara ethnic group that dominated both the Haile-Selassie and Mengistu regimes." Even though "the OLF did not pose much of a military threat," but had a long-standing grievance against the Amhara, they were allowed to play "a role in any effort to make peace."[2]

During the transitional period, between 1991 and 1994, more political parties were created in response to the opening up of the political marketplace so that all ethnic groups could be represented in the federal system. The liberalization of the political marketplace was also a condition that was imposed by Cohen who chaired the London dialogue between 1989 and 1991. The leading participant of the meeting with external legitimacy, TPLF, accepted this condition because it was primarily in the party's interest to allow the creation of multiple political parties. Such a political strategy was designed to diminish the dictatorship of the majority and reduce the dominant role of one party in the federal parliament. That is, the greater the number of political parties competing in a limited political space, the stronger the political clout of the TPLF, which claims to represent one of the minority ethnic groups in Ethiopia.

Organizationally, the structure of the present government appears to be distinct from any other governments that ruled Ethiopia since the unification of the country under Emperor Tewodros (1855-1868). The liberalization of the political marketplace is one of the distinguishing structural features of the present government. Separation of power, stipulated in the constitution, between the executive and the legislature is yet another structural feature of the present government that makes it different from the aristocratic or the military government. More importantly, unlike previous regimes that attempted to redistribute resources equitably between *provinces*, the present government came to power with the view to redress historical wrongs in the distribution of economic and political power between the various *ethnic groups*.

The government of Meles Zenawi adopted a number of strategies (for example, a constitution, new administrative boundaries, civil service reform, and a multiparty political system) ostensibly to rectify maldistribution, misrule, and corruption. In terms of substance, however, the current regime is almost identical to its predecessors. To be sure, conducting multiparty elections regularly is an essential part of the democratization process. Yet, simply because the electorate go to polling stations to cast their ballots for one party or another is not sufficient to suggest that the present political system is substantively different from the aristocratic or military dictatorships. In "the absence of a genuinely open electoral process,"[3] whereby the electorate are given almost uniform choices, the holding of regular multiparty parliamentary elections is as meaningless as elections in a one-party political system. Although elections and civil service reform are intended as self-restraining mechanisms and for rebuilding public confidence, fighting corruption, and improving the delivery of public goods and services, they seem to have resulted in strengthening the political muscle of the ruling party.

The adverse effects of the civil service reform and the extent to which there exists separation of power among the three main organs of the Federal Government are more apparent if one examines the organizational structure of the Federal Government. The organizational structure of the Federal Government is presented below as a starting point for the subsequent critical analysis of the results of the 1995 and 2000 multiparty elections. The discussion concerning the structure and implications of the Federal Government should also give us greater understanding of the substantive changes that could possible emerge as a result of the 2005 parliamentary elections.

The Structure of the Federal Government

The structure of the Federal Government of Ethiopia, as shown in the following chart, is an important starting point to understand the complex and subtle interactions between the various organs of the government. Until the first multiparty parliamentary elections in 1995, all the Ministers were directly and indirectly accountable to the Prime Minister. Following the 2000 elections, however, they became accountable to the House of Peoples Representatives (referred to as Parliament) and supposedly to the people of Ethiopia through their elected representatives. This appears to manifest and confirm one of the most important images of a functioning democratic system.

The government of Ethiopia is formed by the coalition party, the EPRDF, whose members nominate and appoint the Prime Minister for as many terms in office as members of the ruling coalition party. Here, nothing appears out of the ordinary, but since members of Parliament have no term limits the Prime Minster remains in office for as long as the coalition party forms the government. The constitution and electoral laws of Ethiopia also stipulate that "a party or a coalition of political parties obtaining the highest number of seats in the Council" forms and leads "the executive branch of the Federal Government," including appointing the Prime Minister. The Prime Minister, in turn, nominates and presents his candidates for cabinet positions to the Parliament.

Obviously, the executive organ is a critical component of the Federal Government. The Prime Minster is the chair of the Council of Ministers, which is made up of all the ministries shown in the chart and other ministries that are not included in the chart. The Ministry of Capacity Building, the Ministry of Federal Affairs, and the Ethics and Anti-Corruption Commission (not shown in the chart) are new institutions added to the executive branch of the Federal Government. Each ministry establishes an executive committee and appoints its members. The committee is responsible for initiating policies and legislation and is in charge of drafting budget proposals for its respective ministry. Draft legislation and budget proposals are submitted to Parliament for approval, appropriation, or passing into laws.[4]

Members of the Council of the Federation are either directly elected by the people or by the parliament of each regional state government. Each nation or nationality is supposedly represented in the House by one representative, and every additional one million people in a nation or nationality is represented by one additional representative. The powers and jurisdictions of the Council of the Federation include interpreting the constitution and arbitrating disputes between states within the Federal Government. Like the executive branch, the budget of the Council of Federation has to be approved by the Parliament.[5]

Figure 7.1: Organizational Chart of the Federal Government of Ethiopia

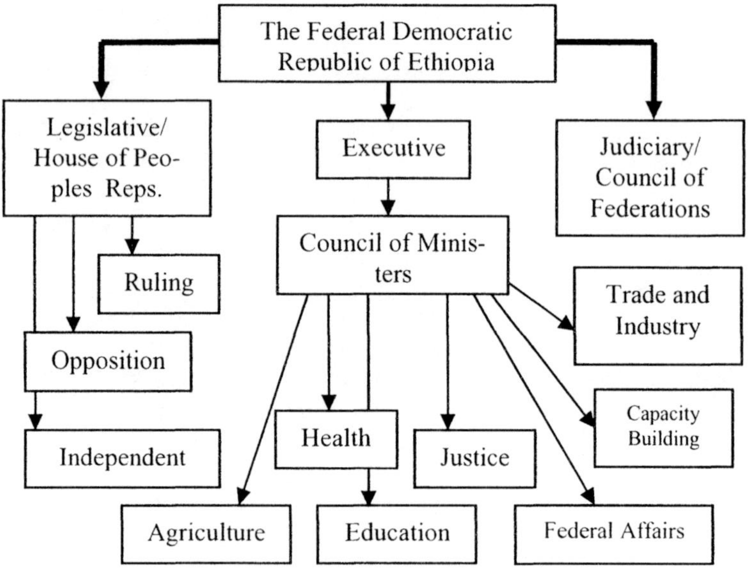

Source: "Ethiopian Constitution," 9 April 2000, at <http//www.sas.upenn.edu: 80/Africa...Hornet/Ethiopian_Constitution.html>. The chart is an interpretation of the constitution.

The organizational structure and limitations on the Prime Minister's term in office suggest that the peoples of Ethiopia are exercising their political rights and that the government is representative of the interests and wishes of the people. However, appearances can be deceiving especially when it does not correspond to substance. Interestingly, in a country where the absence of upward social mobility has been identified as one of the major factors of political instability, the Constitution of Ethiopia says nothing about limiting the House of Peoples Representatives' terms in office. Clearly, this means that members of the present Parliament will indefinitely continue to govern the country. The term of office of the Prime Minister corresponds with that of the House of Peoples Representatives and, by design and default, he remains in power for as long as the coalition party maintains its majority status in the Parliament. Continuity is perhaps a reason for imposing no term limitation on members of Parliament or the Prime Minister, but there is no persuasive argument against imposing term limits on members of Parliament and the Prime Minister and still maintain institutional continuity and political stability.

The opportunity for the emergence of a truly representative democratic government is tainted by the creation of political parties that paid considerable and undue attention to primordial sentiments and parochial interests. These fragmented political strategies deepened segmental cleavages and strengthened the power of the coalition party. And yet, given the absence of a political party that could steer opposition groups away from ethnic politics, either through dialogue or military threat, ignoring the desires of the political elite to exploit the ethnic diversity of Ethiopia for political gains would have been a political miscalculation. The prevailing political condition immediately before and after the collapse of the military regime was conducive to the promotion of ethnic politics and the protection of the right to self-determination. This is perhaps an area that most observers of the political transformation of Ethiopia failed to take into consideration in their harsh criticism of the present regime. That is, it is one thing to protest about the lack of genuine and progressive political transformation, especially during and after the 2000 parliamentary elections, but quite unrealistic to expect the ruling party to forego playing the ethnic card and the establishment of a coalition party in the early 1990s.

Divisions of Electoral Districts

The number of districts in a zone and, by extension, in a region determines the number of representatives in the House of Peoples Representatives. To qualify for representation in the Parliament, a district must have at least 100,000 people who have become registered residents of that district for at least two years. However, when the total number of a minority ethnic group is less than 100,000 and when that group demonstrates its distinctiveness and minority status to the Parliament, then such a group is not subjected to the same quantitative requirements imposed on others.[6]

Therefore, out of the five hundred forty-eight seats, at least twenty seats are reserved for groups that differ from other ethnic groups in some fundamental subjective factors but are unable to meet the minimum "electoral threshold" to compete in an election. When these criteria are satisfactorily demonstrated to the Parliament, such a group or groups can qualify for the special representation clause under the constitution and exercise the right to occupy the "supplementary seats"[7] reserved in the Parliament. The electoral law of Ethiopia appears to contain innovative concepts that attempt to avoid the dictatorship of the majority (which may arise from the majoritarian electoral law adopted in a multiethnic country) and secure the protection of minority rights.[8]

It was also with a preconceived assumption of ethnic homogeneity that the country is divided into nine regional states (Tigray, Affar, Amhara, Oromiya, Somali, Benishangul/Gumuz, Southern Nations and Nationalities Region, Gambella, and Harari), Addis Ababa City Administration and Dire Dawa Administrative Council. Recalling what we stated in the first two chapters, with the exception of the latter two regions, all of them were created supposedly to reflect the dominant ethnic group in each region. The division of the country into nine "ethnic Bantustans"[9] may suggest that these regions are ethnically homogeneous. However, the reality is that the nine regional states are not homogenous; they are heterogeneous in terms of ethnicity, language, and religion. The people of these regions also vary in their settlement patterns and economic as well as political aspirations and choices.

Voting Patterns

Having noted the division of the country, it may be appropriate to discuss the voting patterns and expectation of the electorate and candidates in multiparty elections. In a democratic system, there is a reasonable expectation on the part of candidates and the electorate that the number of ballots partly determines the outcome of elections. There is also some degree of confidence by the electorate and candidates that the electoral organ, which regulates the electoral process to ensure that elections are conducted freely and fairly, is politically non-partisan and impartial.[10] When the electoral organ, namely the National Electoral Board, is non-partisan and impartial, then it basically performs a regulatory function to ensure that ballots are meaningful currencies in the political marketplace. The values of ballots as a currency to reward candidates with political power is contingent on whether the political marketplace is mainly, but not exclusively, governed by the invisible hands of political market forces.

A rational electorate may consider the quality (experiences, visions, education, or even charisma of the candidate) and social and economic returns (efficient delivery of public services of various sorts) that may be derived from casting his/her ballot for a particular candidate. Clearly, one of the fundamental assumptions is that although the country is ethnically diverse, building a democratic system largely depends on the promotion of cross-cutting party memberships, whereby both the electorate and political leaders articulate their interests from an objective point of view.

According to Anthony Downs, the electorate in a democracy can be categorized into agitators, passives, and neutrals. These three types of voters tend to believe that they have enough information about the platforms of each contending political party or candidate and that no additional information is likely to alter their preferences. Downs said that agitators are those voters who use their resources to influence other voters. They are "usually motivated by the desire to see the policies of a specific party enacted, or by gratitude to a party for having carried out some policy they favor."[11] In contrast to these groups of electors, there are many other voters that may be classified as swing-voters.

Swing-voters may not have made up their minds or they may feel that they need additional information to help them decide for which party or candidate to vote. Among these swing-voters are the baffled, the quasi-informed passive, and the quasi-informed neutrals. While the "baffled are those who have not made up their minds ... the quasi-informed passives are those with tentative decisions favorable to some party." The third sub-type of voters among the swing-voters, the quasi-informed neutrals, are those "who have reached a tentative conclusion that there is not significant difference between present parties or between this government and preceding ones." If the neutrals, the baffled, and the quasi-informed neutrals have not made up their minds for which political party to vote, they do not cast their ballots randomly and, therefore, they abstain.[12]

Downs also noted that there are habitual voters who have assessed the various party platforms in preceding elections and decided to vote for the same party in every election "unless some catastrophe makes them realize it no longer expresses their best interests." Habitual voters are of two types: loyalists and apathetic. While loyalists almost always vote for the same party, apathetic voters "always abstain because they believe their party differentials are forever zero."[13] The electorate, whether they vote or not, are assumed to be rational and maximize their own utility. When voters cast their ballots, they are "helping to select the government" which will govern the country until the next election. The electorate is also conscious of the fact that whichever party wins, the ruling party cannot do everything that it says it will do.[14]

The classification of voters based on the information and the political taste they have gathered and developed are important gauges of the political process in western democracies. In a two party system where the electorate and the parties are not sharply divided along irreconcilable platforms, rational voters may or may not cast their ballots based on the policies and programs offered by the two parties or candidates. Except for agitators, the voting patterns and the boundaries between the two party platforms are not rigidly fixed, making the electoral process and its outcomes interesting and unpredictable. On the other hand, as Wilfred David noted, where party platforms are "more or less ideologically similar, there will be no value in voting and most voters will tend to abstain."[15] Similarly, the ways in which political parties are formed in ethnically diverse societies such as Ethiopia minimizes the relevance of voters' classifications purely based on their political taste or as rational utility maximizing actors. Stated differently, in highly segmented societies, the political taste and the voting behavior of the electorate is conditioned by the creation and mushrooming of political parties that claim to protect the interests of their ethnic groups.

Nevertheless, in more established democracies, a candidate expects that his/her leadership experience, skills, knowledge, or even charisma will draw a sufficient number of supporters that rally behind the candidate's political platform. Whatever platform candidates seek to advance, "their primary interest is with increasing their own popularity."[16] Since voters in advanced democracies are assumed to "recognize their self-interests and choose the candidates or parties most favorably evaluated on the basis of this self-interest," the electors are, in effect, "rational actors and candidates respond rationally by designing a policy package to attract enough support to win elections."[17]

Conceptually, the rules governing multiparty elections in Ethiopia resemble to that of the more established and advanced countries of the West, even though both systems are operating in quite different socio-cultural and politico-economic settings. According to the National Election Board of Ethiopia, to compete and win political power, a political party must reflect its own political views, beliefs, and objectives through its party programs and agendas.[18] The electorate would then exchange their ballots for the programs and agendas that seemed to suit their preference. In this regard, ballots help dictate the outcome of elections, but meaningful elections are conducted when consumers of "political ideas" are provided with alternative choices and when there are candidates with a vision that distinguishes them from others.

In competing for political power, party candidates may campaign around some interest-related issues such as health, education, housing, and employment and propose that their party has appropriate strategies to address these issues. In the process, they are not only engaged in winning the hearts and minds of the public but they are also educating the public about the political process as well as sensitizing the electorate about the main issues facing the country. Therefore, even if the market is reasonably free from intervention by agencies of the incumbent party, the electorate must be conscious of the values of ballots. Such "consumers of political ideas" are unlikely to cast their ballots based *primarily* on associations, affiliations, sentiments, and other subjective attributes that differentiates one group from another or the electorate from the candidate. As such, electors force candidates who performed poorly out of office and contribute to improving the opportunity for upward social mobility and elite circulation.

Realistically, in the absence of social security, retirement programs, and limited opportunity for upward social mobility, the provision of basic social services and creation of job opportunities should have overridden political affiliations or strengthening social safety nets by casting ballots based on kinship, ethnic affiliation, or other subjective criteria. However, unable or unwilling to understand the needs of the majority to have accesses even the most basic necessities of life, many political parties defined their party platforms to mirror the ideologies of the leading secessionist party—the TPLF. They did so independent of any influence from electors, civic organizations, and mass media. As such, they leave electors with little or no choices but to compare and contrast whatever is available in the market and cast their ballots for a party or a candidate even if the expected returns of voting is almost zero.

Indeed, except in the Southern Nations and Nationalities Region and in Addis Ababa and Dire Dawa where there are numerous political parties competing for state and federal legislative seats, the electors in other regions had neither a choice in political parties and/or party programs. Consequently, the Tigrays had to vote for the TPLF, the Oromos for the Oromo People's Democratic Organization, the Affars for the Affar National Democratic Front, the Amharas for the Amhara National Democratic Movement, the Hadiyas for the Hadiya National Democratic Organization, and so on.

As we will see later in this chapter, following the May 2000 election, there emerged political party leaders with a vision and strategy to make multiparty elections in Ethiopia more meaningful and unpredictable than it had ever been in previous elections. By creating a coalition party, which crossed over ethnic cleavages, they were able to broaden their political base and help redefine how the political game is played in the 2005 and future elections.

Ballots as Currencies in a Liberalized Political Market

To understand and explain how ballots could be analogous to currencies, we need to make the following few remarks. Depending on the strength of the economy, the currency of a given country can be converted outside its political boundary. Some currencies (such as the U.S dollar, British Pound, Japanese *Yen*) are convertible in many countries while others (for example, the Ethiopian *Birr* and the Sudanese Pound) are not. Generally, unless the political system is fundamentally altered, currencies are accepted as a medium of exchange between economic and non-economic actors. To the extent that a currency is accepted as a legal tender, the only limitation on the use of a particular currency is whether the person can or cannot financially afford to purchase "services" and durable and non-durable commodities.

Unlike currencies, ballots are only useful occasionally within a given political system. Ballots are only valuable during an election period and serve as a medium of exchange between the electorate and candidates or political parties, because a "voting slip, for example, would have printed on it the election for which it was valid."[19] All currencies differ in their values and convertibility. Similarly, the value of ballots differs based on such factors as the level of public confidence, differences or similarities between party programs and policies offered to the electorate, and the effectiveness and impartiality of the institutions that monitor the electoral process in a given political marketplace. Furthermore, a person's ability to purchase varieties of goods and services is affected by the "thickness" of his/her wallet. Similarly, ballots allow electors the means for a possible "control over a specific resource such as a seat in the legislature"[20] by a party or a candidate of his/her choice.

Ballots are useless when not converted in helping a candidate win a seat or when electors fail to exercise their rights to vote on a specific elections day.[21] When the political market is centralized or regulated by political cadres of the incumbent party or by a partisan electoral organ, which often happens in many developing countries, then the power of ballots as one of the deciding factors for the outcome of elections weakens significantly. The value of a ballot in a centralized political marketplace becomes as inflated as the value of a currency in a centralized economic system. Assuming that the electorate is a rational consumer of "political ideas," the political marketplace may experience "inflation"—too many ballots chasing too few political agendas. In such a political marketplace, the casting of ballots hardly influences the outcome of elections and, ultimately, the distribution of political power among competing groups. Indeed, if the political system is "deliberately structured so that the electorate is offered little or no choice as to who it can vote for," then, as John Waisman argued, "the possession of the vote is denuded of most of its significance and the potential for democracy within the system is very dramatically reduced."[22]

Furthermore, unwarranted emphasis on the formation of political parties to reflect segmental cleavages, which may have existed or manufactured, leads to an increase in the number of voters who are agitators, and agitators are less likely to influence party agendas and make the electoral process unpredictable. Thus, in such a situation, the electoral process essentially becomes a passive expression of individual or group loyalty to a certain political party. Party platforms and voters' preferences may not always be reducible to individual or group utility maximization; nor do the electorates always shape party platforms. This is because the political market is open to influence by powerful interest groups, civic organizations, and the like, which are not necessarily organized to ensure that the majority are not shortchanged in casting their ballots for one party or another. Given a fairly competitive political environment and assuming that political parties cross-over ethnic cleavages, the outcome of elections would be difficult to predict and the electors would have the upper hand in determining the outcome of elections.

Democracy without Substance

At the beginning of this chapter, we noted that democracy is a work in progress and that the procession to polling stations becomes ceremonial if ballots have little or no value in determining the outcome of elections. The data on the 1995 and 2000 election results, the highly disputed election of 2005, and the broader political environment in which these elections were conducted suggest that the outcome of multiparty parliamentary elections are fixed. The theoretical and conceptual validity of ballots as currencies in a liberalized political market would have been highly questionable if the outcome of these three consecutive elections confirmed otherwise. That is, in a centralized political system, which we argued to be almost parallel to a centralized economic system, consumers of "political ideas" have virtually no power to decide on their preferences. Just as a monopolistic corporation bullies infant industries to dictate the quality, quantity, and price of goods in a market, a monopolistic party also intimidates rival groups in order to control the political market, limit the choices available to electors, and dictate the outcome of elections.

Consider the following data on the 1995 parliamentary election results, which may give a partial picture of the extent of openness of the political marketplace. The Ethiopian Peoples Republic Democratic Front, which is formed by the coalition of the Tigray People's Liberation Front (TPLF), Amhara National Democratic Movement (ANDM), Oromo People's Democratic Organization (OPDO), South Ethiopia Peoples' Democratic Front (SEPDF) and a few other small parties, had a clear monopoly of legislative power with 88% of seats in Parliament. Various opposition political parties occupied approximately 8% of parliamentary seats while the remaining 1.5% and 2.0% were claimed by independent parties or were vacant due to boycotts in some parts of the S.N.N.R and Somali regions. From Table 7.1, it can be inferred that in the 1995 parliamentary elections the coalition party not only dominated the legislature but also the executive organ of the government. Due to the disproportionate percentage of the seats it won, the coalition party can dictate the social and economic policies of the country and decide what percentage of the federal budget should be earmarked for each and every executive branch. It can also determine which region deserves the maximum federal budget for reconstruction and development.

Table 7.1: House of Peoples Representatives Election Results, 1995

Political Party Affiliation	Number of Representatives
Ethiopian Peoples Republic Democratic Front	483
Various Regional Opposition Parties	45
Independents	8
Vacant	11
Total	**547**

Source: CIA World Fact Book, "Political Resources on the Net," 25 April 2000, at <http://www.agora.stm.it/elections/ethiopia.htm>.

Budget proposals and policies on such politically charged issues as the construction of public schools, clinics, roads, and the like in any region are formulated and presented to the Parliament by a selected group of executive committees. From a practical point of view, any proposal concerning the division of Ethiopia's ever shrinking national pie among the regions and the various branches of the Federal Government are likely to be approved by the parliament without major challenges, amendments, or inputs by non-coalition party members. As a result, the ruling coalition party dictates what is best for each region, including regions that may have categorically rejected the ruling party's ideology and development policy and strategy. Here, the federal system which presupposes the granting of a fairly broad sovereignty for state and local governments to decide on social programs, inter-regional investment, and other related matters seems to provide alternative avenues for designing and executing region-specific policy and strategy. Yet, parties that are appendages of the EPRDF rule the majority regional states, making the notion of regional state sovereignty almost meaningless.

Table 7.2: Registered Voters, Votes, and Absentees in the 1995 Elections

Region	Registered Voters	Votes	% of Absentees	No. of Reps.
Addis Ababa	564,378	445,058	21.1	23
Affar	574,616	503,483	12.4	8
Amhara	5,447,236	5,268,501	3.3	138
Ben/Gumz	213,665	195,487	8.5	9
Dire Dawa	100,551	82,328	18.1	2
Gambella	52,487	32,228	38.6	3
Harari	60,357	52,412	13.2	2
Oromiya	6,191,826	5,855,598	5.4	178
Somali	2,294,497	2,086,869	9.0	23
S.N.N.R	4,473,679	4,204,693	6.0	123
Tigray	1,364,087	1,341,850	1.6	38
Total	**20,712,644**	**19,571,031**		**547**

Source: The National Electoral Board, "Results of the 1995 Election of House of People's Representatives, List of Candidates, Party Affiliation, and Votes," (Addis Ababa: National Electoral Board, n.d).

Nothing is controversial about the fact that the country was at its initial phases of political transformation from a single-party rule to a multiparty democracy when the first elections were held. The outcome of the first elections and the implication of monopoly of power by the coalition party may not be alarming signals of a serious derailment of the process towards democracy. The results of the 1995 elections combined with the percentage of voters and absentees (see Table 7.2 below) could help us measure the progress that has been made towards sustainable democratic rule. To the extent that the dictatorship of the ruling party is explained away by the historical conditions of the country, the next election would have to show a slight, if not a major, improvement in the distribution of meaningful political power among competing groups.

Even with such acknowledgment of the country's stage of political development and poor communication systems, it is interesting to note that a few political parties seem to have won overwhelming public support and were able to increase voter turnouts while others did not. However, the same cannot be said at the national level. The total population of Ethiopia in 1995 was approximately 55 million; approximately 3 million were between the ages of 0 and 19 and the remaining 52 million were over the age of 20.[23] With the exception of Gambella, Dire Dawa, Addis Ababa, and to a lesser extent, Affar and Harari, the percentage of voter turnouts, compared with the number of registered voters, was notably high. Indeed, the average absentee (5.5%) in the country was negligible. However, when this data is compared with the number of eligible voters who were at least 18 years of age at the time of registration as electors,[24] it becomes evident that almost 62% of the people were left out of the political process.

Some of the reasons for the high percentage of non-participation in the 1995 elections may include poor infrastructure and communications, which impede the timely delivery of election materials as well as party programs and agendas, and candidates' inability to mobilize political support. Additionally, some may have felt betrayed by the previous governments and, therefore, lost confidence in the system. Nevertheless, the exclusion of a significant proportion of the electorate from the political process cannot support the assertion that the Parliament is dominated by representatives of the people and that the executive branch carries out the wishes of the people as expressed in the voices of parliament.

The data in Table 7.1 only shows the numerical distribution of political power, measured by the number of seats claimed by each political party. The scope and depth of under-representation becomes even more alarming when one examines the second multiparty parliamentary election results. Before examining the 2000 election results, however, it is important to note that since political parties are formed with the notion of homogeneity of membership and sharp segmental cleavages, the majority of the ethnic groups may be silenced from voicing alternative views on community affairs or, generally, their views on how they want to be ruled.

As stated earlier, the percentage of the population of each ethnic group determines the number of districts and, consequently, the number of representatives. Therefore, the statistical data in Table 7.3 seems to suggest that, except for the vacant seats, the diverse interests of each ethnic group is effectively insulated from rival interest or ethnic groups. However, hidden behind the numerical data is the fact that, with the exception of independent and the various political parties (mainly in the S.N.N.R), the rest are members of the ruling coalition party. That is, the listing of the EPRDF in the table should not be confused as if it is an independent party in and of itself.

Table 7.3: Parliamentary Election Results, 2000

Party Affiliation	No. of Reps.
Affar National Democratic Party	8
Amhara National Democratic Movement	137
Benishangul Gumz Peoples Democratic Unity Party	8
Ethiopian Peoples Revolutionary Democratic Front	19
Gambella Peoples Democratic Front	3
Oromo People's Democratic Organization	173
South Ethiopia People's Democratic Front	3
Tigray Peoples Liberation Front	38
Various Parties (mainly in the S.N.N.R)	131
Independent	12
Vacant	15
Total	**547**

Source: CIA Wold Fact Book, "Political Resources on the Net," <http://www.agora.stm.it/elections/ethiopia.htm>.

What is taking place here is that the coalition party competes for parliamentary seats in its own right and at the same time serves as an "umbrella" organization for the rest of the parties listed in Table 7.3. This is precisely the reason why the government is formed by EPRDF, which also has the constitutional mandate to elect the Prime Minister, for it has obtained the majority of seats (over 70%) in Parliament. Those fragmented and ethnically inclined political parties in the S.N.N.R as well as in a few other electoral districts, won approximately 24% while independent parties only secured an insignificant percentage (less than 3%) of parliamentary seats. If the parties in the S.N.N.R find a middle-ground for cooperation and coalition and became swing voters in legislative debates, as opposed to block voters, they will have posed a serious challenge to the ruling party and contributed significantly to providing alternative policy frameworks. The fragmentation, in and of itself, is a cause for concern for cooperation and competition at the federal and regional level.

The implication of the continued dominance of the parliament seats by the EPRDF is clear in that any legislation, annual budget, and social and economic policy that are proposed by any branch of the Council of Ministers will certainly be approved without substantial challenge by opposition political parties. Similarly, having a monopoly of the decisionmaking body, the parliament will almost automatically confirm any candidate for presidency and vice-presidency of the Federal Supreme Court, ministerial, and commissioner posts that are nominated and presented to it by the Prime Minister. The criteria for the nomination of Ministers and Vice-Ministers are, for instance, "individual political competence,"[25] which amounts to nothing more than advancing a uniform political outlook of the EPRDF.

The Prime Minister's nomination and presentation of candidates to parliament is essentially a formal exercise and a symbolic process of accountability and separation of power. In effect, the criteria trivializes the need for appointing individuals to high-ranking posts based on their level of education, experience and work ethic, ethical and moral disposition, or other qualities that are desirable and necessary for the political and economic development of Ethiopia.

Had the coalition party not been formed, some minority political parties would have played an important role in the country's political direction as well as social and economic policymaking processes, perhaps even influence the country's foreign policy agenda. On the one hand, it needs to be recognized that, given the politicization of ethnicity, the competition for dominance of the political space between the two majority ethnic groups (Amhara and Oromo) would have been fierce. The intensity of the competition for safeguarding the interests and securities of each ethnic group in Ethiopia could have been more violent than what has occurred during the transitional stage. Even though violent clashes among the various ethnic groups has been more or less minimized, the absence of overlapping membership and "swing voters" both at the level of the electorate and political party leaders, has derailed the democratization process. As Michael Bratton and Nicolas van de Walle argued, "Cracks in the edifice of autocracy should not be mistaken for fully fledged transitions to democracy."[26]

The monopoly of political power by the coalition party has also a far-reaching ramification than is apparent in the statistical data shown above. For instance, there is an absolute consensus on social, economic, and political agendas even though the party is a host of political parties that proclaim to represent diverse interests, which arguably emanates from the diversity of the ethnic groups that underpinned the very creation of these political parties.

The consensus between parties within the coalition party are not simply on fundamental issues such as whether or not the government should maintain a leading role in ensuring equity, both qualitatively and quantitatively, in the distribution of health and education services. Members of the coalition party supposedly agree on such specific issues as the strategies for ensuring the delivery of social services as well as ethnic factors as a measure for appointment of individuals for civil service posts. These are critical points in understanding the problems of consensus between members of political parties of the EPRDF on issues that may differ across regions and ethnic groups.

The political, economic, and social programs and strategies as well as the foreign policy of the EPRDF are the programs, strategies, and policies of, for example, the Amhara National Democratic Movement and other members of the coalition, but the converse is not true.[27] It shows that with the exception of perhaps the TPLF, each political party member to the EPRDF are preoccupied with maintaining political solidarity than safeguarding the interests of their constituents. An example of why this is a political miscalculation on the part of minority political parties of the coalition is the agreement on the appointment of public service officers to reflect the dominant ethnic makeup of a given regional state. That is, irrespective of whether the person is competent, credible, or posses the leadership skills, individuals are awarded high-ranking public posts simply because they pay allegiance to the ruling party's political agenda, including a recognition that Ethiopia's problems are mainly ethnic in nature.

This is also the main reason why the Ethiopian People's Democratic Movement (EPDM), which was founded in 1981 to advance a nationalist agenda and oppose the military dictatorship, was transformed into the Amhara National Democratic Movement in 1989/90 and became a member of the EPRDF.[28] The Prime Minister has been criticized for appointing Genet Zewde (an Amhara) as Minister of Education who lacked the necessary experience and credentials to oversee the functions of educational institutions including the highly acclaimed Addis Ababa University. She is nonetheless appointed mainly for her conviction to advance the ruling party's political ideology. Such rules of appointment reigned high until opposition parties such as the EDP and the AEUP complained about the implication of attempting to converge public service appointments with ethnicity, especially on the development potential of regions that are dismally short of experienced and educated persons.

Redefining the Rules of Political Game

The struggle for political freedom and equitable access to social services and economic opportunities were the driving forces behind the first major coup attempt of the early 1960s, the social upheaval of the 1970s, and the resurgence of a more organized movement of the 1990s. Leaders, which may have been genuinely committed to improving the lives of ordinary citizens, have come and gone, leaving behind significant contributions or irreversible damages to the making of contemporary Ethiopia. Each incoming regime holds the outgoing regime responsible for the destitute conditions of the people, destroys almost everything associated with the previous regime, and begins charting a new direction for the development of the country.

By and large, there has been little or no behavioral and attitudinal changes in how Ethiopian elite understand the sovereignty of the state, public property, or the holding of political offices. To many of them, the sovereignty of the state is not relative to other states or subject to the people's transferring of allegiance to the state, but it is an absolute authority and power to carry out policies as the elite see it fit. They see public properties or political offices as private properties in the sense that they take their power and authority for granted and hold everyone else accountable, but themselves. The demolishing of monuments and historical sites or unilaterally deciding on what is best for the people are manifestations of paternalistic attitudes that have also defined the Ethiopian elite cultures.

Throughout these symbolic or substantial changes in political system and economic policy, the people of Ethiopia continue to demand political freedom, equity, and greater economic opportunities. Ethiopians have come to believe that the ruling elite cannot be trusted and that the political system should be structured in such a way to restrain the state from becoming overbearing. This is partly because the Ethiopian political history is fraught with the rise of elite that tend to behave and act as paramount chiefs and believe that the public office they hold is given to them by some divine power. This has not been restricted to the upper echelon of the political class, but it also included individuals from the lowest to the highest ranks of the policymaking apparatus. It is also partly because the wishes, desires, and expectations of the people remain unfulfilled, making each emerging leadership in Ethiopia in the past four decades nothing more than a collectivity of hypocritical elite.

To be sure, Ethiopians no longer live in a constant state of fear of persecution and uncertainty. Additionally, human demands are completely unattainable and, depending on the internal and external economic and political dynamics, it is almost impossible to meet even the very basic demands of mankind. This is especially true for democracy, which is built upon the notion of distrust and adversarial system of checks and balances. Its inherent characteristics and Ethiopia's unique economic and social conditions could, arguably, make it difficult to take a significant step towards democracy. From these assumptions, however, it does not follow that the people of Ethiopia should settle for less. Indeed, the horrifying experience of the past should not be used to explain away the lack of progress to meeting the basic demands of the people, such as exercising their political rights to freely elect their leaders. This is true even if the opening up of the political marketplace since the early 1990s is recognized as a positive contribution of the present government to the political development of the country. Yet, it should be noted that "while credit must be given to leaders for genuine efforts, [one] cannot allow the weight of their past contribution to burden the future."[29]

Accepting democratization as a work-in-progress is one thing, but it is quite short sighted and backward looking to argue that the West did not democratize overnight and that the people of Ethiopia are now living in a much better political environment than they were during the military regime. Even though there were numerous allegations of electoral fraud, the 1995 and 2000 elections were certified as "free and fair" mainly because opposition parties were unable to sink their differences and form a coalition party to generate domestic and international support. The international community also recognized the holding of elections every five years in May as positive sings of developments toward democracy.

As the Ethiopian saying goes, *Yageruin Serdo Bageru Berie*, opposition parties, which were formerly fragmented, finally realized that a suitable approach to compete for power in a relatively liberalized political market is to form a coalition of opposition parties. Among these newly formed coalition parties is the Coalition for Unity and Democracy (CUD), which was established in 2004 by a merger of the Rainbow Ethiopia, Movement for Democracy and Social Justice, the Ethiopian Democratic League, the All Ethiopian Unity Party, and the United Ethiopian Democratic Party-Medhin. Collectively, they mobilized not only domestic and international support but also exposed that the 2005 parliamentary elections were as fraudulent as the previous elections. During the previous elections, there were of course loyal oppositions such as the All Ethiopian Unity Party, the Ethiopian Democratic Party, and the United Ethiopian Democratic Forces (UEDF). However, they were unable to influence the behavior of the electorate, the ruling coalition party, or block any legislation that seemed unfavorable to their political survival or the interests of their constituents.

The formation of the Coalition for Unity and Democracy fundamental shifted the Ethiopian political landscape. It unraveled the degree
to which the people of Ethiopia are able to sink their parochial differences in the struggle for democracy, development, and unity. The coalition of opposition parties is also instrumental in redefining the rules
governing the 2005 and future multiparty parliamentary elections, and
it will have a significant influence over the policymaking and legislative process. How this is possible can be elaborated by analyzing the
2005 preliminary election results.

On May 15, 2005, almost 90% of Ethiopians marched to polling
stations to express their desires, demands, interests, and discontents
through the ballot box.[30] Provisional results of the elections indicated
that opposition parties, mainly the CDU and the UEDF, had gained a
unanimous support of the electorate in the "self-governing" city of Addis Ababa. Initially, the ruling party admitted that opposition parties
have won all 23 seats in the capital, Addis Ababa. Despite losing seats
in the capital city, however, the Minster of Information, Bereket Simon,
told reporters that the ruling coalition party had won more than half of
the seats in parliament.[31] Preliminary election results also confirmed
that opposition parties, which had only 12 seats or less since the 1995
multiparty elections, had done remarkably well in elections outside the
capital. "Results released July 8 for more than half the seats showed the
ruling party and opposition in a virtual tie."[32]

By the first week of June 2005, university students, opposition
party leaders, and taxi drivers in the capital city protested that the election had been rigged and that there were numerous incidences of intimidation, imprisonment, and harassment of voters and opposition
party leaders and candidates. On June 7, 2005, students at Addis Ababa
University staged a peaceful demonstration, which turned violent when
the police fired directly at them. This unfortunate clash left at least one
student dead and over 500 arrested.[33] The following day, Ethiopian
police forces fired into crowds, killing at least 27 people and arresting
over 700 protestors.[34] The chairman of the CDU, Hailu Shawel, and the
Ethiopian Democratic Party senior official, Lidetu Ayalew, were also
placed under house arrest or, according to the government, "put under
surveillance as a precautionary measure."[35]

The harsh measures carried out against unarmed civilian protestors
provoked the Government of Britain to freeze "20 million British
Pounds ($35.2 million)" in aid to Ethiopia. Subsequently, the European
Union brokered an agreement between the two sides to resolve the dispute through dialogue and negotiation and to "cooperate with the National Electoral Board and investigate about irregularities in the election results of 299 constituents."[36] Until the first week of August 2005,

there were no official results for the highly contested parliamentary elections of 2005. Some reports indicated that the National Electoral Board "found evidence of irregularities at more than 100 polling stations. . . . The number of re-elections could go up as probes are carried out in 40 other constituencies."[37]

Excluding those polling stations under investigation, partial election results show that the ruling coalition party, the Coalition for Unity and Democracy, the United Ethiopia Democratic Front, and a few other opposition parties had won 139, 93, 42, and 33 seats in the Federal Parliament, respectively. The city Council of Addis Ababa will also be entirely controlled by opposition party members.[38] Except perhaps in the Tigray Regional State, it is very unlikely that members of the ruling coalition party would be able to dominate the state legislature in other regional states. The implication of the 2005 elections on the political and economic future of the country is profound. For the first time since the rise of the TPLF to power, the United States government had unsettling and mixed perception of the Ethiopian government, which was partly ignited by the expulsion of election observers from the National Democratic Institute and the International Republican Institute. The European Union had already expressed its dissatisfaction over the indiscriminate shooting of demonstrators and predatory electoral activities of the ruling party.

However the National Electoral Board (NEB) investigation turns out, the Board would have to be too partisan to throw out all complaints of electoral irregularities and fraud as illegitimate. The NEB will ultimately award some votes to the ruling party and some to opposition parties. Since the NEB "found evidence of irregularities in at least 100 polling stations," it would not be overly speculative to suggest that at least 50% of the votes in the disputed constituents may be distributed among the various opposition parties. This would make their collective parliamentary representation above and beyond the minimum threshold (181 votes) required to block any legislation. Such a projection is, of course, based on the assumption that the CUD, UEDF, Independents, and others would have mutually reinforcing agenda. Possibly, they may also form a temporary grand-coalition among opposition parties to defend their collective interests. Alternatively, assuming that occasional differences and legislative wrangling arise among opposition parties, each party would have to cross to the other side of the isle and secure the backing of other party members to pass legislation.

Comparatively, the EPRDF may not be confronted with insurmountable political bickering and maneuvering, lobbying, or engage in arm twisting activities to achieve its goals. Yet, the effectiveness of the party and even its very survival depends on the leadership's ability to demonstrate that it can provide relevant and meaningful alternative policy choices to move the country forward. The 2005 elections clearly show that playing the ethnic card is no longer a viable political strategy and that the ruling coalition party would have to come up with innovative platforms to alter the "political taste" of the electorate. Since too many ballots are not "chasing" to few political platforms, the values of ballots have come to be useful currencies as a means of exchange between party candidates and the electorate during the 2005 elections.

No country leaves the political market in the hands of market forces. What makes elections unpredictable is not that the political market is regulated by the invisible hands of the market, but primarily due to the changing preferences of the electorate and the formulation of innovative party programs. Even though the coalition of opposition parties have fundamentally shifted how the 2005 and future multiparty elections are conducted, having an independent and non-partisan regulatory agency is also critical to bring about democracy and development in Ethiopia.

Summary and Conclusion

The early 1990s London dialogues set the stage for the consolidation of political power in the hands of the ruling coalition. The various political parties that mushroomed immediately before and after the liberalization of the political market seemed to legitimize the claim that the coalition party advances a nationalist agenda while protecting the interests of minority ethnic groups. To be sure, the collapse of the military regime left a political vacuum that needed to be filled by a party with credible military threat. Except for the TPLF, which had the support of the United States administration, none of the contending parties were able to flex their military muscle or muster a broad-based acceptance and recognition among many Ethiopians or Western powers. It is against this background that the chairman of the TPLF, Meles Zenawi, became President while Tamrat Layne of the EPDM was installed as Prime Minister of the transitional government.

In the early days of the transitional period, the government was beginning to cover up its systematic exclusion of individuals and political leaders who expressed dissenting views on almost all of the TPLF's agenda and policy. The transitional period also served as a time for structuring the government so that new parties could emerge and play to the tunes of the ruling party. Because the various political parties in the coalition are careful not to disturb the balance of power within the grand-coalition, perhaps for fear of the consequences, they generated little or no alternative strategies to address development challenges that may be unique to their constituents. The member parties of the coalition are essentially appendages to the dominant party, the TPLF, within the coalition. There is, therefore, a faulty assumption that the needs, desires, and interests of each of the ethnic group are expressed and protected under the umbrella organization, collectively, or by each political party, individually.

Furthermore, since one party dictates regional and national development policies, the establishment of a Federal Government is out of touch with the principles of regional state sovereignty. Regional state governments are merely symbolic parts of the Federal Government. To the extent that they remain appendages and symbolic parts of the EPRDF, minority political groups (minority in terms of meaningful political power) do more harm than good to the democratization process in Ethiopia. Had it not been for the politically subordinate parties of the coalition, the TPLF would have been unable to deny the dictatorship of the majority.

In the long run, some members of the coalition party may come to realize that their minority status is neither beneficial for achieving their personal goals or to effectively respond to the long overdue demands of the people for real political, economic, and social transformations. The international and domestic political current of the early 1990s was characterized by uncertainty, uncertainty over what the new international order would usher in. There was also a growing sense of relief among the general public about the end of military rule, which also provided ample opportunity for the consolidation of power in the hands of a few elites. The memories of the recent past concerning the main factors that brought about the demise of the military regime remain fresh in the minds of many Ethiopians. The scenario that the public could once again expresses its discontent silently, as it was the case in 1991, is not far-fetched. Given the 1960 and 1974 uprisings and the collapse of the military regime in 1991, the peoples of Ethiopia have shown that they could either silently or openly demand for a fundamental change in how they want to be ruled. The June 2005 mass demonstration is a clear example of the increasing discontent and frustration among the general public.

The formation of a coalition party in a country that was arguably divided along irreconcilable differences and the concession of real political power to the chairman of the minority ethnic group that represents a mere 5 or 6 percent of the population of Ethiopia defy realistic expectation. On the one hand, engineers of the coalition party maintained that the political system of the constitutional monarchy, followed by the dictatorial military government, was at the core of Ethiopia's dismaying economic backwardness. Thus, they crafted a multiparty system as one of the major steps toward democracy. On the other hand, the fear of losing political power to the demographically dominant groups, the leadership of the TPLF managed to create a coalition party which denied an equitable political space to members of the coalition as well as opposition parties.

It seems to be a short sighted perception of reality that minority members (in terms of influence) of the coalition party fear that breaking away from the EPRDF would result in political chaos and the break-down of the country into fragments and unstable formation of multiple "ethnically" defined states. The fear that this would occur is not necessarily that the EPRDF is an integrative force, but what the TPLF has induced as a mechanism for the consolidation of political power created the conditions for the erosion of national unity and identity. Alternatively, it should also be clear that as regional economic growth disparities become more unacceptable and the people of the neglected regions become increasingly frustrated, subordinate political groups could internalize their status as meaningless and may walk away from the coalition.

Furthermore, if the crises in Ethiopia were essentially ethnic in their nature, then there is obviously the need to diffuse the super-ordinate/subordinate social hierarchy in order to bring about peace, democracy, and development. However, empirical and historical data on the relationships between ordinary members of the various ethnic groups refute the notion of super-ordinate/subordinate socio-cultural, economic, and political stratification. Additionally, the assumption could also be refuted by the formation of the coalition party, which is apparently a host for political parties of the diverse ethnic scepters.

The adoption of a majoritarian electoral law was perhaps the most difficult challenge to the ruling political party, which represents an ethnic minority. Clearly, under a proportional or majoritarian electoral arrangement, any political party of a minority ethnic group, such as the TPLF, would have automatically ceded political power to one of the political parties with an Oromo or Amhara emblem. This is precisely one of the reasons for the formation of the coalition party, whereby the TPLF became the dominant political party. Changing the electoral law from a majoritarian to a proportional system may not be essential to pave the way for a genuine democracy. Realizing democracy with substance is partly contingent upon the rise of leaders with vision and commitment who sacrifice their individual interests to that of society's. The formation of political parties that encourage trans-ethnic membership also makes regular elections more meaningful.

The lack of distributive justice in real political power and the inability of the government and regional political parties to deliver on the

promises of economic and social justice will be, sooner or later, re-
sented by the public at large. The low voting turnouts in Addis Ababa
where the percentage of literate is high, communication infrastructure
is better, and public and private print media circulate news on a daily
basis may be a sign of dissatisfaction about the predictability of previous election outcomes. The 2005 election dispute and civil disobedience are clearly major signs open expressions of discontent. More specifically, it shows that the electorate have realized that they would no
longer be spectators of the beauty contests between political parties that
dress up in ethnic costumes with almost identical political objectives.

One of the most important lessons from the 2005 elections for the
ruling coalition party and opposition parties is that turning off their
listening devices of the heartbeats of the general public will be a political miscalculation. Irrespective of the final vote counts, the Ethiopian
political landscape will never be the same. Moreover, as indicated at
the beginning of this chapter, democracy needs to be understood from a
holistic perspective. It is a work-in-progress and that the transformations of a one-party state into a multiparty political system is simply the
tip of the iceberg in the transition to democracy.

Of course, one has to be cognizant of the internal social dynamics,
the role of super powers in the internal affairs of Ethiopia, the unreli-
able infrastructural basis, and the disappointing role of the Ethiopian
mass media as some of the major factors that may hinder any genuine
effort towards democracy and development. However, these and other
conceivable explanations would have nothing to do with allowing citizens to exercise their freedom of assembly, civil disobedience, or going
to polling stations to cast their ballots to whichever candidate they
choose. To paraphrase Wole Soyinka's observation, the Ethiopian
elite's past contribution such as opening the political market for the
establishment and competition of political parties is not necessarily
derived from their benevolence and, even so, it should not inhibit the
public from expressing their wishes.[39]

A final remark is to note that when examining the outcome of elections in developing countries and most certainly in Ethiopia, one needs
to be aware of whether the electoral commission or board is partisan or
non-partisan. More often than not, the incumbent party may have had a
sweeping majority in parliament which would enabled it to hand-pick
officers of the commission or the board, whichever may be the case.
Since opposition parties who competed in previous elections were
likely to be overwhelmed by the power of the ruling party, they may
have had little or no choices but to participate in elections under the
rules, conditions, procedures, and regulations envisioned by the ruling
party and its electoral agents. In such regulatory frameworks, it would

be difficult to have a fair and acceptable adjudication of electoral disputes.

How regulatory institutions and agencies stay away from partisan
politics to maintain their independence and credibility is a complex
issue. Nevertheless, one of the first legislative agenda for the State
Council and the Federal Parliament in Ethiopia should be reexamining
and taking corrective policy measures to equip the NEB with the necessary financial and human capital so that it would carry out its mandates
without any fear of retaliation. Additionally, questions such as the factors that influence the electorate to cast a ballot for one candidate and
not another need to be examined in future researches. Whether the majority of the electorate are rational consumers of political agendas is
also another area of research interest that needs a much more in-depth
analysis than has been presented in this study.

Notes

1. Brian Smith, *Understanding Third World Politics: Theories of
Political Change and Development* (Indiana: Indiana University Press,
1996), pp.199-200.

2. Herman Cohen, *Intervening in Africa: Superpower Peacemaking in a
Troubled Continent* (New York: St. Martin's Press, 2000), p.23.

3. Richard Joseph, "Oldspeak vs. Newspeak," *Journal of Democracy* Vol.
9, 4 (1998): 55-61.

4. "Ethiopian Constitution," 9 April 2000, at <http://www.sas.upenn.edu:
80/Africa...Hornet/Ethiopian_Constitution.html>.

5. Ibid.

6. "Electoral Law of Ethiopia," *Negarit Gazeta*, Proclamation 64/1993,
No. 56 (Addis Ababa: Berhanena Selam Printing Press, 23 August 1993).

7. Arend Lijphart, *Democracies Patterns of Majoritarian and Consensus
Government in Twenty-One Countries* (New Haven, CT: Yale University Press,
1984), p.155.

8. "Electoral Law of Ethiopia," *Negarit Gazeta*, Proclamation 64/1993,
No. 56.

9. Congress, House, Committee on Foreign Relations, "Human Rights
Progress in Ethiopia: Hearing before the Committee on Foreign Relations,"
105th Cong., 1st Sess., June 4, 1997.

10. Ibid.

11. Anthony Downs, *An Economic Theory of Democracy* (New York:
Harper and Row, 1957), p.84.

12. Ibid., p.85.

13. Ibid., p.85.

14. Ibid., p.39.

15. Wilfred David, *The Political Economy of Economic Policy* (New York: Praeger Publishers, 1988), p.191.

16. Ibid., p.192.

17. David Knoke, *Political Networks: The Structural Perspective* (New York: Cambridge University Press, 1990), p.37.

18. National Election Board of Ethiopia, "*Yepartiwoch Mina Bedemocratic Mircha*," (The Role of Political Parties in Democratic Election) (Addis Ababa: National Electoral Board, n.d).

19. James Coleman, *Individual Interests and Collective Action* (New York: Cambridge University Press, 1986), p.171.

20. Ibid., p.169.

21. Ibid.

22. John Wiseman, *Democracy in Black Africa: Survival and Revival* (New York: Paragon House Publishers, 1990), pp.4-5.

23. Central Statistical Authority, "Statistical Abstract 1997," (Addis Ababa: Central Statistical Authority, 1998), p.76.

24. "A Proclamation to Provide for the Electoral Law of Ethiopia," *Negarit Gazeta*, 52nd Year, No. 56 (Addis Ababa: Berhanena Selam Printing Press, 23 August 1993).

25. "Meles Announces New Cabinet," *Daily Monitor*, (17 October 2001).

26. Michael Bratton and Nicolas van de Walle, "Toward Governance in Africa: Popular Demands and State Responses," in *Governance and Politics in Africa*, eds., Goran Hyden and Michael Bratton (Colorado: Lynne Rienner Publishers, 1992), p.29.

27. Amhara National Democratic Movement, "The Programs and By-laws of the Amhara National Democratic Movement," (Addis Ababa: Mega Publishing Enterprise, 2000).

28. Jenny Hammond, *Fire From the Ashes: A Chronicle of the Revolution in Tigray, Ethiopia, 1975-1991* (Lawrenceville, NJ: The Red Sea Press, 1999).

29. Wole Soyinka, "Of Sacred Cows . . . ," *Mail & Guardian* (Johannesburg) 26 July 2005.

30. "Ethiopia ruling party claims win," *BBC News*, (17 May 2005), 14:31 GMT.

31. Ibid.

32. "Feeling is not good after Ethiopia vote," 20 July 2005, at <http://www.usatoday.com>.

33. "Ethiopian policy, protestors clash," 07 June 2005, at <http://english.aljazeera.net>.

34. "Annan calls for peace in Ethiopia," 10 June 2005, at <http://english.aljazeera.net>.

35. "House arrest for Ethiopia rivals," 11 June 2005, at <http://newswww.bbc.net.uk>.

36. "Ethiopia to return elections," 22 July 2005, at http://www.news24.com.

37. "Ethiopia to repeat elections in 20 regions," *Standard* (23 July 2005).

38. Elections in Somali were scheduled for 21 August 2005.

39. Soyinka, "Of Sacred Cows . . . ."

Chapter VIII

Institutional Reform
and the Erosion of Public Confidence

Institutions undergo morphostatis and morphogenesis transformations to cope with changes that occur within or without their boundaries. However dormant they appear, institutions are made up of components that constantly act and react to certain endogenous and/or
exogenous stimulants. They comprise components that perform various
functions, and each component or element largely maintains symbiotic,
interdependent relationships with one another. The degree of relevance
and performance of each component to the proper and efficient functioning of the institution varies from one element to another.

Some components are as useless to the proper functioning of the
system as a dog's tail is to the survival and well-being of the organism.[1]
Other elements of the institution perform a critical role that could affect
changes in the internal dynamics of the system or diffuse disturbances
to the structural integrity of the institution that emanate from one or
more of the components. Indeed, some parts of an institution may be
more important to maintaining the status quo or the structural integrity
of the system than other components. Defects in one or more parts of
an institution could also cause other sub-systems or the components
within them to behave in such a way as to insulate the general system
(economic, socio-cultural, and political) from decaying or collapsing.

At times, structural and functional transformations of institutions
do not turn out as beautifully as the transformation of a caterpillar into
a butterfly. The lack of systemic coordination and interactions among
the various institutions in a system, which characterizes developing
countries' institutions, has both negative and positive consequences.
For instance, weak vertical linkages and interactions between civic in-

stitutions and the state adversely affect the contribution of the former to the development and continuity of the latter. Similarly, at the highest level of institutional hierarchy, the absence of reinforcing interactions among the institutions' specialized agents could affect the entire system's ability to perform inefficiently or less than its optimal capacity.

Institutions may also be perceived as a symphony orchestra. Each member of a symphony orchestra specializes in playing a particular instrument, although some may be flexible and competent in playing different (roles) instruments. While some may naturally prefer playing one instrument more than another, the environment in which each member of the orchestra finds himself/herself could also influence his/her preference and specialization. In any event, to the extent that there is no functional deficiency in any of the instruments, the conductor leads the entire orchestra, for example, by moving his button left and right, up and down, or in a tangential direction. While each member of the orchestra may play his/her instrument perfectly, creating harmony by coordinating the various musicians primarily depends on the experience, skills, and abilities of the conductor.

In our discussion of institutional reform in Ethiopia, we will come across similar developments, including lack of coordination and overlapping roles among the various parts of the executive branches of the government. We will also observe a weak vertical integration between the lowest and highest levels of the institutional hierarchy and an almost non-existent vertical interaction between civic and public institutions. The expected outcome of institutional reform at the executive level is improving the delivery of public goods and services, mediating inter-regional state disputes, and making the executive organ more responsive, transparent, and accountable.

The attempt to create a regional grand-coalition of political parties in the Southern Nations and Nationalities Region strikingly resembles our analogy of the symphony orchestra. The governor of the Region is bent on amalgamating all the political parties in the Region under one regional umbrella organization. The drive towards greater synchronization of the various parties is directly derived from the experience of the ruling coalition party where the TPLF, a party of minority ethnic groups, managed to police everyone else in the coalition, thereby placing itself at the summit of the grand-coalition party.

Both at the regional and federal levels, one of the main purposes of decentralization or undertaking institutional reform is to make sure that the center does not lose touch with the periphery. Vertical integration between the center and the periphery, characterized by top-down and bottom-up interaction, builds public confidence towards the government. However, the various strategies adopted recently have led to the consolidation of executive power, growing frustration among ordinary citizens, and the erosion of mutual trust between the public and the government. It is against this background that we explore the impetus for the government's desire to rebuild public confidence and the implications of administrative reforms that have been undertaken since the second parliamentary elections. The last section analyzes the growing interests in creating a mini-coalition party in the more politically and ethnically polarized state of the Southern Nations and Nationalities Region.

Transforming the Executive Branch

Even though the role of mass media in the democratization and development process in Ethiopia may be over-valued, at times it has exposed some of the corrupt practices and bureaucratic inefficiencies that have taken place across regional state administrations. The result is the closing down of most private print media outlets, following the three-day symposium, in January 2003, which outraged the international community and the Ethiopian Free Press Journalists' Association. In any event, objective criticism of the government by a very few private press, opposition parties in Ethiopia, and international organizations such as Amnesty International swayed the ruling coalition to engage in reforming the public sector. Probing a sense of domestic and international discontent towards the government, the EPRDF shifted gears to become a truly multiethnic party and to promote the concert of nations and nationalities. The state-owned newspaper, *Addis Zemen*, stated that cities that are under EPRDF's control will be reorganized to reflect that the coalition party is a mosaic of political parties of diverse ethnic groups.[2]

From the analysis of the political environment in previous chapters, it is evident that opposition political parties took the view that they were shortchanged in the competition for political power. External and independent observers of the political environment in Ethiopia concurred with the views of opposition parties. Siegfried Pausewang, Kjetil Tronvoll, and Lovise Aalen, who were members of the Scandinavian election observers group, reported that the 1995 and 2000 elections were not free and fair. They noted that there may have been some cultural and economic factors, which made it difficult to evaluate the process of election and election outcomes across the country based on some widely accepted electoral measurements. Even so, they argued that such was the nature of competition in Third World countries where the culture of tolerance is at its infancy and the majority electorate is politically illiterate. Pausewang and company also observed that au-

thoritarian and hierarchical attitudes towards the government and submissiveness to such rule were embedded in the perception of the public.
As Pausewang, Tronvoll, and Aalen observed, this was more evident in
rural Ethiopia. Therefore, although some of the main opposition parties
boycotted the 1995 and 2000 elections, "the electorate ... could be for-
given for assuming that voting to be no more than an expression of
obedience, and that any choice other than favored by the government
might well lay them open to retaliation."[3] There may be other justifications for why opposition parties find it difficult to accept defeat gra-
ciously or why the ruling party engages in predatory strategies to ensure its continued dominance of the political space and, consequently,
the decision-making entities of the government.

Whatever explanations were given, Ethiopian newspaper reports
and the government's reform programs suggested, on the one hand,
whether the 2000 parliamentary elections were free and fair and, on the
other hand, the seriousness of the government in "having its houses in
order." This evidence emerged not only as a matter of widespread disenchantment by the academic community and the general public, but
also because of the government's contradictions in what it did in reality
as opposed to what it claimed rhetorically. By effectively manipulating
election outcomes, the ruling party managed to place individuals in
leadership positions, and some of those appointed in such crucial public
posts as governors, ministers, or commissioners during and subsequent
to the 1995 and 2000 elections had a history of corruption and nepotism.[4] The government has now come to grips with the realization that
the level of public confidence is diminishing, its dismal failure in managing the economy is an open secret, and that its choice of candidates
for elections and political appointment are widely recognized as fla-
grantly incompetent.[5] These are some of the main reasons why the government undertook the Civil Service Reform program. Obviously, the
reform was designed to improve the management of human resources,
management and control of public funds, and the quality of and efficient delivery of public goods and services.[6]

To demonstrate its commitment to improving the bureaucratic efficiency of the public sector and rebuilding the confidence of the public,
the government dismissed regional state administrators at various levels, some of whom were elected while others were political appointees.
Headed by the Prime Minister, the ruling party also made a major reshuffling of its cabinet which resulted in the demotion or promotion of
ministers with a few retaining their old positions. "According to the
state radio, 16 of the 18 new cabinet members are senior officials of the
ruling Ethiopian Peoples Revolutionary Democratic Front."[7] Following
the 2000 election, the government also established the Ethics and Anti-

corruption Commission, the Ministry of Capacity Building, and Ministry of Federal Affairs.

The establishment of the Ethics and Anti-corruption Commission in May 2001 was not simply intended as a safeguard against possible corrupt practices. It was rather created as an institutional instrument to build positive public perception of the government and fight the prevalent corruption that evolved in many of the regional and federal bureaucracies. The Ethics and Anti-corruption Commission was investigating numerous cases of corruption either identified by the commission or tipped by concerned citizens.

The total number of cases under investigation or cases that have been closed since the formation of the Commission are said to be over a thousand. The agencies that are under scrutiny by the Commission include the Ethiopian Privatization Agency, Ethiopian Electric Power Corporation, Commercial Bank of Ethiopia, and the Ethiopian Road Authority. According to the commissioner, Enwey Gebre-Medhin, who is a member of the TPLF, some individuals have already been found guilty and sentenced to one to five years imprisonment. The court also issued an injunction to withhold the properties and finances of those who were charged with corruption but awaiting trial. The estimated value of the properties and finances was over 25 million *Birr* or approximately 3 million dollars.[8]

While the establishment of the Ethics and Anti-corruption Commission (EACC) seems to be a logical step, based on the concept of specialization, to prosecute "white collar" crimes, the Ministry of Justice expressed concern that the EACC trespasses the jurisdictions of the Federal Prosecutors Office and the Ministry of Justice, generally. The President of the Federal Supreme Court, Kemal Bedri, wrote a letter to the Speaker of the House, Dawit Yohannes, complaining that the EACC undermines the independence of the judiciary. The President noted that the Ethics and Anti-corruption Commission is tasked with "fighting corruption and keeping tabs on the mismanagement of government and public funds as well as being given the power of bringing to court peoples suspected of corruption." However well-intended, said the President, the Commission "impinges on the independence of courts and inhibits judges from ruling on cases based solely upon the dictates of law and their consciences." If judges are not impartial, then it would be "impossible to ensure the respect of human rights and ... the public will lose its faith in an independent and impartial judiciary" and, consequently, in the government. The Honorable Kemal Bedri called the attention of the Speaker to take the matter seriously and fix the problem "as soon as possible."[9]

The establishment of the Ministry of Federal Affairs suggests actual or potential inter-regional disputes that may have stemmed from differences in tax laws, trans-boundary water resource utilization rights, and inter-ethnic conflicts over grazing land. During the last week of May 2003, the Minister of Federal Affairs (MFA), the Honorable Abay Tsehaye, convened a conference to introduce and publicize the mandates of his office and impress upon regional state leaders to resolve their differences and disputes through the ministry. Subsequently, the Ministry of Federal Affairs has come to play key roles in bringing the Affar and Oromiya regional governments to a round-table dialogue to resolve disputes between the Affar and Issa trans-boundary ethnic groups. It also served as a mediator between two opposing parties, the Gambella Peoples Liberation Party and the Gambella Peoples Democratic Unity Party (a member of the ruling coalition) over differences in political outlook.

The MFA also arbitrated disputes between the Ethiopian Berta People Democratic Organization and the Benishangul/Gumuz Peoples Democratic Unity Front (a member of the ruling coalition) in Benishangul/Gumuz regional state and between the executive and legislative members of the Somali regional state government. In all these instances, the MFA intervened to resolve disputes between two or more competing trans-ethnic groups or political parties. The MFA was also actively involved in overseeing issues related to rural and urban development and capacity building programs at the state and federal levels.[10]

Along with the establishment of the MFA, the Ministry of Capacity Building has been created with a broad mandate to direct and oversee programs and projects that are directly and indirectly related with capacity building such as improving infrastructural bases (communication and transportation) of development. Economic backwardness and the poor performance of the civil service are explained in light of the inability of the previous regimes to manage the economy and appoint civil servants based on objective criteria such as level of education, skills, and experiences. The previous regimes are often condemned for failing to formulate development policies that were grounded on the realities of the people and for appointing civil servants based on association, family ties, or political inclination and affiliation. Thus, taken at face value, the Ministry of Capacity Building is established with the responsibility and authority to enhance the skills and work ethics of, mainly, civil servants. It is also intended to oversee a shift towards merit-based appointment of civil servants and improvement in the delivery of public goods and services.

The question of whether the expansion of the executive branch leads to a more centralized management of socioeconomic activities is open to debate. What is less controversial is that renewing a positive image of the government among an already distrustful public with fresh memories of unfulfilled promises requires meaningful participation of the public in the decision-making process. The perception among most Ethiopians is that the collapse of the military regime has ushered in the rise of rulers in civilian uniform of the same substance. "Twelve years ago when EPRDF seized power there was hope that things would change for the better." What happened now, says a civil servant, is that "they failed to win the hearts and minds of the people." It is a shame that "what they are doing is to get richer and richer at the expense of us poor. Look at their way of life, the cars they are driving, and the buildings they are putting up."[11]

Like the Ethics and Anti-corruption Commission, the Ministry of Federal Affairs is formed with little regard to the constitution of Ethiopia. According to the new constitution, the Council of Federation is entrusted with jurisdiction to seek solutions to inter-state disputes. In effect, the MFA is encroaching on the rights and duties of regional state governments. The MFA's intervention in regional affairs undermines the role of each state government, which is represented in the Council of Federation, and says a great deal about the expansion of executive power. In addition, it exhausts the assumption that creating artificial boundaries and promoting the creation of political parties is an effective strategy to isolate each ethnic group into geographical enclaves and, subsequently, reduce the intensity and frequency of conflict in Ethiopia.

Furthermore, from the viewpoint of analysis, the MFA, which is part of the executive branch, strengthens executive power and weakens the autonomy and sovereignty of regional state governments. From a practical viewpoint, there is essentially no separation of power and, as a result, the creation of the MFA and other arms of the executive make little or no difference concerning the independence of the judiciary or autonomy of regional states.

Furthermore, the Ministry of Capacity Building may be perceived as much needed as the other newly formed institutions for the country to move forward from underdevelopment to development, from conflict to peace, and from mismanagement of public funds to efficient and accountable allocation of scarce resources. As a political tool, the creation of the Ministry of Capacity Building helps justify why, after a decade of promises for socioeconomic justice, transparency, and accountability, the economy is sluggish and the civil service is infested with inept and corrupt individuals. The establishment of this ministry certainly diverts the attention of the public by attributing social, economic, and political ills to the legacies of the previous regimes that left behind irresponsible civil servants.

If what has transpired is a leadership crisis and mistrust between the public and the government, then the Ministry of Capacity Building may not be able to achieve its objectives alone. In addition, to the extent that public confidence remains low, the Ministry of Capacity Building may turn out to be as ineffective as other branches of the government. Under such political bickering and maneuvering marred by overlapping and conflicting mandates, the Civil Service Reform program, the fight against nepotism and corruption, and improvement in the delivery of public services would become an enormous task to undertake. The failure to achieve these objectives means that the process of democratization and development merely becomes more of an illusion than a reality, making the public more frustrated and disillusioned.

The Socio-cultural Component of Politico-economic Transformation

The roots of apathetic and resigned attitudes of the public towards the government are numerous and complex. Generally, unmet expectations and promises could lead to resignation or frustration. Either way, discontent and disinterest among the general public thwart any genuine attempt at economic and political transformation. Here, the assumption is that individuals act collectively or independent of one another by employing strategies that are rational and at times irrational. Whether we think of them as rational or irrational, Ethiopians have adopted both strategies at different times and situations against unfavorable conditions. Some elements in a socio-cultural system influence individual or collective actions to uphold the *status quo* or to go against the grain in situations that may be inimical to the interests of the group concerned. A few examples may illustrate how tradition, culture, and perception of one's position in the social hierarchy inhibits or contributes to structural transformation.

Donald Levine is among those scholars who correctly pointed out that respect for the rule of law is embedded in the tradition and culture of the Amharas;[12] but like any other group, the Amharas of the peripheral provinces sing happy ballads in the face of socio-economic plight.[13] While diverse ethnic groups maintain their distinct culture, language, and religion, by political necessity the absolutist government of Haile-Selassie elevated the Amhara's culture and language as Ethiopia's distinguishing features, features that were also exploited by Emperor Menelik II for the same purpose.

As David Korten pointed out, there is a major difference between, for example, the Amharas and Tigrays in their interpersonal patterns of communication, "with the Tigrays priding themselves on being more direct and, thereby, more 'honest in their speech." The Amharas, on the other hand, tend to keep personal information secret, often avoiding direct responses to questions of a personal matter, as a means of protecting themselves from such repressive regimes as Haile-Selassie and Mengistu Haile-Mariam. The Amhara also differ sharply, said Korten, from the Tigray in evaluating their honesty on the basis of directness and "from such groups as the Borana, among whom the first topic of conversation between two new acquaintances is to share information on their respective personal histories."[14] No rational authoritarian government would forego the political necessities of selecting a culture whose attributes promote obedience and reservation even though the group claiming ownership of such culture and language does not receive favorable treatment for its cultural and linguistic contribution to the nation.

However, assertions such as the *Amharization* of the Ethiopian polity continue to persist despite the group's economic deprivation and political repression. For example, Amare Tekle entirely ignored the destitute conditions of the Amhara and the ethnic origins of Emperor Atse Yohannis IV (1872-1889), Emperor Menelik, and Emperor Haile-Selassie when he asserted that there was an "attempt to create a polity based on Amhara supremacy and the assimilation of other nationalities." Amare claimed that the *Amharization* was a conscious policy effort of "political repression, social degradation, and economic deprivation," including "the deliberate desecration and vilification, if not obliteration, of the culture, social, and religious values and institutions of other nationalities."[15]

This appears to favor, for example, the OLF's grievances for the right to self-determination and secession of the Oromos based on the allegation of political repression, social degradation, and economic deprivation by the "super-ordinate" ethnic group. Until the publication of an article by John Young, in 1996,[16] the Eritrean elite convinced proponents of self-determination rights that Eritrea was home to a homogenous ethnic group and that the EPLF was fighting for the political, social, and economic freedom of Eritreans. Similarly, the OLF claims to represent the interests of a homogenous ethnic group—the Oromo—and seeks the right to self-determination up to secession. The reality is that within the supposed homogenous ethnic group, there are the Arssi, Borna, Guji, Karaily, Lega, Macha, Afran Kalo, Raya, and Tulama groups that could be further divided into religious and professional groups. "Most would describe themselves as Muslims, Orthodox

Christians, Roman Catholics, Lutherans or Pentecostals."[17] Among the
Arssi Muslims, for example, there are urbanized professionals, nomadic
pastoralists, subsistence farmers, laborers, merchants and traders, and
the like.[18]

If one is to construct a matrix of these variables, one is likely to
find at least fifty combinations of different forms of identities. From
this, it can be inferred that Oromo homogeneity is as socially constructed as most other ethnic group identities in Ethiopia. Furthermore,
even though members of the Oromo People's Democratic Organization
occupy the majority of seats in Parliament, many Oromos are presently
seeking political asylum in the United States and perhaps in Western
Europe as well. This also suggests that either the OPDO is an append-
age to the politically and militarily dominant party of the grand-
coalition or the Oromos have divergent political aspirations.

To be sure, authoritarian rule of the previous regimes, augmented
by the promotion of a rule-oriented culture as their national emblem,
had an adverse effect on the economic and political development of the
country in general and to the Amharas in particular. When subjected to
authoritarian rulers, people tend to be less inclined to explore new ways
of doing things because the system does not create a fertile ground for
innovation. Thus, people remained confined to, for example, traditional
methods of farming or simply recycled and repaired the tools they inherited from their forefathers. As the analysis in chapter six demonstrates, the military regime left behind an atmosphere of fear of change
and mistrust. When few rise to challenge the political establishment and
demand improvement in the economic condition of the poor, the rest
labels them trouble-makers.

The people of Ethiopia are victims of at least three generations of
political and economic misrule and mismanagement by the few that
exploited the cultural and linguistic resources of the "super-ordinate"
ethnic group for their own convenience. This fact is not widely recognized by some elites of competing groups who also find it convenient
to burden the Amhara with shouldering the responsibility for the country's economic and political backwardness. Even though non-Amhara
ethnic groups cannot be exempt, members of the ruling classes from the
Amhara were often indifferent to the political repression and the relative and absolute economic deprivation of other groups.

There are at least two main points that may be extracted from the
above discussion. On the one hand, the political transformation from an
aristocratic to a military dictatorship, and from a military dictatorship
of a single party system to a multiparty political system of the present
regime brought notable changes in the form of personalities. However,
the three political systems simply differ in their choice of names, but

they are practically the same, with some degrees of variations, in the intensity of exploitation and repression. Understandably, therefore, for most of the Haile-Selassie and Mengistu eras the majority were advocates of political stability even at the expense of denying human and political rights.

It appears that the case of Ethiopia is what Samuel Huntington boldly characterized as a traditional society that could be economically poor, politically oppressed, culturally and linguistically exploited, yet prefer to remain stable.[19] What the Ministry of Capacity Building needs to look at seriously is, therefore, whether a cultural transformation is required to build positive attitudes for change such as a culture of tolerance, regenerate interest in participating in the political process, and create conducive environments for invention and innovation.

In the absence of a level-playing field in the political marketplace, opposition parties are likely to be suffocated within a given political space, lose elections, and condemn and hold the ruling party responsible for their defeat. Personal interview with a few leaders of opposition and coalition party members reveal that cadres of the ruling party have allegedly engaged in electoral fraud such as election rigging, ballot stuffing, and the like. Even if the political landscape is fairly open to competition, most opposition parties are politically ill-equipped to put up strong opposition against the ruling party, because they are weakened by their undue emphasis on ethnic assertiveness.

Claims and counter-claims aside, perhaps one of the most revealing aspects of the extent to which both elections were fraudulent are statements published in the state-media on the chronic problems of governance in almost all regional states. Except for the State of Tigray where either the private or the state-owned media has not so far exposed whether the problem of governance is as rampant there as elsewhere, mismanagement of public funds, lack of transparency and accountability, and nepotism spans across regions, making the two multiparty election results almost meaningless.

Regional State Administration Reforms

The following is a summary and analysis of administrative reforms in five of the nine administrative regions and, for lack of data, the Benishangul/Gumuz, Oromiya, Somali, and Tigray regional states are not included in the analysis. The extended discussion and analysis of the Addis Ababa administrative reform is mainly due to the author's exposure to print media and frequent contacts with public officials and residents of the city. Analysis of the reform in the S.N.N.R is treated separately mainly because the reform program in this region includes a crucial development, the formation of a mini-coalition party, which deserves in-depth examination and analysis.

In the Affar regional state, during the last week of May 2003, there was a week-long public meeting organized by the city administrators in the city of *Awash Sebat Kilo*. The meeting was called to identify some of the factors that were responsible for the region's regression from development, accountability, and transparency. Over 700 members of people's representatives of various levels of the state government in Affar issued a communiqué noting that speeding up economic growth in the region requires establishing a transparent and accountable administration. The communiqué further noted that some members of the previous leadership since the 2000 elections were leaches of public resources, corrupt, and narrow regionalists.[20]

The Governor of Affar, Esmael Alisero, also expressed concern over the low rate of private investment in the region. He also noted that private investors recognized the crisis in leadership at the regional level and, therefore, concluded a number of agreements with clan chiefs to purchase or transfer state-owned lands. The leadership crisis in the region not only inspired the clan chiefs to take the law in their own hands – selling and transferring land in violation of the constitution that stipulates public ownership of land – but it also helped diminish the rate of private investment in the region. Of the 124 private investments with a total capital of 2.9 billion *Birr* (approximately $233 million at the current exchange rate of $1 to 8.56 *Birr*) that have been approved by the region's investment bureau since 1993, only 47 had begun operation with 50% of the total capital.[21]

In the Amhara regional state, an application submitted to the Municipality Bureau for a legal transfer of ownership of land or other properties from one individual to another is deliberately delayed through bureaucratic procrastination. Any resident seeking access to public goods and services such as electric power, telephone, and water must submit a request to the appropriate office for the delivery of such services. In other words, the initiative has to come from residents, as opposed to the Municipality Bureau.

The implication of the procedure where a resident takes the initiative to gain access to public services has lent itself to patronage and corruption. Those applicants with financial resources to reward decision-makers or the technicians who are responsible for laying and installing the necessary hardware are given priority. Others who may not be able to afford to be corrupt either for financial reasons or convictions on ethical, moral, and religious grounds become deprived of equal access to public goods and services.

The same is true when a property is in dispute and requires a decision by a legal entity or when the parties who are not in dispute need to formalize a transaction and request the approval of the Municipality Bureau for a legal transfer of the property. Like those officials in the State of Affar and elsewhere in Ethiopia, there are a considerable number of civil servants in the Amhara regional state who are bent on ensuring that their personal interests, rather than the public's, are fulfilled. In many instances, family ties, acquaintance, and affiliation with civil servants supersedes the law of the State. It is precisely such disregard for the rule of law that spurred the need for a public discussion in the State of Amhara in 2003. Participants of the conferences held in many cities and towns of the State of Amhara concluded that the entire administration of the State needed to be restructured. The purpose was obviously to make the bureaucracy efficient by right-sizing it and appointing individuals who are impartial and uncorrupt.[22] Corruption not only breeds corruption, but it also facilitated an environment for incubating a growing number of *Sera Asfetsamiwoch*, which is conveniently referred to in the West as "lobbyists."

Similar development characterizes one of the most neglected regions of the country: the State of Gambella. The Governor of the State of Gambella, Akelo Akuay, said that most of the development programs outlined for the 2002-2003 fiscal year have not been executed effectively. Program evaluations of the first nine moths of the 2002-2003 fiscal year indicate that there were numerous factors that contributed to under-implementation of the region's development programs. He stated that there was a delay in the appropriation of the budget for the implementation of various development programs and projects. Those completed projects were unable to begin their operation due to conflicts between ethnic and nationality groups. For instance, there were intermittent and widespread ethnic conflicts in the State of Gambella in 2002, which helped expose the inability of the State to contain such conflicts and the impartiality of administrative officials and the police force in the conflict.[23]

As a result, a three-day peace and reconciliation conference was held in which participants expressed their deep disappointment "to witness the involvement of some state officials and members of the police in last year's conflict." Consequently, they called for "the establishment of a militia force that has the support and trust of the local people" and a "wise leadership and police force that could assume accountability."[24] Furthermore, some leaders were disappointingly lethargic and incompetent, and focused their energies on running personal chores rather than attending to public interests. Some officials showed little or no regard for administrative rules and regulations in their assessment of project proposals and allocation of budget. More often than not, project proposals and the release of funds for the implementation of programs and projects were carried out in a manner that crossed over their administrative jurisdiction and authority.[25]

In addition, the state-owned newspaper, *Addis Zemen*, noted that in the State of Gambella, over 24 million *Birr* (or approximately $3 million dollars at the 2003 exchange rate) were unaccounted for. The region's Parliament, Ministry of Water Resources, Mining, and Energy, and the Bureau of Agricultural and Urban Development were some of the institutions that failed to produce credible evidence that justified their budget allocation and expenditure. There were irregularities and illegal auctioning procedures as well as fabrication of receipts for services rendered and purchase of material. Bureaucratic inefficiencies and abuse of power has not been limited to those regions discussed so far. The Benishangul/Gumuz, Oromiya, and Tigray regional states have experienced a different sort of setback. For instance, high-ranking officials such as members of parliament from Tigray regional state have been dismissed from their positions for their dissenting views. In Benishangul/Gumuz, police officers have been dismissed or disciplined for using excessive force against civilians.[26]

Since the second multiparty elections, there has been widespread disenchantment by residents of the city of Addis Ababa. Many realistically expect that Addis Ababa, the center of diplomatic initiatives and activities, headquarter of continental and inter-continental institutions, and the capital of the country would, at a minimum, be properly administered. Additionally, since most of the country's resources as well as foreign and domestic private investments are concentrated in the city, the rate of unemployment in the Administrative Region of Addis Ababa would be expected to be lower than in other regions. While regional variation may exist, the national unemployment rate is estimated at over 33% and, given the above reasons, one would anticipate that it would be lower in regions such as Addis Ababa. However, there are more homeless people, beggars, abandoned children, prostitutes, and idle youth and middle-aged people in Addis Ababa than anywhere else in the country, perhaps even in Africa.[27]

The President of the Addis Ababa Chamber of Commerce, Berhanu Mewa, said in a televised interview that the rate of production declined by at least 34% due to interruption, often without notice, and rationing of electricity in Addis Ababa. Pressured by the business community and by the Ethics and Anti-corruption Commission, the Ethiopian Electric Power Corporation attempted to explain away that the frequent interruptions of electricity were due to the clogging of the hydroelectric power generator at Fincha and Koka dams. To justify why there was frequent interruption and the need for rationing of electricity, the Corporation insisted that drought and increased use of water for irrigation caused a decline in the production of electric power.[28]

In the city of Addis Ababa, with the exception of perhaps the office of Immigration and Naturalization Services, many private establishments and governmental institutions are hamstrung by a host of anti-development behaviors and practices. For example, to a large extent, owners and employees of coffeehouses, restaurants, hotels, car rentals, retail trades, and travel agents ignore the simple fact that appeasing each customer would mean increasing the rate of sales and consequently profit. Obviously, a displeased customer is less likely to return to such businesses in order to purchase the goods or services where customer satisfaction is not equated with increasing the rate of profits. Such unfortunate attitudes lead to the closing of businesses and forces employers and employees to join the unemployed work force.

Among government institutions, the police force may be cited as an example that hinders the democratization process in Ethiopia. In the city of Addis Ababa, the police force often fails to take action against persons that violate the human and constitutional rights of law-abiding citizens and foreigners. They deliberately misinterpret the constitutional guarantee that provides for equal protection of citizens as equally applicable to protecting the safety and security of criminal gangs. To be sure, the constitutional guarantees of freedom of movement and protection from unlawful search and seizure as well as prohibition of arrest without a warrant were the results of the woeful experiences of the military regime's armed force that took extrajudicial measures against civilians.

As if they found loopholes in the constitution, some rank-and-file and leaders of the police force are engaged in the business of shielding criminals under their uniform. Furthermore, in many other governmental institutions, the rank-and-file, beginning with front-door guards and receptionists to mid- and upper-level management, subconsciously put up barriers to obstruct the efficient provision of services to clients. For example, at the National Archive in Addis Ababa, to make a copy of a document, a researcher has to see at least four officials of the institution. One has to get a form from one office, take it to another office for signature, pay a cashier the amount for the photocopies, take the signed form to another person who makes photocopies for researchers. Certainly, there has to be a better way of facilitating services to clients or researchers while monitoring corruption.

Nevertheless, experiences gained from regions and cities elsewhere and in Addis Ababa as well as an uproar from the city's residents seem to have provoked the leadership in Addis Ababa and the federal government to make an administrative face-lift of the civil service of the capital city. The administrative reform encompasses all sectors of the civil service from the lowest administrative hierarchy of the *Kebele* Association to the Municipality and the office of the Mayor. In short, Addis Ababa was placed, once again, under a transitional administration system and "about 42,000 employees in 40 different institutions under the city administration would be placed in new organizations in different positions" including the 175 *Kebele* Associations throughout the city.[29]

Elected officers of the *Kebele* Association were replaced by appointed officials who have been transferred, with demotion, from the Ministry of Education, the Bureau of Municipality, and other public institutions. Some elected officials of the *Kebele* Association have been promoted and transferred to other institutions without training or prior knowledge, experience, and skills to perform the work that is demanded by their new employer. Other elected officials of the Association either were not placed elsewhere or were given the lowest job of cleaning the city or monitoring the residents so that garbage was properly disposed in Dumpsters. Many of them expressed their irritation, displeasure, and frustration over the civil service reform program. They disputed the assertion that the reform is genuinely intended to improve the delivery of public services. Generally, there was a sense of insecurity among people who were transferred from one institution to another partly because of the perception that the host organization may not accept them or there may not be vacancies in the host organization. According to the Mayor of the transitional city administration, Arkebe Iqubay, and his deputy, Hilawe Yosef, the restructuring of the administration is "part of the development process"[30] that is necessary for opening opportunities for visionary, able, and responsible persons.

The Mayor of Addis Ababa admitted that there were some inconsistencies in the restructuring of the city administration. For example, "names of former employees, who had either resigned, retired, or died years ago, had also been included in the restructuring program and assigned to take posts" and, as a result of poor record keeping and information flow, others were assigned to positions in more than one institution.[31] Irrespective of these inconsistencies, Mayor Arkebe asserted that "[t]hose who were laid off were found directly involved in mismanagement and corruption." He added that "they were also found to be incompetent . . . [and that] the administration is not in a position to tolerate such employees anymore." The Mayor promised that he would expand the reform measures to clean up the police force, health, and educational institutions as well.[32]

For the Mayor of the city, it may also be equally important to envision the ramifications of replacing elected officials by non-elected officials of the *Kebele* Association, especially with reference to the political and economic transformation of the city. It is also important to look at the ways in which the implementation of the reform program regenerates a positive image of the civil service in the minds of the public. When there are not specific criteria and guidelines open to public scrutiny for appointing public service officials, appointed officers may take their position for granted and, as a result, become as inefficient as their predecessors. In this case, the reform policy is likely to be aborted even before it reaches the stage of implementation.

In terms of improving governance and reorganizing the administrative structure of the city to reflect the end results of institutionalizing a transparent and accountable administrative system, the federal government is infringing upon the right to autonomy of the city government. It may also divert the process of democratization towards authoritarian rule. It does so when it replaces elected personnel with appointed personnel of the *Kebele* Association which was created during the military government and sustained by the current government as a bridge between the people and the government and as a listening institutional device for the heartbeat of the public. The *Kebele* Associations were designed to lift the workload burden off of the office of the Municipality, Judiciary, and others, and to minimize public discontent towards bureaucratic inefficiencies.

The *Kebele* Associations are the most immediate channels of communication between the people and the government. However, since the *Kebele* Associations are staffed by "outcast" bureaucrats whose work ethics earned them demotion with a certificate for incompetence and corruption, the government's strategy for improving the delivery of public services and rebuilding public confidence through decentralization of local administration misses its aims. Nor is it laying the foundation for a transparent and accountable administrative system. Consequently, a possible outcome of the reform policy is not what the government proclaimed to achieve; rather it is the erosion of public confidence, further de-linkage of vertical, top-down and bottom-up, interaction, and the worsening of the provision of public services.

Like the city of Addis Ababa, the city of Dire Dawa was a flourishing business center during the government of Haile-Selassie mainly because of its strategic location. The railroad from Addis Ababa via Dire Dawa to the port of Djibouti passes through it. There was also a spirit of entrepreneurship among the residents who came from different parts of the country. In the past few years, however, the vibrancy of the city is fading. The spirit of entrepreneurship also seems to be distorted by illicit drugs such as *Chat*, a local antidepressant leaf which is usually consumed by persons who are engaged in monotonous jobs or those who look for a temporary relief from their desperate conditions. Such economic and social quagmires necessarily demand energetic and dedicated leadership in Dire Dawa, which is in short supply in many places in Ethiopia.

The *Gimgema* (evaluation) process designed to regularly assess the performance and ethics of civil servants revealed that "corruption and anti-democratic practices" have become commonplace among the leadership in all levels of administration in Dire Dawa. As a result, preparations were underway for the federal government to temporarily and directly administer the city until such time as effective remedies become available to disinfect the civil service from corrupt and anti-democratic practices.[33]

To the extent that regional states and administrative councils are meaningfully autonomous, the recommendation for a temporary and direct administration of the city of Dire Dawa certainly manifests itself in a significant loss of autonomy. Conversely, it needs to be remembered that one of the objectives of the federal system is to allow a two-way interaction between the public and their leaders. Consequently, since regional leaders have become more of an obstacle to achieving this goal, using regional autonomy as a scapegoat to fend off federal supervision and oversight, infringing on the right to regional autonomy has no effect whatsoever on the rights of citizens. This is because the rights and privileges protected under the autonomous status of regional states is not the ordinary citizens, *per se*, but those of upper and mid-level public officials.

In addition, in the absence of a transparent and accountable administrative system, insisting on the right to autonomy may be perceived as an effort to maintain a breeding ground for corruption. Needless to say, primarily because of a lack of a transparent and accountable administration, the city that was once the center of economic activities in Ethiopia has become a run-down peripheral city.

To summarize, the implication of the reform policy is that, on the one hand, the transferring of already demoralized and inefficient bureaucrats from one institution to another will further raise the temperature of discontent and lower the level of public confidence in the government. On the other hand, the replacement of one bureaucrat with another through authoritative procedures and measures breaks down the most fundamental institutional linkages between the people and the government, which effectively undermines the legitimacy of the government.[34] Furthermore, as the discussions above seem to suggest, recycling incompetent bureaucrats with a history of corruption is not an innovative approach to improving governance. Above all, the civil service reform that touches almost all regional state governments demonstrates the difficulties that the federal government has encountered and its inability to reverse the pattern of corruption and abuse of power.

The extent of abuse of power, corruption, including misuse of working hours to run personal chores or coming in to work late and leaving early, seems to be more frequent and widespread in Addis Ababa than in other regions. Perhaps the only difference between Addis Ababa and other regions is that newspapers and radio broadcasting services expose corruption and abuse of power more openly than in other regions. The proximity of media establishments also contributes to accessing and reporting topical news.

Fragmentation leading to Consolidation in the S.N.N.R

What explanations are given for the deteriorating performance of the civil services and the growing tendency towards unaccountability? One way of explaining the problems in many of the regions is the extent of fragmentation or consolidation of political power in the regional parliaments. In all the regions examined so far, except for Dire Dawa where data is not available, a single party is in the majority in the State Parliament. For instance, in the Affar regional state, there are five zones and thirty electoral districts of which the district of Argoba is one. Except in this district where there was one independent and two candidates from the Affar Peoples Democratic Movement (APDM), the rest of the districts fielded candidates from the Affar National Democratic Party (ANDP), which won the majority of votes during the 2000 competition for seats in the State Parliament. Out of the three candidates in the district of Argoba, the independent lost to one of the candidates from the APDM. From the analysis presented in the first part of this chapter, it is clear that the ANDP, as a member of the coalition party at the federal level, essentially deepens the political influence of the coalition in regional affairs as well.

In the Amhara Regional State, there are eleven zones and one hundred thirty-eight electoral districts. Out of the total number of zones, one of them is the Oromiya zone with three electoral districts. Except for these districts where the candidates for the State Parliament were from the Oromo Peoples Democratic Organization, the rest of them were from the Amhara National Democratic Movement (both parties are members of the ruling coalition, EPRDF). Thus, for all practical purposes, the Amhara National Democratic Movement dominates the State Parliament in that regional state.

Furthermore, the parliament of the regional state of Gambella, like its counterparts in other regions, is occupied mainly by a single party, the Gambella Peoples Democratic Front (GPDF). In this region, there are three zones and ten electoral districts, including Gog and Jor. Not surprisingly, the GPDF, a member of the EPRDF, won 80% of the district votes during the 2000 elections for the State's parliament. A similar pattern is also apparent in the Administrative Region of Addis Ababa. That is, out of the twenty-three districts in six zones, there were three political parties, the Ethiopian Peoples Revolutionary Democratic Front, the Ethiopian Democratic Party (EDP), and the All Amhara Peoples Organization (AAPO) participating. Four candidates from the EDP and five from the AAPO won the election to represent their district constituents, often referred to as the Addis Ababa City Council.

The consolidation of political power in the hands of a single party is clearly manifested in the above regions. It is a paradox, however, that there is, on the one hand, the belief that the political marketplace is open to all legal political entities and that they can meaningfully participate in the decision-making process in their respective regions. On the other hand, a party that has very little social basis within its region draws strength from its membership to the coalition party and monopolizes the political marketplace in a region. That most dominant parties in each State parliament belong to the ruling coalition is not a mere coincidence.

As the analysis below suggests, ethnic politics has become a major regressive force in the country's drive towards development and democracy. On the one hand, the fragmentation of political parties has impaired genuine efforts at improving the delivery of public services through strategies such as civil service reform. Political parties in ethnically divided regions tug against one another, and in the process bureaucrats at the state and federal level gain ample opportunities and sufficient time to become corrupt. On the other hand, the consolidation of political power, such as the regional parliament noted above, leads to a political system that is functionally authoritarian. Interestingly, both fragmentation and consolidation seem to retard the transformation of the political system towards democracy. The struggles between regionalized and *ethnicized* political parties to retain supremacy over regional or national affairs have become politically and economically unproductive activities.

As Donald Williams correctly pointed out, such struggles for domination "have led to a general paralysis of productive political activity, a demobilization of participatory institutions, and the seemingly ineluctable turn toward authoritarian mechanisms of rule."[35] This seems even more pronounced in the Southern Nations and Nationalities Region where the ethnic heterogeneity of the region provided a breeding ground for the establishment of political parties that appeal to ethnic sentiment.

Strengthening of Political Muscle

The majority ethnic groups and about 20% of the population of Ethiopia are in the S.N.N.R. Since 1991, there emerged over twenty political parties in that region that are symbolic expressions of the region's ethnic diversity and illustration of the assertion that an ethnic group's interest is best protected by a "representative" political party of each ethnic group. In the S.N.N.R, there are 9 zones and 131 electoral districts and each of the following political parties won seats mainly in the electoral districts that are reflected in the name of the party.

The nine political parties occupy 113 of the 131 seats in the State Parliament, while the remaining seats are distributed among at least five other parties. In all cases, the political parties proclaim to represent the interests of the ethnic group(s) in whose name they were established. There were no candidates from the EPRDF in any of the districts. To the disappointment of EPRDF, the South Ethiopia People's Democratic Front, a member of the coalition, brings little or no political leverage in EPRDF's favor either in regional or national political or socioeconomic legislative affairs.

Table 8.4: Regional Parliament Election Results in the S.N.N.R., 2000

Party Affiliation	No. of Seats	Comment
BMPDO	8	Exclusively in Bench Maji district
GPUDM	7	Exclusively in Gedio district
GNDM	12	Mainly in Gurage district
HNDO	8	Exclusively in Hadiya district
KSPDO	9	Exclusively in Kafa Shaka district
WGGPDO	31	In various districts
SPDO	18	In various districts
KPDO	5	Mainly in Ka'te district
SEPDF	15	In various districts

Source: The National Electoral Board, "Results of the 2000 Election of House of People's Representatives, List of Candidates, Party Affiliation, and Vote," (Addis Ababa: National Electoral Board, n.d).

On May 24, 2003, Haile-Mariam Desalegn, Governor of the
S.N.N.R, who is also a member of the South Ethiopia People's Democratic Front (SEPDF), announced that there were widespread problems
of governance in the region due to lack of competent political appointees coupled with the ways in which the state government are structured.
The organization of the state government and political parties are structured in such a way as to discourage transparency and accountability
and cooperation between nationalities. In the past ten years, some nationalities were prohibited from participating in any capacity in the
administration of cities. According to him, these were some of the major forces that impeded the region's progress towards development.[36]

A week later, in a televised interview with a group of reporters, the
Governor declared that the SEPDF needed a fundamental organizational restructuring and reevaluation of its leadership at all levels: local,
district, zonal, and regional. A committee assessing the party's programs, achievements, and challenges found that a considerable number
of its members had not only been incompetent but they had also been
involved in activities that deliberately undermined the effective implementation of the party's programs. Those activities that retarded the
delivery of public services included bribery, partiality, and unnecessary
bureaucracy, thereby diminishing the level of public confidence towards the party and, consequently, towards the government. The Governor further claimed that the existence of many of the parties in the
region was indeed inimical to the region's progress towards development and democratization.[37]

Haile-Mariam further stated that in response to the regional leadership's multi-faceted problems, a transitional government had been set
up and will remain in effect until the upcoming elections. Meanwhile,
the leaders of the transitional state government were to be appointed
based on their level of education, ability to take initiatives, and positive
attitudes towards change. The appointment was to be based on a demonstrated commitment for impartiality in their views of nations and
nationalities and ability to discharge their responsibility effectively.
The Governor held the view that the formation of a mini-grand-
coalition that embraced the various parties in the region, whether members of the grand-coalition or opposition to the ruling party, was necessary for collectively voicing matters of federal and regional affairs.[38]

Such an approach to improving the delivery of public services or
representation of the interests of the multi-ethnic region, on the one
hand, accepts the notion that these parties are merely symbolic and
practically a hindrance to the development of the region. On the other
hand, it indicates that although the region is home to diverse ethnic
groups their interests can be, after all, articulated by a coalition party

which has to come up with a common agenda, making the mini-coalition essentially a single party. The proposition of the Governor also contradicts the ruling party's initial assumption that inter-ethnic hostilities are irreconcilable not only in the S.N.N.R but also in the entire nation.

The EPRDF, following the demise of the military regime, was formed with the view to stabilize the political system and to guarantee the rights of minority ethnic groups to representation, participation in the political process, and the right to vote for a party of their choice. This innovative political stabilization scheme has been emulated by the Council of Alternative Forces for Peace and Democracy in Ethiopia (CAFPDE), a party that finds its social and political base mainly in the South. It has also stimulated discussions between the All Ethiopian Unity Organization, Oromo National Congress, Ethiopian Democratic Party, and Council of the Alternative Forces for Peace and Democracy in Ethiopia to form a mini-coalition party. At least three political parties in the State of Affar have also formed a united front, which may have been advocated by the people of the region. Nevertheless, the formation of a united front among the parties there ultimately resulted in the concession of power to the Affar National Democratic Front (ANDF). Whether by design or default, the merger brought an additional layer of political muscle to the EPRDF, a layer of political muscle derived from ANDF's membership in the grand-coalition.

The SEPDF has certainly acquired valuable lessons from these and other party leaders' political maneuvers to model the creation of a mini-coalition party around the idea of forming a stronger collective voice in federal affairs and consensus on regional issues. The need for creating a mini-coalition may be justified in many other ways. However, what is clear is the inconsistency between the original assumption of establishing political parties as a reflection of the "irreconcilability" of interests and the shift towards reconciling differences between parties for the purpose of forming a regionally grand but nationally mini-coalition.

Indeed, if the relationship between the diverse ethnic groups in Ethiopia was historically marred by tension and irreconcilable interests and demands, then the strategies of the government are radically innovative in shifting the attitudes and perception of political elites towards cooperation and reconciliation within a decade. Nonetheless, taking into consideration the overriding factors for the formation of the grand-coalition, it is erroneous to suggest that the SEPDF is driven by the interest to improve the delivery of public services any more than by the factors that inspired the formation of the grand-coalition. In other words, the proposition to unify the various political parties in that region is a political maneuver to strengthen the political muscle of the ruling coalition.

There are also other reasons for the SEPDF's interest in incorporating other political parties in the region. If the SEPDF is successful in casting its net over other parties in the region and creating a mini-coalition under its leadership, then the CAFPDE, whose political base is mainly in the S.N.N.R and is one of the most outspoken opposition parties, may weaken its political muscle. Additionally, the parties of the region have, in the past few years, been allegedly instigating violent demonstrations by students and farmers that demand curative measures to mitigate the impact of the decline of coffee price on the peoples of the region. The reluctance of many peasants to repay the government for the price of fertilizer, which was distributed in previous years, is also attributed to opposition parties' anti-government propaganda. Driven by their own political agenda or not, opposition parties in the S.N.N.R are annoying the ruling party by boycotting elections and re-sisting being in the shadows of a regional mini-coalition party.

Summary and Conclusion

The various political strategies of the EPRDF has successfully si-lenced the voices of the people of Affar, Amhara, and Oromo by por-traying political parties in their image and casting its nets over their respective political parties (ANDF, ANDM, OPDO, and the SEPDF). Therefore, drawing a lesson from the ruling party's schemes of political maneuver, the concept of forming a mini-coalition by SEPDF is hardly surprising.

However, the formation of another mini-coalition party would not have made a significant difference in terms of the ruling coalition party's monopolization of power, improvement in the delivery of pub-lic services, or reduce the incidence of corruption. This is because some of the strong opposition parties were in a position simply to comment and suggest alternative approaches on the agendas and policies of the ruling party. They were short of the necessary votes to have their agen-das discussed in parliament or change the content of the ruling party's agendas or policies. In this respect, the unification of the parties in the S.N.N.R neither weakens nor strengthens the leverage of those truly opposition parties. As the previous chapter shows, what has changed the balance of power is the emergence of a coalition of opposition par-ties and their effective strategies to widen their political base.

The political marketplace in the S.N.N.R has not been a fertile ground for the centralization of power in the hands of a regional politi-cal party or the ruling coalition party. Practically, most opposition and members of the coalition party from this region are less preoccupied with fending for the interests of their constituents. Rather, they are more concerned with the calculation that the formation of a party entails, at a minimum, an opportunity for a few to rise to political power at the federal or regional level. In the package to rising to political power are generous salaries, amenities, and privileges, and possibly some kickbacks. These manifest in the transfer of public properties and contracts of large projects to companies owned by a few members of the coalition party and by the level of corruption that arguably annoyed Haile-Mariam Desalegn to undertake drastic reform measures.

Of all the reforms undertaken in the above-discussed regional states' administrations, the steps taken in the S.N.N.R to ameliorate the lack of good governance also seem to reveal the interests of the ruling coalition and the SEPDF in squeezing opposition parties out of the political marketplace. Given the fragmentation of political parties along ethnic lines, the parties in the S.N.N.R have essentially become toothless watchdogs. The degree of mismanagement of public funds and lack of accountability and transparency may not be greater in the S.N.N.R when compared with others. But the formation of a mini-coalition in that state to correct its multiple problems is as dangerous as the fragmentation of the parties there or, for that matter, in many parts of the country.

In the final analysis, the remedies to rectifying inequities in the distribution of political power are marred by numerous contradictions and inconstancies. Prime Minister Meles, in presenting his cabinet for confirmation following the 2000 elections, reminded the parliament that the criteria for selecting members of his cabinet is the nominees' ability to take initiatives, their competency, and, most importantly, their political outlook. Ironically, these criteria were ignored until after the second multiparty elections. Prior to the second elections, the ruling party advanced a policy of segregation on various fronts, including delimitation of regional borders, consolidation of ethnic Bantustans, and appointments of individuals to important public posts.

Initially, the ruling coalition took bold steps to use ethnicity as a point of reference to redress historical distortions in the distribution of political power. It now seems to have taken yet another radical step to facilitate the creation of mini-coalition parties, which suggests that ethnicity is no longer a relevant point of solidarity nor is it a determining factor in the distribution of legislative and executive powers. It is important to reiterate that institutional morphostatis and morphogenesis do not always produce the expected outcomes. The transformation of the civil services alone or reconfiguration of the ways in which regional or national political parties are organized could hardly bring about a more favorable condition to improving the general welfare of society. Any genuine attempt at improving the quality and delivery of public goods and services requires leaders with vision and political will.

Notes

1. Georgios Anagnostopoulos, "Sustainability and Ways of Achieving It," in Gunnar Skirbekk (ed.), *The Notion of Sustainability and its Normative Implications* (Stockholm: Scandinavian University Press, 1994), p.133.

2. "EPRDF is executing its policy of reorganization of the party," *Addis Zemen*, (5 June 2003), p.1, col. 1.

3. Siegfried Pausewang, Kjetil Tronvoll, and Lovise Aalen, eds., *Ethiopia since the Derg: A Decade of Democratic Pretension and Performance* (New York: Zed Books., 2002), XVI.

4. Ledetu Ayalew, interview by author, tape recording, Addis Ababa, 29 October 2002.

5. Admasu Mulaw, interview by author, tape recording, Addis Ababa, 25 November 2002.

6. "Tinkering with Public Fund," *Fortune*, (27 April 2003), p.20.

7. "Meles Announces New Cabinet," 20 June 2002, at <http://allafrica.com/stories>.

8. "What the Anti-corruption Commission is doing," *Addis Zemen*, (21 May 2003), p.2, col.2.

9. "Judiciary's grave concern on its independence," *The Reporter*, (7 May 2003), p.13.

10. "The 2003 Annual Journal on Ethiopia," (Addis Ababa: Berhanena Selam Printing Press, 2003), pp.274-7.

11. "Confidence in Ethiopian government declines," *The Sub-Saharan Informer*, (30 May 2003), p.1, col.2.

12. Donald Levine, "Ethiopia: Identity, Authority, and Realism," in *Political Culture and Political Development*, eds., Lucian Pye and Sidney Verba (Princeton: Princeton University Press, 1965), pp.248-9.

13. Joseph Lapalombara, "Italy: Fragmentation, Isolation, Alienation," in *Political Culture and Political Development*, eds., Lucian Pye and Sidney Verba (Princeton: Princeton University Press, 1965), p.305.

14. David Korten, Planned Change in a Traditional Society: Psychological Problems of Modernization in Ethiopia (New York: Praeger Publishers, 1972), p.64.

15. Amare Tekle, "Continuity and Change in Ethiopian Politics," in *The Political Economy of Ethiopia*, Marina Ottaway, ed. (New York: Praeger Publishers, 1990), p.48.

16. John Young, "Ethnicity and Power in Ethiopia," *Review of African Political Economy*, Vol. 23, 70 (December 1996): 531-42.

17. Ibid.

18. P.T.W. Baxter, "The Creation and Constitution of Oromo Nationality," in *Ethnicity and Conflict in the Horn of Africa*, eds., Katsuyoshi Fukui and John Markakis (Athens, OH: Ohio University Press, 1994), p.167.

19. Samuel Huntington, *Political Order in Changing Societies* (New Haven, CT: Yale University Press, 1968), pp.41-2.

20. "Speeding up the process of development in Affar is said to have required a transparent and accountable leadership," *Addis Zemen*, (31 May 2003), p.9, col.4.

21. "The Governor stated that the development goals have not been achieved as expected due to limited private investors' participation in Affar," *Addis Zemen*, (25 May 2003), p.9, col.4.

22. "Proclamation for reorganizing city administration in the Amhara Regional State is being drafted," *Addis Zemen*, (25 May 2003), p.9.

23. "Execution of plan is low in Gambella Regional Bureau," *Addis Zemen*, (25 May 2003), p.9.

24. "Conference participants call for establishment of peace, democratic order," *Ethiopian Herald*, Sunday Edition, (6 July 2003), p.1, col.2.

25. "Execution of plan is low in Gambella Regional Bureau," *Addis Zemen*, (25 May 2003), p.9.

26. "In Gambella, over 24 million *Birr* has been unaccounted for," *Addis Zemen*, (31 May 2003), p.2.

27. Ethiopian Television News, (9 July 2003), 10 p.m. news.

28. Ibid.

29. Emrakeb Assefa, "City starts reshuffling employees," *The Reporter*, (7 May 2003), p.3.

30. Ibid., p.18.

31. "City Administration Claims Success in Reshuffle of Officials," *Addis Tribune*, (16 May 2003), p.1.

32. Ibid., p.13, col.3.

33. "Dire Dawa, Like Addis Ababa, will be governed by a transitional administration," *The Reporter*, (5 May 2003), p.11.

34. Abebe Tadesse, "The new melody: civil service reform, *The Reporter*, (7 May 2003), p.5.

35. Donald Williams, "Accommodation in the Midst of Crisis? Assessing Governance in Nigeria," in *Governance and Politics in Africa*, eds., Hyden and Bratton (Colorado: Lynne Rienner Publishers, 1992), p.97.

36. "Strengthening public support is needed to promote good governance in the South," *Addis Zemen*, (25 May 2003), p.1, col.2.

37. "Close-up," Ethiopian Television, (31 May 2003), 9:30p.m.

38. *Addis Zemen*, (25 May 2003), p.11.

Chapter IX

Summary and Conclusion

Annual reports by the United Nations Development Programme and the World Bank and numerous studies by policymakers and scholars indicate that approximately one out of every two Ethiopians lives below the poverty line of $1 per-day. However one prefers to interpret the data, the reality in Ethiopia is far from what these statistical data seem to suggest. The statistical data here does not reflect the depth and incidence of poverty and the extremity of the regional differentials in access to the most basic necessities of life.

For example, access to health and education services, which are essential for improving the standard of living of a society, are measured in terms of how far a person lives from these service centers. Yet, there are many families in Ethiopia who live near the location of health centers or hospitals who do not receive medical treatment for their illness because they cannot afford to purchase gloves, syringes, prescription medicines, bandages, and the like. In 1998, for example, a couple accompanied by one of their sons went to one of the well known hospitals in the country so that the doctors would perform surgery on the mother who had been diagnosed with cancer. When the doctors finally admitted the patient, after five months of waiting, the husband was told to send his son to town to buy bandages and syringes. However, these items could not be found in any of the pharmacies, health centers, or clinics in town and, as a result, the son had to travel more than 200 miles (which takes more than four hours by bus) to buy the basic but necessary items for the surgery.

In many places outside the capital of Ethiopia, the medicine cabinets in the pharmacies, clinics, and hospitals are gravely under-stocked. There were a number of cases observed where doctors had to give children's medicine to adult patients. The only difference, they say, is the amount of intake and the solution to such chronic shortage of medicine is to double the dosage of the medicine when prescribing to adult patients. Such chronic shortage of medicine and low rates of growth in health and education facilities suggest that one may be above the poverty line but may also be denied the basic necessities of life. If political freedom and civil liberties were included as components in the calculation of the wellbeing of the society, then the percentage of people who enjoy a decent standard of living would decline dramatically.

In the final analysis, however, there are those privileged ones who received quality health and education services, had access to employment opportunities and reliable road networks, and dominated the decisionmaking processes and apparatus. Thus, the question becomes whether or not one can establish a strong correlation between ethnicity, on the one hand, and the monopoly of socioeconomic resources, on the other. Were there diversions of resources from one province dominated by the "subordinate ethnic groups" to improve the quality of life in the provinces largely inhabited by the alleged "super-ordinate" ethnic group? From a historical and comparative perspective, to what extent has political power been in the hands of the super-ordinate ethnic group? If so, has the monopoly of political power resulted in the economic exploitation and political repression of the "subordinate" groups?

Furthermore, to the extent that there was super-ordinate and subordinate division in the distribution of resources and political power during the reigns of Haile-Selassie, can one claim and provide empirically and analytically plausible evidence that the Mengistu regime maintained the status quo? All said and done, the question also boils down to examining the strategies and effectiveness of the policies of the current government to equitably redistribute socioeconomic resources and political power among the various ethnic groups and/or regions.

In many of the scholarly works undertaken to investigate the sources and persistence of ethnic conflict in Africa, it is not unusual to find assertions that dichotomize the conflict in Ethiopia in terms of "the ruling ethnic group" versus the rest of the society. Overtime, myths became realities to such an extent that the protracted secessionist and irredentist movements as well as the poor performance of the Ethiopian economy are attributed to misrule and centralization of the political system in the hands of the supposed "ruling ethnic group," the Amhara. Many scholars had little, if any, hesitation in asserting that the distribution of socioeconomic resources and political power in Ethiopia during the governments of Haile-Selassie and Mengistu Haile-Mariam was biased in favor of the Amharas, mainly because they rely on questionable premises and narrow theoretical lenses.

However, until recently the term "Amhara" did not refer to a particular ethnic group, but it was rather used to identify whether a person was Christian or Muslim. This was not unique to the people who are now lumped together as "Amhara." Others also identify themselves on the basis of their religion or geographical origin. Thus, a person from Tigray, Wollo, Gojjam, or Harar province may be an Amhara or a Muslim. He/she identifies himself/herself geographically as a *Tigrea*, *Wolloye*, *Gojjame*, or *Harere*. One need not necessarily delve into a stock of material to differentiate myths from realities.

Myths about the distribution of socioeconomic resources and political power have been perceived and promoted as realities, primarily because many of the studies on Ethiopia were not based on objectivity and the use of appropriate theoretical frameworks. They included little, if any, statistical and empirical data and, as a result, the assumptions and conclusions which suggest that socioeconomic resource allocations and political power distributions were historically biased in favor of one ethnic group have been patently erroneous.

Unfortunately, the dominance of the primordial school of thought in academic discourses helped dichotomize as though the distribution of economic resources and political power were along ethnic lines. In effect, it intensified the civil war in Ethiopia and paved the way for recognizing Issayas Afewoki's demand for the secession of Eritrea as a legitimate grievance. This happened even though Eritrea was the second largest beneficiary of industrial activities and social services until its separation from Ethiopia, which should have seriously weakened secessionist claims on the basis of economic deprivation. Nonetheless, the international community's recognition of Eritrea as an independent and viable state was supposed to open Pandora's box for separatist movements in other conflict-ridden regions of the continent. The fact that Pandora's box has not opened in other parts of the continent is surely a setback to elites with secessionist inclinations in Ethiopia and other parts of Africa.

To the disappointment of scholars and policymakers who advocated the interpretation of conflict through the prisms of the primordial theoretical tool, Issayas continued to subject the people of Eritrea to a far more wretched economic condition and political repression than when they were citizens of Ethiopia. In 1998, before the people of the two countries recovered from the thirty-year devastating civil war, the regimes in Addis Ababa and Asmara declared war against each other over a piece of land that is unsuitable for farming or possesses little, if any, mineral resources. Whether Issayas or Meles was the aggressor is of no relevance here. What is more important is that the people of the two countries were subjected to relive the experiences of their forefathers during the secessionist war from the mid-1960s until the collapse of the Soviet Union which ushered in the rise of formerly separatist parties to power. Even after the end of the border dispute, Ethiopians and Eritreans wake up everyday only to realize that there has not been much progress towards peace, security, freedom, or in their livelihood.

To make matters worse and more complicated, the government of Meles implemented an ambitious policy of "ethnic federalism" as if conflict over the distribution of resources and abuse of power could be resolved by dividing the country into ethnically segregated communities. In the end, although the government has not admitted the kind of problems it encountered when implementing its policy of "ethnic federation," it nonetheless achieved at least two major political objectives. First, it pitted one ethnic group against another so that a demographically minority ethnic group dominates the decisionmaking apparatus.

Second, the current government facilitated the mushrooming of political parties that are allegedly formed to defend the interests of their ethnic groups. After the redrawing of the administrative regions, each individual identifies himself/herself on the basis of ethnicity, for example, when registering for school, elections, and appearing before the court of law. To make the segregation of Ethiopians along ethnic lines a more effective political tool, each person is issued an identification card that includes information about the person's ethnicity and permanent residency. Thus, the federal system not only sharpened pre-existing notions of ethnic-based hostility, conflict, and discrimination, but it also made it difficult to relocate civil service personnel from one region to another.

The term "ethnic federalism" to refer to the Ethiopian political system is now grossly and widely used and abused by scholars and policymakers alike. There is nothing practical, which suggests that the political system or the division of administrative regions in Ethiopia reflects ethnic federalism. To say that the political system and the division of administrative regions are based on ethnic markers is to deny, for example, the Agew in Amhara and Tigray, the Shinasha in Benishangual, the Nuer in Gambella, the Sodo Guragie and the Arusi in Oromiya, or the Kunama in Tigray the right to establish their own state and to be ruled by their own ethnic kinsmen. Since there are not as many regional states as there are ethnic groups, notwithstanding its impracticality, it is erroneous to assert that the division of the administrative regions is based on ethnic markers.

Furthermore, as explored in chapter one in greater detail, the four criteria (consent of the people, language, settlement patterns, and iden-

tity) adopted to redraw the administrative regions are arbitrary and misleading at best. Perhaps one may need to look at the chronology of
events to understand the extent to which the regional administrative
boundaries are arbitrary, misleading, and authoritatively demarcated.
That is, the mapping of administrative regions and the promulgation of
the constitution (with particular reference to freedom of expression and
choice) took place in that order of chronology. The drafting and promulgation of the new constitution occurred later than the division of the
regional boundaries. The same is also true for the granting of Eritrea's
independence by the current ruling elites. Why these are so important
issues is because there are those who emphatically reject the illegiti-
macy of the regional boundaries as well as Eritrea's separation from
Ethiopia.

In any event, if the problems in Ethiopia were ethnic in nature,
then it is unlikely that the Oromos, which are a majority in the Harari
regional state, would have consented to be ruled by the minority Harari
ethnic group in that state. Likewise, the use of the Amharic language as
the official language of the states of Benishangul/Gumuz, Dire Dawa,
and Gambella would have been rejected by the Berta, Oromo, and the
Nuer ethnic groups that are a majority in these regional state.

From the statistical data presented in this study, it can be concluded that there were major distortions in the regional distribution of
health and education services as well as manufacturing establishments
across provinces or regions. Indeed, until the early 1990s, the establishment and expansion of manufacturing establishments as well as
health and education facilities gravitated towards Addis Ababa and
Asmara. Accordingly, health personnel and teachers were disproportionately congregated in these two cities in the country.

The data also suggest that the assertion that there were diversions
of resources biased in favor of the "ruling ethnic group" against others
during the previous two regimes is erroneous. The data on revenue and
expenditure by province indicate that there were no diversions of resources from one province for the development of other provinces. By
and large, there was equilibrium between revenue from and expenditure
to each province. Furthermore, although there was inequity in the distribution of socioeconomic resources, such disproportional distribution
of wealth was not between ethnic groups. It was rather between provinces or regions which were ethnically heterogeneous. The provinces of
the "super-ordinate" ethnic group were as marginalized as the provinces of the "subordinate" ethnic groups.

Having said this, it should not come as a surprise that after five
decades since the establishment of the maintenance districts, two of the
major cities, Gonder and Debre Markos, still have the lowest density of

asphalt roads in the country. The only exception is Wollo in the now Amhara Regional State where there was increase in the construction of gravel and asphalt roads. This may be explained by the fact that the city of Kombolcha, Wollo province, was a link between the cotton growers in the Affar region and the port of Assab and the city of Addis Ababa. What is equally disappointing is that since the early 1990s, there has been little, if any, investment in expanding the transportation networks that could allow greater interactions among peoples of the various regions and between producers and consumers.

In addition, agricultural productivity failed to catch up with population growth and meet the possible demands of the industrial sector for agricultural raw materials. To a large extent, the few industries that operate in Ethiopia were dependent on imported raw material. The volatility of the agricultural sector may explain the high ratio of imported to total raw material consumed by some of the industrial subsectors. Under these conditions, it is difficult to meet the growing demand for food and perhaps more difficult to realize the Agriculture-Development Led Industrialization (ADLI) scheme of the present regime.

The objectives of ADLI are made unnecessarily difficult to achieve for at least three main reasons. First, there is neither an agricultural or industrial policy in place to guide public and private investments to enhance the productivity of the agricultural and industrial sectors. Second, the absence of policy allows the office of the Municipality and other agencies involved in granting land lease rights to be arbitrary, thereby inducing corruption of the bureaucracy. Finally, to talk of the importance of small-scale credit schemes to improve the economic welfare of the largely agrarian Ethiopian society and, at the same time, maintain land as a public property makes little or no economic and political sense.

Therefore, what prevailed prior to the early 1990s was the exploitation of the majority by a few ruling elites. The supposed preferential treatment of the government of Emperor Haile-Selassie or Colonel Mengistu in the delivery of educational and health services to the largely Amhara regions of Gojjam, Gonder, and Wollo provinces neither quantitatively nor qualitatively exceeded the services delivered to the presumably neglected regions. Many political entrepreneurs and scholars insisted that the previous governments of Ethiopia advanced a conscious policy of economic deprivation. They asserted that these policies were biased in favor of the "crudely imperialist and expansionist Amhara ethnic group" of the Ethiopian highlands, even though there they produced no statistically significant evidence to support their claims.

Some of the scholars who insist on dichotomizing the division of resources and political power between the Amhara, on the one hand, and non-Amharas, on the other, were primarily carried away by the dominant discourse of the 1960s and 1970s. As a result, the search for the sources of and the solution for the conflicts in Ethiopia were evaluated through the prism of a primordial theoretical lens. Others simply ignored the internal dynamics that shaped the socio-cultural, economic, and political systems of Ethiopia. There are also mistaken assumptions that the super-ordinate group was expansionist and that it mainly inhabits the Ethiopian highlands in and around the capital city.

However, conflict over the distribution of resources was not between people that live in and around the city of Addis Ababa and people in other parts of the country. Most of the political leaders that surrounded the monarch and the military regime may have acted and behaved as what has become known as "Amhara." As a result, many confuse Emperor Haile-Selassie's ethnic identity as purely Amharan. And, this is not just about Emperors Haile-Selassie and Menelik II but also about Emperor Fasiledes (1632-1667) who ruled the northwestern part of Ethiopia and established his capital city in the predominantly Amhara province of Gonder.

In fact, since the expansionist expedition of the Oromo in the early 16th century, the genealogical distinctions between the various ethnic groups continued to blur through cross-ethnic marriages. Lest these facts are ignored for political convenience, it is inaccurate to conclude that resources were distributed purely along ethnic lines and that the primordial theoretical tool is suitable to examine, understand, and explain the sources of conflict and cooperation in Ethiopia. Furthermore, Eritrea is an interesting case where the data on social services, manufacturing industries, and transportation reveal the inconsistency of the assumptions and conclusions of some scholars who deliberately sought to establish a linear correlation between ethnicity and the distribution of resources. Hence, it follows that the notion of super-ordinate/subordinate socioeconomic relationships between ethnic groups was nothing but a catalyst to play one ethnic group against another. However, the fact that the majority members of the "super-ordinate" ethnic group are as economically marginalized as other ethnic groups in the country does not mean that "one nationality group" could not have dominated the political space or controlled the machinery of the state.

Even though the government of Haile-Selassie took an unprecedented step in 1957 to decentralize power among district representatives, the first as well as the subsequent parliamentary elections were only symbolic as far as genuine representation and decentralization of power were concerned. The 1957, 1961, and the 1965 parliamentary elections were meaningless political gestures, but they were useful as processes of electing members of an advisory board to the Crown Council and ministries. Notwithstanding the weaknesses of the elected members of parliament in serving the interests of the electors, eligible voters in all the provinces were given equal rights to elect and be elected for parliamentary posts. Thus, it does not follow that the political rights and civil liberties of some ethnic groups were protected at the expense of politically repressing others.

To be sure, the political system was designed to oppress the majority of Ethiopians by a few ethnically diverse elites who were unified by their loyalty to the monarch and submissiveness to his authoritarian rule. Indeed, a few of the available biographical data on the political appointees of the Haile-Selassie government suggest that ethnic sentiments were not overriding guidelines; rather, it was loyalty and competence that seemed to have been crucial in the Emperor's appointment of his political officers.

The symbolic elections and the failure of the Haile-Selassie government to lift the people of Ethiopia out of their dreadful social and economic conditions led to a growing frustration and, ultimately, to the downfall of the monarch. Following the downfall of the aristocratic regime, the people of Ethiopia hoped for equal treatment under the law and for greater and more equal access to education and health services as well as redistribution of land based on fairness and equity. Instead, they found themselves ruled by one of the most brutal military regimes in the political history of Ethiopia which controlled not only their meager resources but also their physical movement and place of residence. The Mengistu regime flexed its military muscle on opposition political groups and its subjects without any consideration to the ethnic affiliations of its prey.

In fact, the military regime was composed of junior and high-ranking military officers that transcended ethnic boundaries; and as such it sought to stimulate a nationalist rather than parochial sentiment. Membership of the dictatorial regime was not based on the tracing of lineage to a royal dynasty, romanticized lineage to King Solomon of Israel, or one's place in the social hierarchy. Contrary to pre-existing traditions, it dismantled the systems of property inheritance and indiscriminately executed members of the royal family, cabinet, and the nobility. There is little, if any, evidence to suggest that the military government entertained grievances built upon ethnic sentiments and loyalty, or that it was sympathetic towards some ethnic groups but not to others. Witness, for example, the execution of Aman Michael Andom (a Tigrae), Teferi Banti (an Oromo), Atnafu Abate (an Amhara) and the mass executions of students in Bale, Gonder, Addis Ababa, and Gojjam provinces that caused divisions within the military clique and between the regime and the masses. Additionally, it was not the ascendancy of the elect of God but the dictatorship of the proletariat that reigned supreme in the early days of the revolution.

While the military regime sought to enforce compliance through its coercive instruments, it also conducted elections to appoint officials of the *Kebele* Associations. However, these elections were closely monitored and regulated by cadres of the military government to ensure the appointment of individuals who internalized the principles of socialism with a potential to translate the Marxist-Leninist theory into practice. To a large extent, members of the associations were centrally nominated and "elected" for their allegiance to the principles of socialism and the dictatorship of the proletariat, which was ironic because Ethiopia was and still remains an agrarian society in which less than 5% of the population are industrial laborers. Such criteria ran through the entire system, from the lowest local elections up to the highest ranks of the government. The fundamental criterion for appointing cabinet members was either commitment to the advancement of socialist ideology, above and beyond primordial attachments and patronage, or membership in the military establishment. One could not, either as a member of the military regime or as a civilian, hold an opposing political view and expect leniency and tolerance from the military regime.

Undoubtedly, efforts were made to link the masses with their rulers through such mechanisms as the establishment of *Kebele* and urban associations and elections of their officers. However, the authoritarian characteristic of the system did not allow the rise of a truly vibrant civic organization to voice the desires and wishes of the masses. As a result, development policies were formulated at the highest level of the government without any input from the masses. Not surprisingly, the military government's horrifying and arbitrary rule as well as the top-down administrative system intensified a sense of resignation, frustration, and suspicion towards the government. In a sense, Donald Rothchild, Aaron Tesfaye, and some members of the current ruling elite and their academic clients may have been correct if they claim that the military regime maintained the *status quo* concerning the division between the masses and the political elite. But, it is utterly inaccurate to suggest that the Amharas dominated the decisionmaking organs of either the Haile-Selassie or the Mengistu regimes.

The notion of super-ordinate/subordinate economic and political relationships has given the impetus for the emergence of political parties that claim to represent and defend the interests of ethnic groups. One cannot be objective and, at the same time, deny the destitute conditions under which Ethiopians were subjected during the Haile-Selassie and Mengistu regimes and the need for an incoming government to take corrective measures. To avoid the resurgence of conflict and to improve the socioeconomic conditions of the majority in Ethiopia, any corrective measure should necessarily include equitable distribution of political power. It must also ensure that elections are meaningful, that the leadership is accountable, and that the system is transparent. All of these conditions, at a minimum, should help restore public confidence in the present government.

The present government came to power claiming that its objective is to rectify historical distortions in the distribution of socioeconomic resources and political power. However, an examination of the statistical data in chapter four and five strongly suggest that the present government, like its predecessors, has been unable to improve the economic and social conditions of the people and equitably allocate the necessary incentives to induce the flow of private investments in each region. Policymakers of the present government attribute the disproportionate private investment flows among the regions to the legacy of the previous regimes and "the invisible hands" of the market. As if the market has built-in censors to recognize the legacy of the previous regimes, Ethiopian policymakers of the present regime insist that the market, not the government, dictates the kind and amount of investment in each region.

Apparently, most Ethiopian public officials do not seem to recognize the inconsistencies in their explanation for the lack of balanced investment and growth between the regions. On the one hand, the regions that presently lag behind (Affar, Amhara, Benishangul/Gumuz, Gambella, and Somali) inherited poor infrastructure and human capital—prerequisites for attracting private investments. On the other hand, the role of the state in guiding public and private investments to the neglected regions through incentive schemes and expansion of public goods (energy, roads, hospitals, and housing) are conceded to the invisible hands of the market. Thus, give the policy analysis in Chapter IV, it would not be presumptuous to argue that contemporary Ethiopian policymakers have become "prisoners of paradigm," woefully attempting to fit Ethiopian realities into a theoretical framework supplied by the advanced nations of the North.

Additionally, the fact that land is owned by the state, perhaps as a political instrument, suggests that indirectly the state is impeding rather than facilitating agricultural productivity, thereby distorting balanced economic growth among the regions. There may be a host of other ramifications in attributing the persistence of inequity among the regions to the failure of free market economics. Suffice it to say that the

continued investment in Addis Ababa and a few other regions demonstrate not only the failure of the government to achieve its objectives of
redistribution with equity, but it also reveals the tainted perception of
the dominance/dependence paradigm exponents.

In the scramble for claiming the territories with a better infrastructure and natural resources, the Oromiya Regional State successfully
pressed the constitutional assembly of 1993 to grant the State of
Oromiya a special privilege to utilize the resources in Addis Ababa. As
a result, the Bureau of Oromiya Industry and Urban Development, Investment Office, Office of the Regional Council (parliament), and the
Justice Bureau of Oromiya are located in the capital city of Ethiopia.
No other regional state government is given a similar privilege. Ironically, even though the Oromo is the largest group in the Harari Regional State, the leaders of the group saw no material gain or historical
ties to claim either part of the land or the human and physical capital of
the Harari Regional State.

The adoption of a multiparty political system, whereby elections
for seats in the Federal Parliament are governed by a majoritarian electoral law, was to accommodate the transition from an authoritarian to a
multiparty democratic system. Before making some concluding remarks on the outcome of the 1995, 2000, 2005 parliamentary elections,
it may be appropriate to mention a few of the paradoxes in the formation of the grand-coalition party and the electoral law.

In spite of its problems, the division of the regional states was
based on the assumption that geographically isolating the diverse and
often "hostile" ethnic groups would reduce the intensity and frequency
of conflict between them. And yet, when opportunities presented themselves for the former secessionist parties to rule the entire nation, they
managed to cross over segmental cleavages and formed the Ethiopian
Peoples Revolutionary Democratic Front (EPRDF). Members of the
grand-coalition included political parties that supposedly held antagonistic ideological outlooks and represented the interests of ethnic
groups that were once considered rivals. Other political elites of the
lower order followed suit and the result became the congestion of the
political marketplace with numerous political parties that are essentially
identical in their interests and political agenda.

Clearly, the framers of the electoral law preferred the majoritarian
to the proportional system to regulate and manage the increasing number of political parties and perhaps to avoid repeating the experience of
Somalia in Ethiopia. According to some politicians, the majoritarian
electoral law was designed to avoid unnecessary complications and
problems that may have emanated if the proportional system was
adopted. All signs indicate that the proportional electoral law regulates

the competition for political power, but what seems to be at work is the majoritarian electoral system.

Whichever electoral law governs the competition for political power, one of the parties of the two demographically dominant ethnic groups (the Oromo or the Amhara) would have had greater leverages over legislative issues and the composition of the executive organ of the government, including the post of the Prime Minister. It is, there-fore, ironic that the Prime Minister belongs to one of the minority eth-nic groups (the Tigray) whose term in office is unlimited and whose power ranges from appointing individuals to core positions in the gov-ernment to suspending the constitution and dissolving the parliament.

The Prime Minister is so powerful that none of his "nominees" for cabinet posts have been rejected for any reason whatsoever. Members of the parliament collectively have no political clout to make meaning-ful contributions to the legislative processes on the parliament floor. Indeed, a few of the opposition parties such as the All Ethiopian Unity Party, the Council of Alternative Forces for Peace and Democracy in Ethiopia, and the Ethiopian Democratic Party are paralyzed by keeping their individual or combined votes at about twelve. As a result, they have been unable to have any say in any policy or program even if it directly affects the interests of their constituents.

The structure of the government and the multiparty elections in 1995, 2000, and 2005 obviously distinguish the present regime from both the Haile-Selassie and Mengistu regimes. Functionally, however, it is markedly similar to both governments and continues to reflect the same behavior as it builds layers of political clout to strengthen its mo-nopoly over the political marketplace. In both the 1995 and 2000 par-liamentary elections, the common thread was the dominance of the Ethiopian Peoples Revolutionary Democratic Front which claimed al-most seven of every eight seats in the House of Peoples Representa-tives. In the 1995 elections, the ruling coalition claimed more than 85% of the seats, which declined by about 10 percentage points in 2000.

The 2005 elections, for which results were not available when the manuscript was completed, were completely different from previous elections in at least three main respects. First, a few opposition party leaders surpassed the expectation of many, including members of the ruling party, by developing strategies to compete effectively in a politi-cal market that was controlled by the ruling coalition. Second, for the first time since the first elections, election observers from the European Union and even the NEB accepted opposition parties' claims of elec-tion irregularities as legitimate complaints deserving of investigation. Finally, the formation of a coalition of opposition parties demonstrated that the same tools utilized for the monopoly of political power could also be used to make multiparty elections more meaningful.

Until the 2005 elections, similar patterns characterized the regional state parliaments as well. For instance, The Regional Parliaments in Addis Ababa, Affar, Amhara, Dire Dawa, Oromiya, and Tigray are largely, and in some cases entirely, dominated by a single political party. At the level of analysis, the domination of regional parliaments by a single party is a contradiction of the principle of democratic governance: freedom of choice. It is this contradiction that brought about a major split among members of the TPLF Central Committee in late March 2001. Therefore, it appears that there could be no opposing views on matters of sub-regional issues. The people of each and every regional state, with the exception of the Southern Nations and Nationalities Region, are ruled by a dictatorial sub-national regime.

Apparently, the leaders of the EPRDF seem to be concerned about the insignificant loss of seats in the 2000 elections. Perhaps the most important factor for this decline may be the absence of a mini-coalition party in the third largest populated region of the country, the Southern Nations and Nationalities Region (S.N.N.R). As a member of the EPRDF, the South Ethiopia Peoples Democratic Front (SEPDF) did not bring as many votes to the Federal Parliament as was expected in the 2000 elections. The S.N.N.R is inhabited by diverse ethnic groups, which constitute the largest number of ethnic groups and approximately 20% of the population of Ethiopia. It is also a region with the largest number of political parties, of which the South Ethiopia People's Democratic Front is one of them. In the 2000 election, the party won only three (or approximately 2%) out of the total number of seats reserved for the region.

In early 2003, the Governor of the S.N.N.R, Haile-Mariam Desalegn, claimed that the state government was in need of major structural reforms. As discussed in chapter eight, a substantial number of appointed and elected members of the state government were allegedly involved in corruption and anti-democratic activities that discouraged cooperation among the various ethnic groups. He proposed the establishment of a coalition party that embraced the various parties in the region and appointment of public officials based on a number of criteria: commitment to impartiality, level of education, ability to take initiatives, and positive attitudes towards change.

Widespread corruption and the need for reconfiguring the state's administrative structure in the S.N.N.R are characteristics of most of the other regional states in the country, including Addis Ababa where EPRDF won the majority vote in both elections. What is unique about the S.N.N.R is, however, the number of votes that has been lost to the

ethnic-based political parties that are not associated with the ruling coalition party. Thus, while the above criteria seem to suggest a genuine
interest in solving the region's multifaceted problems, the formation of
a mini-coalition especially under the custodianship of the SEPDF ultimately leads to the monopoly of political power by the ruling coalition
party, both at the regional and federal levels. In real terms, there is no
need for the EPRDF leadership to fear that their monopoly of political
power is slipping away simply because the people of the Southern Nations and Nationalities Region are overwhelmed by a large number of
ethnic-based opposition parties. They, as their counterparts elsewhere
in the country, are toothless political opponents.

Nonetheless, the ruling coalition insisted on placing some of the
regional states under the direct tutelage of the federal government and
continued to create new institutions such as the Ministry of Federal
Affairs, the Ministry of Capacity Building, and the Ethics and Anti-
corruption Commission. The newly established institutions were designed to fight corruption, improve the delivery of services, and to
work in a synergetic fashion. However, they are faced with problems of
overlapping responsibilities and jurisdictions of authority and are consequently contending against each other to assert and broaden their
scope of influence and authority. In effect, there is less energy expended and resources allocated in dealing with the very problems that
brought about the need for institutional transformations.

Furthermore, from the current widespread civil service reform program, two substantial characteristics of the present government seem to
be reflected. On the one hand, the government is besieged by inept and
corrupt individuals, which is partly a result of appointing people to important posts based on their ethnic identity. On the other hand, the current government is characteristically similar to its predecessors as it is
composed of certified corrupt civil service officials. This is one of the
reasons why the current regime is engaged in duplicating institutions to
distort public perception of the sources for the discouraging performance of the economy and dwindling delivery of public services.

The assumption that the sources of conflict, political instability,
and economic underdevelopment were rooted in the aggrandizement of
scarce resources and political power by the alleged hegemonic ethnic
group certainly distorted the perceptions of members of the constitutional assembly in 1993 and political leaders of the present regime. The
mushrooming of political parties following the liberalization of the
political market in the early 1990s is deliberately intended to mask the
essential characteristics of the present political system, which is an authoritarian system that tolerates the formation of fruitless political parties.

However, given the political situation at the time (nationally, continentally, and globally) and given the long-held assumption that exercising the right to self-determination brings a lasting solution to "ethnic conflict," political parties that aspire for national unity with an overlapping membership would have been on the losing side of the political game. To be sure, it would have been disastrous to challenge the setting up of a government that recognizes the rights of minority ethnic groups and to concede significant political space to the party with substantial military hardware and personnel. No rational political elite would have preferred duplicating the experiences of Somalia in Ethiopia.

Similarly, no visionary leader would continue to perpetuate maldistribution among the regions and deliberately shift the conflict over resources to ethnic conflict to facilitate fertile grounds for mutual annihilation and suspicion between ethnic groups. It is this deliberate political action that made it difficult to relocate a skilled and experienced labor force from one regional state to another. Relocating manpower from one region to another has been difficult primarily because an increasing number of people are being conditioned to internalize a sense of hostility towards members of "immigrant" ethnic groups. There is also the fear that the mobilization of civil servants from one region to another is a deliberate effort to place individuals loyal to the ruling party in politically and strategically significant positions.

The Way Forward

The way forward may include a number of short- and long-term policies that can enhance the development and democratic processes in Ethiopia. One has to begin with a pragmatic look at why a federal system with loosely defined ethnic boundaries was a necessary step to maintain political stability in the country. The historical context within which the present regime came to power did not allow renouncing the right to self-determination or abandoning power-sharing among ethnically-inclined political elites as irrelevant to the Ethiopian political situation. For example, the lack of popular support of the 1960 coup, the resurgence of movements against aristocratic rule in the early 1970s, and the rise of a military junta in 1974 were conditioned by the dynamics of the socio-cultural and economic systems of the time.

The silence of the people in the late 1980s and the collapse of socialist regimes in most parts of the world helped secessionist groups to topple the military regime of Ethiopia in 1991. Had the military regime made a genuine effort to accommodate adversarial views, secessionist or nationalist groups would have had little or no reason to take their fight to the jungle or gain external sympathy and military support. The main point here is that the ways in which the present regime came to power and the subsequent enactment to redraw administrative regions, frame a new constitution, and promote the formation of political parties with ethnic emblems were dictated by the prevailing conditions of the time.

Having said that, it can be argued that in the short-term, public ownership of land may appear an effective political muzzle to make farmers feel a sense of dependency and vulnerability on the will of the ruling elites. In the long-term, public ownership of land would have environmental, economic, and political consequences. In the absence of a sense of ownership of land, farmers would tend to see no reason to invest and maintain property that can be taken away from them at any given time, which would have both environmental and economic adverse consequences. Politically, it is sufficient to recall the early 1970s starvation and the 1974 revolution that brought about an end to one of the most revered dynastic systems in Africa. Thus, the current land policy requires a critical rethinking and an immediate action so that its political, economic, social, and environmental consequences could be averted.

Looking ahead may be one of the qualities of visionary leaders, but the lessons of history must be taken into consideration to avoid repeating the political turmoil that engulfed the country in the 1970s. Defining the course of actions necessary to bring about development is not a major undertaking, especially given the current advances in communication technology (print and electronic media, transportation, and telecommunication). All of these are assets that facilitate the collection and dissemination of information, which were not available to policymakers in the early 1950s and 1960. Simply because the previous regimes had comprehensive development policies that did not improve the social and economic conditions of the people does not justify the lack of agricultural and industrial policies by the current regime. The tools that augment the application of policies are useless and could be inefficiently and inappropriately used if there are no visionary leaders, society is handicapped by the fear of the unknown, and if the people shy away from accepting a development-oriented cultural transformation.

Like physical and human capital which could be transferred from one generation to the next, the present government also inherited a dispassionate society with a tendency to be more distrustful towards the government than they were either under the Haile-Selassie or Mengistu regime. If the elite, past and present, managed to manipulate, manufacture, and exploit the socio-cultural components of the system to achieve a set of objectives, then they can also utilize the relevant policy application tools to improve the economic conditions of the people and restore public confidence of the government. They can also deliberately strengthen mutual trust that transcends socially constructed ethnic boundaries, thereby facilitating the conditions necessary for the creation of an economic and political community of states within a modified federal system of government. Mutual trust and civic engagement are critical not only for resolving conflict provoked by an essentialist perception of one ethnic group against another or by the competition for scarce resources, but also for rebuilding the war-torn economy of Ethiopia.

Building public confidence towards the government is also contingent upon whether multiparty elections are symbolic or meaningful. To make both the structure and function of the present government converge, the formation of political parties with overlapping membership needs to be encouraged. Ultimately, the competition for political power bears fruit when the electorate holds both the sticks and carrots which strengthen horizontal and vertical interactions and communications. In addition to encouraging the formation of political parties that sink their regional, linguistic, religious, and other unproductive cleavages, facilitating the political conditions for the rise of indigenous civic associations needs to be included as one of the major components of the political system.

Conventional belief holds that the number of independent newspapers is one of the measurements of freedom of speech and the level of democratization in a country. It is also believed that privately owned and independent media serve as channels to link the state with the society by reporting fairly accurate, relevant, and credible news. This argument could easily be understood from the point of privatization, in particular, and free market economic theory, in general. But when free market economic principles are applied to a certain economic situation, the outcome is not always positive. Similarly, the application of one of the principles of democracy, which is reflected in the privatization of mass media enterprises, has had adverse effects in Ethiopia.

Since 1991, there has been progress towards respect for freedom of speech, not necessarily in peaceful demonstrations and associations but certainly in the privatization of print media. However, the government's policy to unchain the media from the shackles of cultural impediments to development and democracy has been, to a large extent, disappointing. While the constitution guarantees freedom of speech which, in turn, is aimed at nurturing a culture of tolerance for adversarial points of views, the mass media in Ethiopia concentrates on subjective reporting of news, often with a political agenda and contributes little to discussions on social and economic issues. In effect, the media seems to have lost its credibility as an impartial and key player in the democratization of Ethiopia. The majority of pieces published in the local newspapers appear to help many develop a sense of indifference towards the growing number of homelessness, AIDS, rising unemployment, and mismanagement of public funds. Although there is a need for a closer and systematic examination of print media in Ethiopia, preliminary impressions suggest that many of the stories published by the private press were essentially illicit drugs, providing temporary relief but with little or no positive effect on the development and democratization of Ethiopia.

The role of the mass media in the development and democratization processes in Ethiopia could be improved when the state subjects itself to the rule of law, thereby setting examples that no one is above the law. Initially, the government may have been desperate for internal and external legitimacy or to demonstrate its commitment to institutionalize a democratic political system. Consequently, the government may have, in some cases, induced the birth of the private print media. In any case, the number of privately owned newspapers and journals grew exponentially until the Ministry of Information proposed a new press law in 2002. The assumption by most personnel of the private media, some of whom were selling newspapers in the streets of Addis Ababa and had no training in journalism, was that the law provided them with the right to freedom of expression and press. While this is true, no law could be misconstrued and applied to fit the interests of those with chaotic and anarchic motives. As the law provides rights and privileges, it should also contain both carrots and sticks.

It is also extremely important to point out that even though the private press seems to be a disappointment, endogenous civil society associations and representatives of the private press need to design policies to enhance the role of civic organizations and the private press. The government should also formulate guidelines that encourage, rather than undermine, the rise of ethically grounded, socially responsible, and objectively creative journalists. Given the sacrifices made for freedom of expression during the brutal military dictatorship, short of commitment to uphold the rule of law and make contributions to improve the overall well-being of society is, at a minimum, morally and intellectually deplorable. Furthermore, any dialogue to establish standards and ethics of journalism must be grounded in the socio-cultural, economic, and political realities of Ethiopia.

To be sure, both centralized systems of government during aristocratic and military rule damaged the social bases of conflict reconciliation and economic reconstruction that are necessary for development and democratization. Their political legacy has deepened a sense of suspicion, indifference, inertia, and hopelessness especially among

Ethiopian youth. Consolidating political power in the hands of the ruling party, expelling those certified to be corrupt, and opening the same opportunity of mismanagement of the economy and abuse of power to a new brand of elites could hardly reverse the trend from suspicion and inertia to mutual trust and motivation. In this regard, an initial step for political leaders is to redefine their political platform with emphasis on proposing solutions to unemployment, homelessness, and economic stagnation. Doing so would simultaneously help restore public confidence and lay the foundation for economic development and democracy.

Finally, there are four main areas that may be of interest for further research. The list of political leaders of the government of Haile-Selassie and Mengistu Haile-Mariam are provided in the appendix to stimulate a more elaborate and in-depth biographic research than presented in this study. Another area of research interest may be to examine the contents of newspapers published in Ethiopia as they relate to the development and democratization processes in the country. The concluding remarks concerning the role of the mass media in Ethiopia are based on personal interviews and observations. Clearly, this is one side of the story because it does not include the views and opinions of the private media personnel. Thus, newspaper editorial content analysis and interviews with media personnel would help determine the extent to which the mass media plays a role in the development of a country such as Ethiopia.

Additionally, a mathematically rigorous equity model could be developed from the statistical data in chapter five as well as from the data provided in the appendix. This would give policymakers and members of academia a clear understanding of the scope and depth of inequity in the distribution of socioeconomic resources, thereby providing a reliable frame of reference to formulate a development policy with emphasis on equity between regions and among ethnic groups in a given region. Finally, researchers may fill the knowledge gap by further exploring whether political party platforms influence the perception, preference, and decision of electors in plural society such as Ethiopia. One could also further examine if and how the value of ballots depreciates or appreciates in a given political marketplace.

Appendix

Appendix A: Estimate of Area, Yield, and Production of Major Crops

Crop	1962 Area (in '000 ha)	1962 Yield (in qt/ha)	1962 Production (in '000 mt)	1967 Area (in '000 ha)	1967 Yield (in qt/ha)	1967 Production (in '000 tons)
Cereals						
Barley	950.0	8.0	760.0	1,693.2	8.5	1,430.0
Maize	757.7	9.0	682.0	824.4	10.3	853.0
Sorghum	1,352.2	8.0	1,081.0	1,174.0	8.4	988.6
Teff	3,316.0	5.5	1,824.0	2,154.0	6.6	1,304.3
Wheat	371.4	7.0	260.0	1,028.6	7.4	760.0
Dagusa	-	-	-	299.3	5.0	150.9
Ensete	-	-	-	190.8	24.0	458.0
Oil Seeds						
Castor Beans	-	-	-	21.5	5.3	11.3
Ground Nuts	-	-	-	37.9	5.2	19.6
Linseed	102.0	5.0	51.0	115.3	5.0	58.2
Neug	346.6	6.0	208.0	384.2	6.3	240.8
Sunflower	-	-	-	58.5	5.1	30.0
Sesame	76.2	4.0	30.5	115.5	4.4	51.0
Pulses						
Chick Peas	270.0	6.0	162.2	285.3	6.2	176.7
Field Peas	123.9	9.0	111.5	131.8	9.2	121.6
Haricot Beans	86.7	7.0	60.7	91.9	7.4	68.2
Horse Beans	112.7	9.0	101.4	136.0	9.3	125.9
Lentils	152.0	6.0	91.4	169.6	5.9	101.2
Other Crops						
Cotton	-	-	-	62.8	1.6	10.4
Sugar Cane	5.0	1,300.0	650.0	5.9	1,454.0	858.0
Coffee	-	-	-	611.5	2.6	160.0
Average	**573.0**	**98.7**	**433.8**	**457.0**	**127.3**	**379.9**

Appendix A (continued)

Crop	1973 Area (in '000 ha)	Yield (in qt/ha)	Production (in '000 tons)
Cereals			
Barley	940.0	8.0	752.0
Maize	882.0	10.0	882.0
Sorghum	1,012.0	8.6	870.3
Teff	1,686.0	7.0	1,180.2
Wheat	816.0	8.0	652.8
Dagusa	202.0	6.0	121.2
Ensete	-	-	399.0
Oil Seeds			
Castor Beans	8.0	5.1	4.1
Ground Nuts	20.0	7.2	14.4
Linseed	125.0	3.7	46.3
Neug	152.0	3.9	59.3
Sunflower	63.8	3.8	24.2
Sesame	160.4	5.8	93.0
Pulses			
Chick Peas	302.8	7.8	236.2
Field Peas	151.4	4.9	74.2
Haricot Beans	132.4	6.8	90.0
Horse Beans	138.0	8.6	118.7
Lentils	172.0	4.3	74.0
Other Crops			
Cotton	62.1	15.1	94.0
Sugar Cane	6.7	1,606.0	1,075.7
Coffee	-	-	135.0
Average	**370.1**	**91.1**	**333.2**

Note: In the 1972 and 1973 data, the total area cultivated, yield, and production of Millet is added to Sorghum.

Source: Central Statistical Office (CSO), "Statistical Abstract 1964," (Addis Ababa: CSO, 1970), p.7. See also, "Statistical Abstract 1969," (Addis Ababa: CSO, n.d.), pp.42-3 and "Statistical Abstract 1975," (Addis Ababa: CSO, 1975), p.48.

Appendix B: Current Government Expenditure (in Million *Birr*)

	1965	1966	1967	1968	1969
General Service	**244.3**	**209.2**	**200.6**	**206.5**	**213.8**
General Government	13.8	14.8	15.2	17.6	21.3
National Defence	118.6	98.4	86.8	86.8	85.3
Internal Law and Order	89.3	70.7	69.6	75.1	81.8
Foreign Relations	6.4	7.3	7.3	8.0	9.4
Finance and Planning	16.2	18.0	21.7	19.0	16.0
Economic Services	**37.6**	**73.6**	**47.8**	**50.1**	**44.1**
Agriculture and Land Reform	7.9	36.1	9.1	10.0	10.4
Industry, Commerce and Mining	4.0	5.0	4.7	4.8	4.7
Public Works and Communications	25.7	32.5	34.0	35.3	29.0
Social Services	**92.8**	**99.2**	**74.6**	**78.8**	**94.2**
Education and Culture	63.2	68.0	50.8	54.9	69.0
Public Health	25.0	27.0	19.8	18.9	20.6
Social Affairs	4.6	4.2	4.0	5.0	4.6
Pension Fund	**3.2**	**5.4**	**7.1**	**8.7**	**13.8**
Unallocated Expenditure	**12.3**	**28.7**	**112.0**	**110.3**	**107.7**
Total	**390.2**	**416.1**	**442.1**	**454.4**	**473.6**

Source: Central Statistical Office, "Statistical Abstract 1967 and 1968," (Addis Ababa: CSO, n.d.), p.138. See also, Statistical Abstract 1972," (Addis Ababa: CSO, n.d.), p.131.

Appendix C: Sectoral Contribution to GDP, 1965-1973 (at constant factor cost 1960)

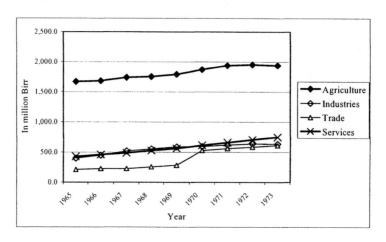

Source: Central Statistical Office, "Statistical Abstract 1970," (Addis Ababa: CSO, 1970), p.125. See also, "Statistical Abstract 1976," (Addis Ababa: CSO, 1977), p.140.

Appendix D: Sectoral Contribution to GDP, 1974 - 1990 (at constant factor cost 1980)

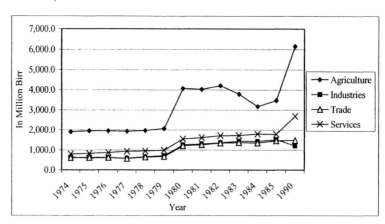

Source: Central Statistical Office, "Statistical Abstract 1976," (Addis Ababa: CSO, 1977), p.140. See also, "Statistical Abstract 1980," (Addis Ababa: CSO, 1982), p.174, "Statistical Abstract 1986," (Addis Ababa: CSO, 1988), p.197, Central Statistical Authority (CSA), "Statistical Abstract 1990," (Addis Ababa: CSA, 1993), p.182, and "Statistical Abstract 1995," (Addis Ababa: CSA, 1996), p.217.

Appendix E: Estimated Population by Province and Rank, 1970

Province	Total (in '000)	Area (in '000 km²)	Population (Per km²)	Rural	% Urban
Shoa	5,051.4	85.2	59.3	4,006.3	20.8
Sidamo	2,369.2	117.3	20.2	2,252.8	4.9
Wollo	2,355.6	29.4	29.7	2,250.7	4.5
Eritrea	1,836.8	117.6	15.6	1,515.3	17.5
Tigray	1,748.7	65.9	26.5	1,625.0	7.1
Gojjam	1,668.7	61.6	27.1	1,589.0	4.8
Gonder	1,294.6	74.2	17.4	1,209.4	6.3
Kaffa	1,224.3	54.6	22.4	1,550.0	5.7
Wollega	1,214.2	71.2	17.1	1,164.6	4.1
Arussi	818.2	23.5	34.8	768.5	6.1
Addis Ababa	795.9	0.2	3,979.5	-	100
Gemu Gofa	668.1	39.5	16.9	635.6	4.9
Illubabor	659.6	47.4	13.9	635.6	3.3
Bale	190.4	124.6	1.6	165.6	12.8
Total	**24,319.0**	**1,221.9**	**19.9**	**22,027.0**	**9.4**

Source: Central Statistical Office, "Statistical Abstract 1970," (Addis Ababa: CSO, 1970), p.26.

Appendix F: Estimated Population by Region and Rank, 1995

Region	Population	Percent
Oromiya	19,158	35.1
Amhara	14,128	25.9
S.N.N.R	10,627	19.4
Somali	3,249	5.9
Tigray	3,203	5.9
Addis Ababa	2,157	3.9
Affar	1,079	2.0
Benishangul/Gumz	470	0.9
Dire Dawa	259	0.5
Gambella	185	0.3
Harari	135	0.2
Total	**54,650**	**100**

Source: Central Statistical Authority, "Statistical Abstract 1997," (Addis Ababa: CSA, 1998), p.70.

Appendix G: Gravel and Asphalt Roads, 1967 and 1974

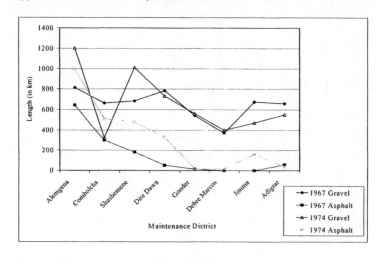

Source: Central Statistical Office, "Statistical Abstract 1970," (Addis Ababa: CSO, 1970), p.74. See also, "Statistical Abstract 1971," (Addis Ababa: CSO, 1979), p.105.

Appendix H: Gravel and Asphalt Roads, 1980 and 1990

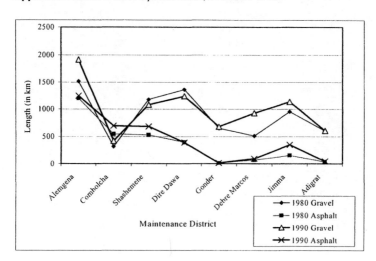

Source: Central Statistical Office, "Statistical Abstract 1982," (Addis Ababa: CSO, 1983), p.103. See also, "Statistical Abstract 1992," (Addis Ababa: CSA, 1994), p.129.

Appendix I: Gravel and Asphalt Roads, 1995 and 2000

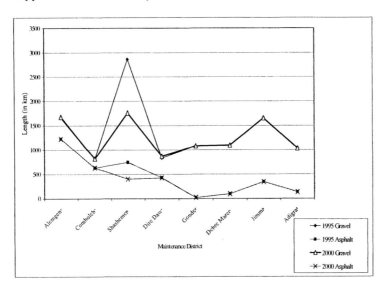

Source: Central Statistical Authority, "Statistical Abstract 2000," (Addis Ababa: CSA, 2001), p.103. See also, "Statistical Abstract 2001," (Addis Ababa: CSA, 2002), p.209.

Appendix J: Short Biographies of Officials Assassinated during the 1960's
Coup Attempt

Ras Abebe Aregai was born in 1896 to Afe Negus Aregai and As-
kale-Mariam Gobena in **Shoa** province. In 1933, he became Maj. General and was appointed Governor General of Shoa province. Retaining
his title, Maj. General Abebe was transferred to Sidamo province. In
less than a year, he was promoted as Minister of Defense and ruled
Tigray until 1941. In 1941, Maj. General Abebe became Minister of the
Interior until he was once again elevated as Let. General, in 1945, and
retained his post as Minister of Defense. By 1950, he became Chairman
of the Council of Ministers while serving as Minister of Defense.

Major General Mulugeta Buli was born to Ato (Mr.) Buli and his
mother Weizero (Mrs.) Ayelech Chere in **Sidamo** province. Major
General Mulugeta was the architect and Commander of the Royal
Bodyguard. He was later appointed Minister of Community Development and held his position until his assassination during the 1960's
coup. Maj. Gen. Mulugeta was one of Haile-Selassie's allies during the
1960's coup attempt by members of the Royal Bodyguard, including
Col. Mengistu Neway.

Ato Mekonnen Habte-Wolde was born in Bisheftu, Kajima, in
Oromiya region, formerly part of the province of Shoa. At age seven,
he entered the Ziquala Monastery traditional school with the intention
to become a priest. During the Italian occupation, Mekonnen was a
refugee in France. There, he established an association of Ethiopian
refugees in Europe through which he was able to help many Ethiopians
acquire residency status and find employment opportunities. He was
also able to collect donations from the community of Ethiopian refugees to help Ethiopian refugees elsewhere in Europe and Africa. On
May 14, 1934, Ato Mekonnen was appointed Minister of Agriculture
and, a year later, he became Minister of Industry. While retaining both
posts, Mekonnen also served as President of the Agricultural Development Bank. On June 21, 1941, Mekonnen was appointed Minister of
Finance, on March 25, 1950, Minister of the Interior, and in 1951, he
became Minister of Planning in the Ministry of Trade and Industry.

Blata Dawit Eqube-Egzi was born in **Eritrea** in January 1906. He
was a journalist by training and profession. After completing his education in journalism in Beirut, in 1929, he returned to Ethiopia and started
teaching at Teferi Mekonnen School in Addis Ababa. A few years later,
he became Director of the Teferi Mekonnen School. Except during the
Ethio-Italian war, Blata Dawit held various positions, including Deputy
Governor of Addis Ababa District, in 1940, and Minister De'ta in the
Ministry of Foreign Affairs, in 1957, which he held until his death in
December 1960. Dawit was a major force in exposing the inhumane

treatment of Ethiopians by Italian forces. As a multi-linguist journalist (Tigrigna, Amharigna, English, French, and Italian), Dawit was on the war front with foreign journalist and the Red Cross, as a reporter and interpreter for foreign journalists and envoys.

Blata Ayele Gebre was born in 1886 to Ato Gebre Andargachew and Weizero Debritu Bisewer in the city of Grawa, district of Gara Muleta, **Harar** province. He was probably one of the few individuals who started from a clerical position and attained ministerial-level posts under the Haile-Selassie government. In 1903, he was a postal clerk at the Dire Dawa Post Office. Six years later, he was promoted as Secretary of the Dire Dawa Custom's Office. In 1926, Blata Ayele was appointed Director of the Addis Ababa Municipal Office, and during the Italian occupation he was imprisoned in Azira concentration center. When the Emperor returned from exile, Blata Ayele was one of the persons who was promoted to high-ranking public posts for his loyalty to the Emperor during and after the Ethio-Italian war. Consequently, Blata Ayele was promoted as Minister of Justice.

Afe Negus Eshete Geda was born in 1904 to Grazmach Geda Mandefro (from **Gamu Gofa**) and Weizero Trufat Yergu in Addis Ababa. In 1940, Afe Negus Eshete was appointed Judge at the Gamu Gofa Superior Court. In 1958, he was promoted to Deputy Minister of National Security in the Ministry of Interior. He held his position until his death in December 1960.

Ras Seyoum Mengesha was born on June 16, 1879, to Ras Mengesha Yohannis (grandson of Emperor Yohannis II of **Tigray**) and Lady Tewabech Wolde-Gebriel of Agew Midir, Gojjam province in Zembre, Agew Midir. During the Italian occupation, Ras Seyoum was prisoner of war (POW) and sent to Rome along with Princes Astede Asfaw, granddaughter of Emperor Haile-Selassie. Both were imprisoned for 26 months and brought back to Addis Ababa where they remained in jail until the occupying forces were defeated. When the Emperor returned from exile, Ras Seyoum was appointed Governor General of Tigray province.

Ato Amde-Michael Desalegn was born in January 1912 to Ato Desalegn Habte-Mariam and Weizero Wolete-Eyesus in Mescha *Kebele*, district of **Tegulet** and **Bulga**, Shoa province. During the Ethio-Italian war, Ato Amde-Michael was Ration and Weapons Comptroller. Between 1942 and 1951, he was Director of the Office of Information, which is now the Ministry of Information and Culture. In 1951, Amde-Michael served as Liaison Officer between the central government and the province of Eritrea. He was later transferred to Somalia where he served as Consular General. A few years later, Amde-Michael returned to Ethiopia and became Chief Prosecutor in the Ministry of Justice. In

1958, he was Deputy Minister of the Ministry of Information. Ato Amde-Michael held his position until he was assassinated in 1960.

Dejazmach Let-Yebelu Gebre was born to a Menze nobility, Ato Gebre Gultu and Weizero Wolete-Selassie Derge in Gino *Kebele*, district of **Menze and Yifat**, in Shoa province. At age eleven, he came to Addis Ababa to serve as a junior attendant to the Emperor. As a gratitude to his services, he was given the traditional title of Balambaras and later became Deputy Chief Aid *de* Camp of the Imperial Palace. In 1937, Dej. Let-Yebelu was promoted as District Governor of Bale and, in 1953, Chief Councilor in the Ministry of Justice.

Liqe-Mekuas Tadese Negash was born in Addis Ababa in April 1908 to a well-known Tigray nobility, Fit. Negash Tesfay, and to Weizero Mulatua Dubale of **Menz** in northern Shoa province. Liqe-Mekuas Tadese and his father were among the renowned patriots who defended their country against Italian aggression. Fit. Negash was killed during the Ethio-Italian war in Tigray province and Liqe-Mekuas Tadese was POW in Rome. He was later brought back to Ethiopia where he stayed in detention until the end of the war. At independence, Liqe-Mekuas Tadese served the government of Haile-Selassie in various capacities, including as Governor of Bale District and Deputy Minister of Land Tenure and Contract in the Ministry of Interior. In March 1957, he was appointed Minister De'ta in the Ministry of Justice and held his position until his death in December 1960.

Ato Lema Wolde-Gabriel was born in 1903 to Kegnazmach Gebre-Mariam Abde and Weizero Wolete-Kidan Gebre-Wolde in the city of Goba, district of **Bale**. Lema is yet another example of the ethnic diversity of the government of Haile-Selassie and the rise of few individuals from ordinary citizenship to a status of national and international recognition. Ato Lema was a local retail trader in Goba. Later he moved to Addis Ababa to serve as Director of the Addis Ababa Polytechnic School. He also served as Chief Inspector and Interim Director in the Ministry of Agriculture. In the mid-1940s, he was appointed Chief Inspector and Deputy General Auditor of the Ministry of Finance. Later, he became Deputy Minister of the Ministry of Mines, a position he held until his death in December 1960.

Ato Abdulahi Mume was born in 1914 to Ato Mume Kelo and Weizero Meymuna Abdulahi in the city of **Harar**. During his teen, Ato Abdulahi was a multi-lingual and a person of ambition. In addition to Amharic, he was fluent in Arabic, French, English, and Italian. After graduating from Alliance Francisco High School, he worked as a mail clerk at the Harar Post Office from the late 1920 until 1934. In 1934, he became Deputy Administrator of the Post Office and, later, transferred to serve as Secretary in the Governor's office of the province of Harar.

Until 1959, Abdulahi held clerical positions in the various branches of the provincial administration. In 1959, however, he was promoted as Vice Minister of Finance. A year later, he was killed during the 1960's coup attempt.

Ato Kibret Astatkie was born in April 1902 in Belewa *Kebele*, **Harar** province. He studied French in Dire Dawa Language School and English and Business Administration when he was in exile in Djibouti. After independence, he returned to Ethiopia and held various positions. A few years before the coup attempt, Ato Kibret was appointed as Assistant Minister of the Interior.

Source: *Menen*, Vol. 5, Nos. 2-3, (Addis Ababa: Commercial Printing Press 1960): 24-35.

Appendix K. Names of Officials Executed by the Military Government, November 14, 1967 (Ethiopian Calendar)

Admiral Eskender Desta, Commander of the Naval Force
Officer Gashaw Kebede, Member of the Police Force
Major Birahanu Mecha, Commander of the Police Force
Maj. Gen. Seyoum Gedle-Giorgis, Commander of the Second Brigade
Lieutenant Gen. Derese Dubale, Commander of the Ground Force
Lt. Gen. Debebe Haile-Mariam
Lt. Gen. Asefa Demse, Chief of Aid de Camp of the Imperial Palace
Lt. Gen. Abebe Gemeda, Commander in the Imperial Bodyguard
Lt. Gen. Yilma Sebsebe, Commander in Chief of the Police Force
Lt. Gen. Haile Baykedagn
Lt. Gen. Belete Abebe, Commander in Chief of the Reserve Army
Hon. Tefera-Work Kidane-Work, Member of the Crown Council
Dej. Kasa Woldemariam, Minister of Agriculture
Honorable Seyfe Maheteme-Selassie, Minister of Education
Ato Asefa Defaye, Director of the Awash Valley Authority
Brigadier Gen. Samuel Beyene, Member of the Senate
Hon. Yohannis Kidane-Mariam, Minister De'ta, Ministry of Justice
Col. Tasew Mojo
Col. Yalemzewd Tesema, Commander of the Air-Born
Col. Yigezu Yemene, Commander of the Army Aviation
Brig. Gen. Mulugeta Wolde-Yohannis, Member of the Police Force
Brig. Gen. Girma Tseyon, Member of the Police Force
Cap. Mola Wakene, Member of the Police Force
Cap. Wolde-Yohannes Zergaw, Member of the Police Force
Maj. Gen. Tafese Lema, Commander in the Imperial Bodyguard
Maj. General Kebede Gebre, Commander of the Ground Force
Hon. Aklilu Habete-Wolde, Prime Minister

Lt. Gen. Abiy Ababe, Minister of Defense (patriot)
Leul Asrate Kasa, President of the Crown Council (patriot)
Ras Mesfin Seleshi, Governor of Shoa Province (patriot)
Lij Engalkachew Mekonnen, Prime Minister (1974)
Ato Abebe Reta, Crown Councilor
Hon. Akale-Work Habte-Wold, Minister of Justice (patriot)
Col. Tamirat Yegezu, Crown Councilor (patriot)
Dej. Kifle Ergetu, Ambassador (patriot)
Lt. Gen. Essayas Gebre-Selassie, Member of the Senate (patriot)
Lt. Gen. Asefa Ayen, Minister of Transportation and Communication
Ato Mulahi Debebe, Minister of Community Development and Social Affairs
Dr. Tesfaye Gebre-Egzi, Minister of Information
Dej. Aemro-Selassie Abebe, Governor General of Gamo Gofa Province
Dej. Solomon Abraham, Governor General of Wollo (1965)
Dej. Sahlu Defaye, Governor General of Arussi
Dej. Werku Enque-Selassie, Governor General of Illubabor
Dej. Legesse Bezu, Governor General of Wollo
Blata Admasu Reta, Minister of State in the Imperial Palace
Col. Solomon Kedir, Minister of State in the Ministry of Interior
Hon. Nebiye Leul-Kifle, Vice-Minister in Majesty's Special Cabinet
Hon. Solomon Gebre-Mariam, Vice-Minister of Pen
Hon. Tegegne Yeteshawork, Vice-Minister, Ministry of Information
Dej. Kebede Ali Wole, Deputy Governor of Wollo
Lij Hailu Desta, President of the Ethiopian Red Cross Society
Fit. Amde Aberra, Private Businessman
Fit. Tadesse Enque-Selassie, Governor of Limu District
Fit. Demssie Alamirew, Governor of Gore District
Kegnazmache Yilma Aboye, Member of the Imperial Chief de Camp
Ato Hailu Teklu, Member of the Ministry of Foreign Affairs
Cap. Belay Tsegay, Army Aviation Pilot
Lieutenant Tesfay Tekle, Army Aviation Pilot
Lance Corporal (?) Aekman Fitwe
Corporal Bekele Wolde-Giorgis, Member of the Military Engineering
Lance Corporal Tekle Haile, Member of the Military Engineering
Fit. Kifle Enque-Selassie, (patriot)
Ato Ababe Kebede, General Manager of Haile-Selassie I Foundation

Note: The names are presented here as they appear in the memorial monument at the Ethiopian Trinity Church.

Source: Ethiopian Trinity Church, "Memorial Monument," Addis Ababa.

Glossary

Afe Negus	A title similar to speaker of the house.
Ato	Mister.
Awraja	An administrative unit between a district and a province.
Bitwedede, Bit.	A title of nobility equivalent to earl.
Blata	A title associated with learned men and councilors from the lesser nobility.
Dejazmach, Dej.	Literally "commander of the gate," a title of nobility equivalent to count.
Enderase	Largely a symbolic title given to a person to act on behalf of the Emperor on provincial matters.
Fitawrari, Fit.	Literally "leader of the vanguard," a tittle of nobility equivalent to viscount.
Gasha	A traditional unit of measurement of land between thirty and fifty hectares.
Kebele	The lowest administrative unit, next to a sub-district.
King of Kings	A title equivalent to Emperor.
Lij	Literally "child," a title reserved for sons of high-ranking nobility.
Ras	Literally "head," equivalent to duke.
Sefera	Settlement
Tibeka Guad	Security Comrade (*Guadoch*, plural)
Arso Ader	Farmer
Gibrena	Farming

Bibliography

Books

Ake, Claude. *Democracy and Development in Africa*. Washington, DC: The Brookings Institution, 1996.

Alemseged, Ayhun. *Fana Wogi*. Addis Ababa: Bole Printing Organization, 1991.

Amhara National Democratic Movement. *The programs and By-laws of the Amhara National Democratic Movement*. Addis Ababa: Mega Publishing Enterprise, 2000.

Anagnostopoulos, Georgios. "Sustainability and Ways of Achieving It." In Gunnar Skirbek. ed. *The Notion of Sustainability and its Normative Implications*. Stockholm: Scandinavian University Press, 1994.

Bates. Robert. "Modernization, Ethnic Competition, and the Rationality of Politics in Contemporary Africa." In Donald Rothchild and Victor Olorunsola. eds. *ThePolitics of Cultural Sub-Nationalism in Africa*. Boulder, CO: Westview Press, 1983.

Baxter, P.T.W. "The Creation and Constitution of Oromo Nationality." *Ethnicity and Conflict in the Horn of Africa*. In Katsuyoshi Fukui and John Markakis. eds. Athens, OH: Ohio University Press, 1994.

Bratton, Michael and Nicolas van de Walle. "Toward Governance in Africa: Popular Demands and State Responses." In Goran Hyden and Michael Bratton. eds. *Governance and Politics in Africa*. Boulder, CO: Lynne Rienner Publishers, 1992.

Brinkerhoff, Derick, and Benjamin Crosby. *Managing Policy Reform: Concepts and Tools for Decision-Makers in Developing and Transitioning Countries*. Bloomfield: CT: Kumarian Press, 2002.

Brass, Paul. *Ethnicity and Nationalism, Theory and Comparison*. Newbury Park, CA: Sage Publications, 1991.

Chazan, Naomi. "Ethnicity in Economic Crisis: Development Strategies and Patterns of Ethnicity in Africa." In Dennis Thompson and Dov Ronen. eds. *Ethnicity, Politics, and Development*. Boulder, CO: Lynne Rienner Publishers, 1986.

Clark, Barry. *Political Economy, A Comparative Approach*. Westport, CT: Praeger Publishers, 1991.

Cohen, Herman. *Intervening in Africa: Superpower Peacemaking in a Troubled Continent*. New York: St. Martin's Press, 2000.

Coleman, James. "The Politics of Sub-Saharan Africa." In Gabriel Almond and James Coleman. eds. *The Politics of the Developing Areas*. New Jersey: Princeton University Press, 1960.

_____. *Individual Interests and Collective Action*. New York: Cambridge University Press, 1986.

_____. *Foundations of Social Theory*. New York: The Belknap Press of Harvard University Press, 1990.

Cummings, Robert. "Religious Beliefs and Economic Behavior in Contemporary Africa, South of the Sahara: Linking Religion and Development." in Jacob Neusner. ed. *Religious Belief and Economic Behavior: Ancient Israel, Classcial Christianity, Islam,and Judiasm, and Contemporary Ireland and Africa*. Atlanta: Scholars Press, 1999.

Cummings, Ilijah. "Proceedings And Debate of the 105th Congress." First Session. *Congressional Report*. Vol. 143 (June 4, 1997).

Dahl, Robert. *Democracy, Liberty, and Equality*. New York: Norwegian University Press, 1986.

David, Wilfred. *The Conversation of Economic Development: Historical Voices, Interpretations, and Reality*. New York: M.E. Sharpe, 1997.

_____. The Political Economy of Economic Policy. New York: Praeger Publishers, 1988.

_____. "The Bretton Woods Policy Paradigm Revisited: Between Economic Adjustment and Human Development." Baltimore, MD: University Press of America, 2004.

Deutsch, Morton. *Distributive Justice, A Social-Psychological Perspective*. New Haven: Yale University Press, 1985.

De Vos, George. "Ethnic Pluralism: Conflict and Accommodation, The Role of Ethnicity in Social History." In Lola Romanucci-Ross and George De Vos. eds. *Ethnic Identity: Creation, Conflict, and Accommodation*. Walnut Creek, CA: AltaMira Press, 1995.

Downs, Anthony. *An Economic Theory of Democracy*. New York: Harper and Row, 1957.

Ethiopian Democratic Party. *Ethiopian Democratic Party Program.* Addis Ababa: St. George Publishers, 1999.

Ezeala-Harrison, Fidelis. *Economic Development, Theory and Policy Implications*. Westport, CT: Praeger Publishers, 1996.

Fukui, Katsuyoshi and John Markakis. *Ethnicity & Conflict in the Horn of Africa*. Athens, OH: Ohio University Press, 1994.

Fukuyama, Francis. *The End of History and the Last Man*. New York: The Free Press, 1992.

Furnivall, John. *Netherlands India: A Study of Plural Economy*. New York: Macmillan Publishers, 1944.

Ganguly, Rajat and Raymond Taras. *Understanding Ethnic Conflict: The International Dimension*. New York: Addison-Wesley Educational Publishers, 1998.

Gashaw, Solomon. "Nationalism and Ethnic Conflict in Ethiopia." In *The Rising Tide of Cultural Pluralism: The Nation-State at Bay?* Crawford Young. ed. Madison: The University of Wisconsin Press, 1993.

Guralnik, David. ed. *Webster's New World Dictionary of the American Language.* Cleveland, OH: William Collins + World Publishing, 1976.

Gurr, Ted Robert. *Minorities at Risk: A Global View of Ethnopolitical Conflicts.* Washington, DC: United States Institute of Peace Press, 1993.

Gurr, Ted Robert and Harff, Barbara. *Ethnic Conflict in World Politics.* Westview Press, 1994.

Hadenius, Axel. *Democracy and Development.* New York: Cambridge University Press, 1992.

Haile-Selassie, Emperor. *Hewotiena YeEthiopia Ermja, II Tiraz,* (My Life and Ethiopia's Progress, Vol. II). Addis Ababa: Berhanena Selam Printing Press, 1941.

Hammond, Jenny. *Fire From the Ashes: A Chronicle of the Revolution in Tigray, Ethiopia, 1975-1991.* Lawrenceville, NJ: The Red Sea Press, 1999.

Haynes, Jeff. *Religion and Politics in Africa.* New Jersey: Zed Books, 1996.

Hechter, Michael. *Principles of Group Solidarity.* Berkeley: University of California Press, 1987.

____. Quoted in Alexis Heraclides. *The Self-Determination of Minority in International Politics.* Portland: Frank Cass, 1991.

Huntington, Samuel. *Political Order in Changing Societies.* New Haven, CT: Yale University Press, 1968.

____. "Democracies Third Wave." In *The Global Resurgence of Democracy.* Larry Diamond and Marc Plattner. eds. Baltimore: Johns Hopkins University Press, 1996.

Kebede, Messay. *Survival and Modernization, Ethiopia's Enigmatic Present: A Philosophical Discourse.* New Jersey: The Red Sea Press, 1999.

Keyes, Charles. ed. *Ethnic Change.* Seattle: University of Washington Press, 1981.

Knoke, David. *Political Networks: The Structural Perspective.* New York: Cambridge University Press, 1990.

Knoke, David and Nancy Wisely. "Social Movements." In *Political Networks: The Structural Perspective.* David Knoke. ed. New York: Cambridge University Press, 1990.

Knutsson, E. Karl. "Dichotomization and Integration, Aspects of Inter-ethnic Relations in Southern Ethiopia." In *Ethnic Groups and Boundaries, The Social Organization of Culture and Difference.* Fredrik Barth. ed. Massachusetts: Little, Brown and Company, 1969.

Korten, David. *Planned Change in a Traditional Society: Psychological Problems of Modernization in Ethiopia.* New York: Praeger Publishers, 1972.

Lapalombara, Joseph. "Italy: Fragmentation, Isolation, Alienation." In *Political Culture and Political Development.* Lucian Pye and Sidney Verba. eds. Princeton: Princeton University Press, 1965.

Lemarchand, Rene. "Ethnic Violence in Tropical Africa." In *The Primordial Challenge, Ethnicity in the Contemporary World.* John F. Stack Jr. ed. New York: Greenwood Press, 1986.

Lenin, V. I. 2nd ed. *The State and Revolution, Marxist Teaching on the State and the Task of the Proletariat in the Revolution.* London: Communist Party of Great Britain, 1925.

Levine, Donald. "Ethiopia: Identity, Authority, and Realism." In Lucian Pye and Sidney Verba. eds. *Political Culture and Political Development.* Princeton: Princeton University Press, 1965.

Lewis, Herbert. "Ethnicity in Ethiopia: The View from Bellow (and from the South, East, and West)." In *The Rising Tide of Cultural Pluralism: The Nation-State at Bay?* Crawford Young. ed. Madison: University of Wisconsin Press, 1993.

Lijphart, Arend. "Consociational Democracy." In *Consociational Democracy: Political Accommodation in Segmented Societies.* Kenneth McRae. ed. Toronto: McClelland and Stewart, 1974.

____. *Democracies Patterns of Majoritarian and Consensus Government in Twenty-One Countries.* New Haven, CT: Yale University Press, 1984.

Lijphart, Arend & Carlos Waisman. eds. *Institutional Design in New Democracies: Eastern Europe and Latin America.* New York: Westview Press, 1998.

Mair, Peter. "Electoral Markets and Stable States." In *The Market and the State, Studies in Interdependence.* Michael Moran and Maurice Wright. eds. New York: St. Martin's Press, 1991.

Marcus, Harold. *Haile-Selassie I, The Formative Years: 1892-1936.* New Jersey: The Red Sea Press, 1998.

____. *The Politics of Empire: Ethiopia, Great Britain and the United States, 1941-1974* Lawrenceville, NJ: The Red Sea Press, 1995.

____. *A History of Ethiopia.* Los Angeles: University of California Press, 1994.

Mutahaba, Gelase and Jide Balogun. *Enhancing Policy Management Capacity in Africa*. West Hartford: CT, Cumarian Press, 1992.

Mattes, Robert and Amanda Gouws. "Race, Ethnicity, and Voting Behavior: Lessons from South Africa." In *Elections and Conflict Management in Africa*. Timothy Sisk and Andrew Reynolds. eds. Washington, DC: United States Institute of Peace Press, 1998.

Mazrui, Ali. *Cultural Forces in World Politics*. Portsmouth, NH: Heinemann Educational Books, 1990.

Mbiti, John. *African Religions and Philosophy*. New York: Anchor Books, Double-day and Company, 1969.

Mengistu, Berhanu. "Governance and Sustainable Development Policy: An Interpretive Analysis." In *Globalization and the New World Order: Promises, Problems, and Prospects for Africa in the Twenty-First Century*. Felix Moses Edoho. ed. Westport, CT: Praeger Publishers, 1997.

Mohammed, Mhathir. Speech delivered at the Asia Pacific Economic Cooperation forum. Vancouver, Canada, November 1997.

Matsuda, Hiroshi. "Annexation & Assimilation: Koegu & their Neighbors." In *Ethnic & Conflict in the Horn of Africa*. Katsuyoshi Fukui and John Markakis. eds. Ohio: Ohio University Press, 1994.

Mutahaba Gelase and Jide Balogun. *Enhancing Policy Management Capacity in Africa*. West Hartford: Connecticut, Cumarian Press, 1992.

Nahum, Fasil. *Constitution for a Nation of Nations: The Ethiopian Prospect*. Asmara: The Red Sea Press, 1997.

Nkrumah, Kwame. *Revolutionary Path*. New York: International Publishers, 1973.

Nyerere, Julius. Quoted in Arend Lijphart. "Consociational Democracy." In *Consociational Democracy: Political Accommodation in Segmented Societies*. Kenneth McRae. ed. Toronto: McClelland and Stewart, 1974.

Nyong'o, Peter. "The Implication of Crises and Conflict in the Upper Nile Valley." In *Conflict Resolution in Africa*. Fancis Deng and William Zartman. eds. Washington, DC: Brookings Institution, 1991.

O'Donnell, Guillermo. "Horizontal Accountability in New Democracies." In *The Self-Restraining State: Power and Accountability in New Democracies*. Andreas Schedler, Larry Diamond, and Marc Plattner. eds. Colorado: Lynne Rienner Publishers, 1999.

Office of the United States Trade Representative. *1991 National Trade Estimate Report on Foreign Trade Barriers*. Washington, DC: US Government Printing Office, 1992.

Osaghe, Eghosa. *Ethnicity and Its Management in Africa: The Democratization Link*. Lagos, Nigeria: Malthouse Press Ltd, 1994.

Ostrom, Elinor. "Social capital: a fad or a fundamental concept?" In *Social Capital: A Multifaceted Perspective*. Partha Dasgupta and Ismail Serageldin. eds. Washington, DC: World Bank, 2000.

Pausewang, Siegfried, Kjetil Tronvoll, and Lovise Aalen. eds. *Ethiopia since the Derg: A Decade of Democratic Pretension and Performance*. New York: Zed Books Ltd., 2002.

Putnam, Robert, Robert Leonardi, and Raffaella Nanetti. *Making Democracy Work*. Princeton, NJ: Princeton University Press, 1993.

Rabie, Mohamed. *Conflict Resolution and Ethnicity*. Westport, CT: Praeger Publishers, 1994.

Ramsay, Jeffress. *Global Studies: Africa*, 5th ed. Guilford, CT: Dushkin Publishing Group, 1993.

Rapley, John. *Understanding Development, Theory and Practices in the Third World*. Boulder: Lynne Rienner Publishers, 1996.

Rothchild, Donald. "Hegemonial Exchange: An Alternative Model for Managing Conflict in Middle Africa." In *Ethnicity, Politics, and Development*. Dennis Thompson and Dov Ronen. eds. Boulder: Lynne Rienner Publishers, 1986.

____. *Managing Ethnic Conflict in Africa: Pressures and Incentives for Cooperation*. Washington, D.C: Brookings Institution Press, 1997.

Ryan, Stephen. Quoted in Ganguly Rajat and Raymond Taras. *Understanding Ethnic Conflict: The International Dimension*. New York: Addison-Wesley Educational Publishers, 1998.

Said, Ali. "Afar Ethnicity in Ethiopian Politics." In *Ethnicity and the State in Eastern Africa*. Mohamed Salih and John Markakis. eds. Stockholm, Sweden: Elanders Gtab, 1998.

Scarritt, James. "Communal Conflict and Contention for Power in Africa South of the Sahara." In *Minorities at Risk, A Global View of Ethnopolitical Conflict*. Ted Robert Gurr. ed. Washington, DC: United States Institute of Peace Press, 1993.

Schmitter, Philippe and Terry Lynn Karl. "What Democracy Is ... And Is Not." In *The Global Resurgence of Democracy*. Larry Diamond and Marc Plattner. eds. Baltimore: The John Hopkins University Press, 1996.

Smith, Brian. *Understanding Third World Politics: Theories of Political Change and Development*. Indiana: Indiana University Press, 1996.

Smith, M.G. Quoted in Ganguly Rajat and Raymond Taras. *Understanding Ethnic Conflict: The International Dimension*. New York: Addison-Wesley Educational Publishers, 1998.

Stiglitz, Joseph. *Globalization and Its Discontents*. New York: W.W. Norton & Company, 2002.

Tadess, Kiflu. *The Generation, Part II, Ethiopia Transformation and Conflict, The History of the Ethiopian People's Revolutionary Party*. New York: University Press of America, 1998.

Tekle, Amare. "Continuity and Change in Ethiopian Politics." In *The Political Economy of Ethiopia*. Marina Ottaway. ed. New York: Praeger Publishers, 1990.

Tesfaye, Aaron. *Political Power and Ethnic Federalism: The Struggle for Democracy in Ethiopia*. Lanham, MD: University Press of America, 2002.

Todaro, Michael. 5th ed. *Economic Development*. New York: Longman, 1994.

Tripp, Aili. "The Political Mediation of Ethnic and Religious Diversity in Tanzania." In *The Accommodation of Cultural Diversity*. Crowford Young. ed. New York: St. Martin's Press, 1999.

United Nations Development Programme. *Human Development Report 1998*. New York: Oxford University Press, 1998.

Wagaw, Teshome. *The Development of Higher Education and Social Change: An Ethiopian Experience*. Michigan: Michigan State University Press, 1990.

Weissberg, Robert. "The Democratic Party and the Conflict over Racial Policy." In *Do Elections Matter?* Benjamin Ginsberg and Alan Stone. eds. New York: M. E. Sharpe, 1986.

Widner, Jennifer. "Building Judicial Independence in Common Law Africa." In *The Self-restructuring State: Power and Accountability in New Democracies*. Andreas Schedler, Larry Diamond, and Marc Plattner. eds. Boulder, CO: Lynne Rienner Publishers, 1999.

Williams, Donald. "Accommodation in the Midst of Crisis? Assessing Governance in Nigeria." In *Governance and Politics in Africa*. Goran Hyden and Michael Bratton. eds. Colorado, CO: Lynne Rienner Publishers, 1992.

Wiseman, John. *Democracy in Black Africa: Survival and Revival*. New York: Paragon House Publishers, 1990.

Woldemikael, Tekle. "Eritrean Nationalist Movements." In *The Rising Tide of Cultural Pluralism, The Nation-State at Bay?* Crawford Young. ed. Madison: The University of Wisconsin Press, 1993.

World Bank. *Building Institutions for Markets*. New York: Oxford University Press, 2002.

____. *The State in a Changing World*. New York: Oxford University Press, 1997.

____. *World Development Report 1991*. New York: Oxford University Press, 1991.

Yohannes, Dawit. Quoted in Kjetil Tronvoll and Oyvind Aadland. *The Process of Democratization in Ethiopia – An Expression of Popular Participation or Political Resistance.* Oslo: Norwegian Institute of Human Rights, 1995.

Young, Crawford. "Evolving Modes of Consciousness and Ideology: Nationalism and Ethnicity." In *Political Development and the New Realism in Sub-Saharan Africa.* David Apter and Carl Rosberg. eds. Virginia: University Press of Virginia, 1994.

Young, A. Ralph. "States and Markets in Africa." In *The Market and the State.* Michael Moran and Maurice Wright. eds. New York: St. Martin's Press, 1991.

Zewde, Bahru. "The Problems of Institutionalization in Modern Ethiopia: A Historical Perspective." In *Institutions, Resources and Development in Ethiopia, Proceedings of the Ninth Annual Conference on the Ethiopian Economy, October 8-9, 1999.* Alemu Mekonnen and Dejene Aredo. eds. Addis Ababa: Addis Ababa University Press, 2000.

_____. *The History of Ethiopia1855-1973.* Addis Ababa: Addis Ababa University Press, 1996.

United Nations Development Programme. *Human Development Report 1998.* New York: Oxford University Press, 1998.

Government Documents

Central Statistical Authority (CSA). "Report on Large and Medium Scale Manufacturing and Electricity Industries, 2001." Addis Ababa: CSA, 2002.

_____. "Report on Large and Medium Scale Manufacturing and Electricity Industries Survey, 1998." Addis Ababa: CSA, 1998.

_____. "Report on Large and Medium Scale Manufacturing and Electricity Industries Survey, 1997." Addis Ababa: CSA, 1997.

_____. "Results of the Survey of Manufacturing and Electricity Industries, 1985/86." Addis Ababa: CSA, 1989.

_____. "Results of the Survey of Manufacturing Industries 1979/80." Addis Ababa: CSA, 1982.

_____. "Statistical Abstract 2001." Addis Ababa: CSA, 2002.

_____. "Statistical Abstract 2000." Addis Ababa: CSA, 2001.

_____. "Statistical Abstract 1997." Addis Ababa: CSA, 1998.

_____. "Statistical Abstract 1995." Addis Ababa: CSA, 1996.

_____. "Statistical Abstract 1992." Addis Ababa: CSA, 1994.

_____. "Statistical Abstract 1990." Addis Ababa: CSA, 1993.

Central Statistical Office (CSO), "Statistical Abstract 1986." Addis Ababa: CSO, 1990.

____. "Statistical Abstract 1986" Addis Ababa: CSO, 1988.

____. "Statistical Abstract 1982." Addis Ababa: CSO, 1984.

____. "Statistical Abstract 1982." Addis Ababa: CSO, 1983.

____. "Statistical Abstract 1980." Addis Ababa: CSO, 1982.

____. "Statistical Abstract 1976." Addis Ababa: CSO, 1977.

____. "Statistical Abstract 1975." Addis Ababa: CSO, 1975.

____. "Statistical Abstract 1972." Addis Ababa: CSO, n.d.

____. "Statistical Abstract 1971." Addis Ababa: CSO, 1979.

____. "Statistical Abstract 1971." Addis Ababa: CSO, 1972.

____. "Statistical Abstract 1970." Addis Ababa: CSO, 1970.

____. "Statistical Abstract 1969." Addis Ababa: CSO, n.d.

____. "Statistical Abstract 1967 and 1968" Addis Ababa: CSO, n.d.

____. "Statistical Abstract 1966." Addis Ababa: CSO, 1966.

____. "Statistical Abstract 1964." Addis Ababa: CSO, 1970.

The Federal Democratic Republic of Ethiopia. *Yegeter Lemat Policiwoch Strategewochina Seltoch.* (Rural Development Policies and Strategies) Addis Ababa: Ministry of Information and Culture, November 2001.

____. "Education Statistics Annual Abstract 2000/01." Addis Ababa: Ministry of Education, 2001.

Imperial Government of Ethiopia. *The Second Five Year Development Plan,1962/63-1976/77.* Addis Ababa: Berhanena Selam Printing Press, 1962.

Ministry of Information. *Rural Development Policies and Strategies.* Addis Ababa: Ministry of Information and Culture, November 1995.

____. Ministry of Information. *BeEthiopia YeDemocracy Sirat Ginbata Gudayoch* (Issues of Building Democracy in Ethiopia). Addis Ababa: Ministry of Information, 1994.

The Transitional Military Government of Ethiopia. "National Revolutionary Production Campaign: First Year Plan, 1978/79." Addis Ababa: Berhanena Selam Printing Press, 1978.

U.S. Congress. House. Committee on Foreign Relations. "Human Rights Progress in Ethiopia: Hearing before the Committee on Foreign Relations." 105th Cong., 1st sess., 4 June 1997.

Journals

All Amhara Peoples Organization. *All Amhara Peoples Organization Journal.* Addis Ababa: Bole Publishing Enterprise, 1992.

Fukuyama, Francis. "The Primacy of Culture." *Journal of Democracy* Vol. 6, 1 (1995): 7-14.

Harbeson, John. "A Bureaucratic Authoritarian Regime." *Journal of Democracy* Vol. 9, No. 4 (1998): 62-69.

Henze, Paul. "A Political Success Story." *Journal of Democracy* Vol. 9, No. 4 (1998): 40-54.

Joseph, Richard. "Oldspeak vs. Newspeak." *Journal of Democracy* Vol. 9, No. 4 (1998): 55-61.

Krugman, Paul. "Space: The Final Frontier." *Journal of Economic Perspectives*, Vol. 12, No. 2 (Spring 1998): 161-174.

Loury, Glenn. "Discrimination in the Post-Civil Rights Era: Beyond Market Interactions." *Journal of Economic Perspective.* (Spring 1998): 117-126.

Makki, Fouad. "Nationalism, State Formation and the Public Sphere: Eritrea." *Review of African Political Economy* No. 70 (December 1996): 475-497.

O'Donnell, Guillermo. "Do Economist Know Best?" *Journal of Democracy* Vol. 6, No. 1 (1995): 23-28.

Nyerere, Julius. "African Socialism: *Ujamaa* in Practice." *Black World* (March 1974): 211-218.

Menen. (Addis Ababa), 1960; 1965; 1967; 1971.

Young, John. "Ethnicity and Power in Ethiopia." *Review of Africa Political Economy* Vol. 23, No. 70 (December 1996): 531-542.

Internet Sources

Africa Watch. "Ethiopia and Eritrea: Fratricidal Conflict in the Horn." At [http://www.iss.co.za/Pubs/ASR/7.5/Africa%25Watch.html]. 4 August 2000.

CIA World Fact Book. "Political Resources on the Net." At [http://www.agora.stm.it/elections/ethiopia.htm]. 24 April 2000.

____. "Political Resources on the Net." At [http://www.agora.stm.it/ elections/ethiopia.htm]. 16 September 2000.

"CPJ Urges African Union to Guarantee Press Freedom." At [http://www.internews.org/mra/mrm/oct02/oct02_story11.htm]. 20 September 2003.

"The Constitution of the Federal Democratic Republic of Ethiopia." At [http://www.civicwebs.com/cwvlib/constitutions/ethiopia/constituti on_1994.htm#Chapter4]. 15 November 2001.

Department of Justice. "Statement of Subject Matter and Appellate Jurisdiction." At [http://www.usdoj.gov/atr/cases/f1900/1947.htm]. 8 November 1999.

"Ethiopian Constitution." At [www.sas.upenn.edu/African_Studies/ Hornet/Ethiopian_Constitution.html]. 25 July 2000.

"Ethiopian Constitution." At [http//www.sas.upenn.edu:80/Africa
...Hornet/Ethiopian_Constitution.html]. 9 April 2000.

"Ethiopian press freedom symposium held without press." At
[http://www.afrol.com/News2003/eth002_press_law.htm]. 3 October 2003.

Human Rights Watch. "Human Rights Curtailed in Ethiopia." At
[http://www.hrw.org/press97/dec/ethiop.htm]. 11 October 2001.

____. "Human Rights Development." At [http://www.hrw.org/world
report99/africa/ethiopia.html]. 11 October 2001.

"Journalists in prison - press freedom under attack." At [http://www.
africaaction.org/docs98/east9804.html]. 20 September 2003.

"Intimidation and Harassment Escalates in the South." *Ethio Time*, 11
March 2000. Quoted in "Ethiopian Election Newsflash." At
[http://www.mesob.org/elect/parties.html]. 9 May 2000.

"Letter to President Isaias From Eritrean Professionals And Academics." At [http://www.telecome.net.et/~walta/conflict/articles/article
1407.html]. 13 October 2000.

"Letter to the President of the Republic of South Africa and Chair of
the African Union." At [http://www.ifjafrique.org/english/dern ou-
velles/ 200603_5.htm]. 3 October 2003.

Lussier. "Continued Victimization of the Kunama 1991-?." In "A Day
to Celebrate a Mass Murderer." At [http://www.geocities.com/~
dagmawi/News/News_Sep1_Awate.html]. 4 December 1999.

"Meles Announces New Cabinet." At [http://allafrica.com/stories].
20 June 2002.

"The Parliament of the Federal Democratic Republic of Ethiopia." At
[http://www.ethiospokes.net/Backgrnd/b0409981.htm].   9   April
2000.

"The Regions of the Federal Democratic Republic of Ethiopia." At
[http://www.ethiospokes.net/Backgrnd/b0311981.htm]. 4 December 1999.

Newspapers

Assefa, Emrakeb. "US diverts food aid from Iraq to Ethiopia." *Reporter*
(14 May 2003), p.1.

Demissie, Melaku. "Ethiopia becomes world's 15th largest food aid
recipient." *Reporter* (21 May 2003), p.1, col. 4.

"The European Union granted 9 million *Euros* for the implementation
of the food security program." *Addis Zemen*. (31 May 2003), p.1,
col.1.

"Inadequate Planning of Resettlement Leads to Unnecessary Suffering." *Addis Tribune*, (16 May 2003), p.1, col. 3.

"Relief distributed among 49,000 needy." *Ethiopian Herald*. (22 May 2003), p.1, col.1.

Soyinka, Wole. "Of Sacred Cows ...." *Mail & Guardian*. 26 July 2005.

Tadesse, Abebe. "Drought imposes social crisis, number of severely affected drought victims increases." *Reporter* (14 May 2003), p.1.

The Transitional Military Government of Ethiopia. "Government Ownership and Control of the Means of Production." *Negarit Gazeta*, Proclamation No. 26/1975. Addis Ababa: Berhanena Selam Printing Press, 11 March 1975.

———. "Public Ownership of Rural Lands," *Negarit Gazeta*, Proclamation No. 31/1975. Addis Ababa: Berhanena Selam Printing Press, 29 April 1975.

———. "Government Ownership of Urban Lands and Extra Houses." *Negarit Gazeta*, Proclamation No. 47/1975. Addis Ababa: Berhanena Selam Printing Press, 26 July 1975.

"United States announces additional food contribution." *The Reporter* (14 May 2003), p.3.

"What the US gives its farmers each year is equivalent to total annual global assistance." *Ethiopian Herald*. (22 May 2003), p.3, col. 3.

"World Bank grant." *Ethiopian Herald*. (13 May 2003), p.3, col.1.

Television News

BBC World Service. "Ethiopian ruling party confirms divisions." (23 March 2001), 15:02 GMT

Ethiopian Television. "Close-up." (27 May 2003),10 p.m.

Unpublished Documents

Collier, Paul, Ibrahim Elbadawi, and Nicholas Sambanis. "Why Are There So Many Civil Wars in Africa? Prevention of Future Conflict and Promotion of Inter-Group Cooperation." Paper prepared for the UNECA Ad Hoc Experts Group Meeting on "The Economics of Civil Conflicts in Africa." Addis Ababa, Ethiopia. 7-8, April 2000.

David, Wilfred. "The Bretton Woods Policy Paradigm Revisited: Between Economic Adjustment and Human Development." Maryland: University Press of America, in print.

The Federal Democratic Republic of Ethiopia. "Ethiopia: Interim Poverty Reduction Strategy Paper 2000/01-2002/03." A report prepared for the World Bank (Addis Ababa). November 2000.

The Ministry of Education. "National Development Goals, Priorities, and Policies for the Third Five Year Plan." Addis Ababa: Ministry of Education Archive, December 1967.

____. "The Second Five Year Development Plan, 1962-1966." Addis Ababa: Ministry of Education Archive, n.d..

The Ministry of Finance and Economic Development. "Ethiopia, Sustainable Development and Poverty Reduction Program." A report prepared for the World Bank (Addis Ababa), July 2002.

Mulat Demeke and others. "Market and non-market transfers of land in Ethiopia: Implications for efficiency, equity, and non-farm development." A study conducted for the World Bank (Washington, DC). January 2003.

Mulaw, And Alem. "The Role of Development Planning and International Assistance in Post-World War II Ethiopia, 1941-1988: A Comparative Analysis." Ph.D. Dissertation, Howard University, 1990.

The National Electoral Board. "Results of the 1995 Election of House of People's Representatives, List of Candidates, Party Affiliation, and Votes." Addis Ababa: National Electoral Board Archive, n.d.

____. "Yepartiwoch Mina Bedemocratic Mircha." (The Role of Political Parties in Democratic Election). Addis Ababa: National Electoral Board, n.d.

____. "Results of the 2000 Election of House of People's Representatives, List of Candidates, Party Affiliation, and Vote." Addis Ababa: National Electoral Board Archive, n.d.

Nega, Berhanu and others. "Tenure Security and Land-Related Investment: Evidence from Ethiopia." A study conducted for the World Bank (Washington, DC) 2001.

Office of the Planning Commission. "Strategies Outline for the Fourth Five Year Plan, 1974/75-1978/79." Addis Ababa: Ministry of Education Archive, April 1973.

The Transitional Military Government of Ethiopia. "YeIndustry Kifle Economy YeAser Amet Meri Ikid (Rekik), Meskerem 1975." (A Ten Year Industrial Policy Principal Plan (Draft)). Addis Ababa: Ministry of Education Archive, September 1984.

____. "Yebeheyrawi Abiyotawi Yemirt Zemecha Yemejemeria Amet Ikid, 1971." (National Revolutionary Production Campaign: First Year Plan, 1978." Addis Ababa: Ministry of Education Archive, 1978.

United States Agency for International Development. "Basic Education System Overhaul Program Assistance Approval Document and Project Paper." Addis Ababa, Ethiopia: USAID/Ethiopia, September 1994.

____. "Basic Education System Overhaul Program Assistance and Project Paper." Addis Ababa: USAID/Ethiopia, September 1994.

World Bank. *Education Sector Public Expenditure Review 1993.* Cited in USAID. "Basic Education System Overhaul Program Assistance and Project Paper." Addis Ababa, Ethiopia: USAID/Ethiopia, September 1994.

Index

food aid, 93, 94, 95
freedom
   of expression, 66, 191-193
   political, 55, 190
   press, 14, 67, 245
Fukuyama, Francis, 52
Furnivall, John, 27

Gamu Gofa, 253
   education, 115
   health, 118, 123
   revenue, 119
Gambella, 4, 253
   drought, 93
   education, 126, 127
   ethnic groups in, 4
   health, 129
   industries, 113, 124
   see also conflict, corruption
Gebeyehu, Workneh, 155
Gebre, Kebede, 156
Gebre-Medhn, Enwey, 205
   see also Ethics and Anti-
   corruption Commission
Gestapo, 162, 173
Ghana, 35
Gojjam, xiii, 4, 6, 253
   education, 115
   health, 118, 123
   industries, 84, 113
   revenue, 116, 127
   road density, 137
   see also Amhara
Gonder, xiii, 253
   education, 115
   health, 118, 123
   industries, 84, 113
   revenue, 116, 127
   road density, 137
   see also Amhara
Gouwns, Amanda, 60
Great Britain, 192
Gross Domestic Product, 73

GDP (contd.)
   77, 98, 106, 124, 125, 126
Gross Enrollment Ratio, 115
Gurr, Ted Robert, 5

Hadenius, Axel, 53
Haile-Mariam, Mengistu, xii,
   1, 3, 7, 10, 81, 109, 113,
   117, 119, 143, 158, 164,
   167-168, 230
   see development policy
Haile-Selassie, Emperor, xii,
   xiii, 3, 5, 8, 9, 76, 82, 99-
   100, 146, 155, 158, 230
   see development policy
Hailu, Ras of Gojjam, 147
Hailu, Remamo, 153
Harari (Hararghe), 84, 107,
   113, 253
   education, 115, 126, 127
   ethnic groups, 107
   health, 118, 129
   industries, 113, 134
   revenue, 116, 119
Harbeson, John, 58
Harff, Barbara, 5
Hechter, Michael, 38
Henz, Paul, 58
holistic perspective, xv, 13, 20,
   74, 106, 197
Homan, George, 37
Horowitz, Donald, 60
Houphouet-Boigny, 42
House of Peoples
   Representatives, 10, 11, 58,
   175-177, 184, 185, 240
Human capital, 244
Human poverty index, 1
Huntington, Samuel, 4, 52

Identity, 31, 32, 33, 35
Illibabor, 4, 253
   education, 115

About the Author

Dr. Kasahun Woldemariam is a Lecturer in the African Studies Department at Howard University. He is also Director of Academic Affairs and Curriculum Development and member of the Board of Directors for a non-governmental organization, Education for Everyone in Ethiopia. Kasahun has served as a member of the Steering Committee for the United Nations Development Programme during the planning of the Pan-African Youth Leadership Summit, Dakar, Senegal, and as a Political Analyst for the Voice of America radio broadcasting service.

Kasahun is a recipient of numerous awards, including the Sasakawa Young Leaders Fellowship, Howard University, Visiting Fellowship from the University of Witwatersrand, South Africa, a research fellowship from the Institute for the Study of World Politics, Washington, DC., and a scholarship from the United Nations High Commissioner for Refugees in Khartoum, Sudan.

Dr. Woldemariam has published articles, including on "The Border ruling between Ethiopia and Eritrea," "The Real Power of Ballots," "Selling Investor-friendly Image of Africa," "Public Support is Needed for War against Poverty," and "NEPAD Needs NGOs to work." He is currently working on his second book on social capital and African development.